JB JOSSEY-BASS

Tools for Teaching Health

Interactive Strategies to Promote Health Literacy and Life Skills in Adolescents and Young Adults

Shannon Whalen
Dominick Splendorio
Sal Chiariello

BICENTENNIAL
1807
WILEY
2007
BICENTENNIAL

John Wiley & Sons, Inc.

Library of Congress Cataloging-in-Publication Data

Whalen, Shannon.
    Tools for teaching health : 100+ interactive strategies to promote health literacy and life skills in adolescents and young adults / Shannon Whalen, Dominick Splendorio, and Sal Chiarello.
        p. cm.
    Includes bibliographical references and index.
        ISBN-13: 978-0-7879-9407-5 (alk. paper)
        1. Teenagers—Health and hygiene—United States. 2. Health education—United States. 3. Health promotion—United States. I. Splendorio, Dominick, 1949- II. Chiarello, Sal, 1945- III. Title.
    RA564.5.W46 2007
    613'.0433--dc22   2006101794

Printed in the United States of America
FIRST EDITION
PB Printing   10 9 8 7 6 5 4 3 2 1

Tools for Teaching Health

CONTENTS

CHAPTER 1

TOBACCO

CHAPTER 2

ALCOHOL

Contents

CHAPTER **3**

DRUGS

CHAPTER **4**

NUTRITION

CHAPTER **5**

SEXUALITY EDUCATION

CHAPTER **6**

VIOLENCE PREVENTION

CHAPTER **7**

PHYSICAL ACTIVITY

Thank you to our colleagues, students, and the workshop participants who encouraged us to finally publish a textbook of our own!

About the Authors

Dr. Shannon Whalen is an Associate Professor in the School of Health, Physical Education and Recreation at Springfield College. She received her baccalaureate degree in health and physical education from the University of Delaware, a Masters degree in health education from New York University, and a Masters and Doctorate of Education degrees in health education from Columbia University, Teachers College. Prior to joining the faculty at Springfield College, Dr. Whalen taught health, physical education, and athletic training courses at Adelphi University, The College of Mount Saint Vincent and John Jay College, CUNY. Dr. Whalen has also worked as a health teacher in the Clarkstown Central School District and the Yonkers Public School System and has served as an adjunct lecturer and supervisor of student teaching in the Department of Health and Behavior Studies at Columbia University, Teachers College. She serves as a consultant for many private and public schools health-related organizations. She is currently working as an advocate for health education on state and national committees. She presents health education workshops at many conferences each year and has been publishing her writing and research efforts in health education journals and textbooks.

Dominick Splendorio received his baccalaureate degree in Health Education from the State University College at Brockport and his Masters degree in Humanistic Studies from the State University College at New Paltz. He taught middle and high school health education for over thirty years in the Clarkstown Central School District in Rockland County, New York. He is owner and operator of Prime Time Health, an educational consulting firm specializing in health-related presentations for schools, state education departments, and corporations.

Mr. Splendorio has presented workshops at many regional and national conferences on issues related to sexual harassment in schools, male-female communication, comprehensive sexuality education, HIV/AIDS, alcohol, tobacco, and other drugs, and humor. Mr. Splendorio has twice been selected as New York State Health Teacher of the Year (NYSFPHE 1994 and NYSAHPERD 2001). He has been involved in the production of educational videos related to child abduction-prevention, alcohol abuse, HIV/AIDS, sexual harassment, Skin Cancer Prevention, and Comprehensive Sexuality Education. He has served as chairman of the Content Advisory Committee for the New York State Teacher Certification Exam in Health Education and is president of the Health Section of the New York State Association of Health, Physical Education, Recreation, and Dance (NYSAHPERD). He serves on the Advisory Board of PE Central, an on-line resource for health and physical education teachers. Mr. Splendorio is also a Health Education Consultant with the Bureau of Educational Research and is author of their health education teaching manual entitled *Outstanding Strategies to Optimize Your Health Education Instruction.*

Sal Chiariello received his baccalaureate degree in Health and Physical Education from Hunter College, his Masters in Health Education from Lehman College, and his Professional Diploma in Administration & Supervision from Fordham University. He was a health educator in New York City for 22 years. In 1990 he became the Health Coordinator for the Clarkstown Central School District. Sal was one of the original writers of Goals 2000 Grant in Health Education. He is a frequent presenter at State and Eastern District AHPERD conferences. Sal has been honored as NYC Teacher of the Year, NYS Federation of Professional Health Educators Distinguished Award, and with the NYS AHPERD Exceptional Leadership Award for a School Health Education Coordinator.

Notes to the Teacher

This book is a compilation of classroom-tested, ready-to-use activities. The activities encompass the following six areas: tobacco use, sedentary lifestyle, dietary patterns, sexual behaviors, alcohol and drug use, and behaviors that result in intentional and unintentional injury. Although there are many content areas in which educators can deliver health instruction, these six areas were specifically chosen as a result of the CDC research on behaviors that are leading causes of death and disability among adolescents. Since all of these risk behaviors are preventable, it is imperative that students are taught to reduce their risk by practicing health-promoting skills and behaviors.

The rationale behind developing this book was two-fold. First, there was a need for a book that provided stimulating health education lessons. Rather than assisting children in being healthy, presentation of boring, teacher-centered lessons can turn a child away from healthy behavior. This book was developed to provide teachers with strategies that will enhance the classroom health education experience. All activities are hands-on, student-centered, and interactive. These activities make learning health education fun and exciting.

Second, there was a need for a text that provided teachers with activities that focus on health behaviors. In the past, health educators focused on teaching health knowledge. Over time, research has indicated that health knowledge is not necessarily translated into healthy behaviors. The activities in this text do not merely address the cognitive, or knowledge-based, domain of learning, but they also include the affective (emotional) and behavioral domains of learning as well.

How to Use This Book

The purpose of this book is to offer teachers "pick and choose" teaching strategies to supplement or update an existing health curriculum. It is intended to be used to enhance a coordinated, sequential, comprehensive, health education program. Although it does address the cognitive, affective, and behavioral domains of learning, it does not provide the instructor with an abundance of factual information. With the availability of the Internet, almost any information can be readily available with the click of a mouse. What it *does* provide are the *teaching strategies* that reach young people to interest and engage them in the health education curriculum.

Notes to the Teacher

This book is a valuable resource to the undergraduate student or new teacher who is looking for exciting, stimulating health education activities to liven up his classroom. It is equally valuable to the veteran teacher who has taught health for years in a traditional way and is looking for new ideas to make her health education classes more interesting, relevant, and exciting. This book can also be used by social workers, student assistance counselors, church or other support groups, peer education advisors, or anyone else who works in a group setting with pre-adolescents, adolescents, or young adults.

Icebreakers

Most educators think of icebreakers simply as activities at the beginning of a semester or year to help the students and teachers to get to know each other. We have capitalized on the icebreaker format in this book to create a different outcome. Icebreakers are not just a way to get to know people's names, they are a wonderful way for a teacher to get to know students' prior knowledge. They also assist in motivating and exciting students about the unit under study and are helpful in capturing the students' interest in the subject. Each chapter in this book will include an icebreaker that can be used as a transition into the new topic area.

Functional Knowledge

Some health educators complain that they simply do not have enough time to "dispense" all the information in their curriculum in a typical semester or quarter. One of the advantages of this book is that it encourages educators to switch from a content-driven to a skills-driven curriculum.

When planning curriculum, instruction, and assessment, teachers must constantly ask themselves two very important questions: What do students really need to know, and what do students really need to be able to do? *Functional knowledge* is a term that is being used more and more by health educators to replace *content areas* or *content units*. It refers to specific research-based knowledge that "cuts to the chase." It attempts to separate the need-to-know information from the nice-to-know information. For example, if a student realizes that she has an alcohol problem, she does not need to know the chemical formula for alcohol. It might be nice to know; but what she really needs to know is who to go to for help with her problem.

Skills-Based Model

Recent research has demonstrated that students are more likely to adopt healthy behaviors if they are taught health behaviors. Although this may seem obvious, for many years health educators taught health knowledge rather than health behavior. Every chapter in this curriculum has multiple lessons that promote generic health behaviors, such as stress management, communication skills, assertiveness, refusal skills, goal setting, resource management, media analysis, and that discuss advocating for personal, family, and community health. Each chapter also includes lessons that teach health behavior specific to the conceptual area, such as reading food labels in the nutrition chapter or pollution control in the environmental health chapter. The skills addressed in this book attempt to promote self-confidence, respect for self and others, and risk reduction.

National Health Education Standards

By focusing on the National Health Education Standards, teachers can concentrate on what is essential for students to know and be able to do. It is the belief of the authors that the real value of this book is in using the lessons and activities to address the affective and behavioral domains of learning. In the affective domain, the authors hope to provide opportunities for teachers to reinforce positive attitudes and values related to health. In the behavioral domain, the research-based, interactive, student-centered activities will encourage pro-social and other specific health skills. These skills, as outlined in the National Health Education Standards, are referenced in each lesson.

Interactive, Student-Centered Activities

The lessons in this book are all based on a student-centered model. One of the problems with conventional educational lessons is that the teacher is the focus of the lesson. Traditionally, the teacher lectures and the students take notes. Recent pedagogical research has found that students are more likely to retain information if lessons are taught in a student-centered way. The lessons in this curriculum were specifically created to be student-centered.

Many of the activities in this book use the group process. It may take the form of an ice-breaker or other community-building activity. Over time, groups learn to build trust, solve conflicts, and ultimately create products or performances (demonstrations) that reflect what they know and are able to do. The group process itself teaches social skills by requiring that participants work cooperatively to apply learned knowledge and skills in relevant, real-life situations. In order to be effective, health education must provide authentic, problem-based scenarios to students. In processing those problems and repeatedly practicing skills to deal with those problems, students can develop enduring understandings that apply to all content areas.

Home–School Connection

Each chapter in the book contains a Home–School Connection activity. Again, research indicates that to really make a difference in behavior, it is imperative that we consider other external influences in a young person's life, especially family influences. Giving take-home assignments involving parents or other caregivers keeps the lines of communication open between family members. The Home–School Connection activities in the book give students an opportunity to share ideas, opinions, and values with significant role models in their lives and foster health-enhancing beliefs, attitudes, values, and behaviors.

Parents and other caregivers are an integral part of the development of a child's health behaviors. Unfortunately, one of the behavioral characteristics of adolescence is that the older a child gets, the less they want to share their life with their parents and caregivers. Communication can be enhanced and reinforced with the institution of Home–School Connection activities. Each chapter contains a homework assignment, related to the unit under study, that family members and students complete together.

Traditional Assessment

Shifting from program-based results to standards-based results required new thinking about student assessment. Measuring student progress toward a health standard involves not only recall of content but also demonstrated use of skills. All chapters have a traditional test with a multiple choice and a constructed response (essay) question. The constructed response question generally involves a scenario that requires some basic facts or functional knowledge that the students must include in their answer. The other component of their answer should demonstrate some understanding of the basic skill or skills involved in dealing with the scenario. In this way, students can be assessed not only on what they know, but also on what they need to be able to do.

Alternative Assessment

Recently there has been a movement toward alternative assessment. Experts in education have realized that excellence on written exams does not necessarily demonstrate full comprehension of a subject area. Educators have begun to use alternative methods of assessment, such as papers, presentations, and projects.

In addition to a traditional test, many of the lessons in this text incorporate other ways to assess student acquisition of knowledge and skills. At minimum, each chapter in the book includes a lesson plan and directions for a project in which students will apply the chapter's objectives. Some of the projects are individual, and some require group work. Some projects may be done during class time, and others require time outside of class to complete. The project assignments incorporate Howard Gardner's theories of multiple intelligence regarding how students learn best according to their own personal learning style. Most of the assignments allow students to have some input in how they wish to go about creating their end product, so that they can use their personal learning style to their advantage. Rubrics are included with each project to assist with completion and grading of the project.

Product or performance assessment, selected response questions, teacher observation, student self-assessment, and portfolios are all ways that teachers can monitor student progress. Rubrics have been provided in several lessons in the book to assist teachers in evaluating student work. In other lessons, where teacher flexibility in developing forms of assessment might be more suitable, suggestions about designing formal or informal assessments are provided.

Health Can Be Fun

Perhaps the most important feature of this book is that the majority of lessons and activities encourage a caring, respectful, organized classroom environment and promote a positive, rather than negative, view of health. The activities promote cooperative learning, social interaction, creativity, and a mutual atmosphere of trust, respect, and a joy for learning. If students are shown what positive health behaviors look like and are given the knowledge and skills to practice those behaviors, amazing changes can occur. Health education *can* be effective and—the secret is out—*health can be fun!*

Tools for Teaching Health

CHAPTER 1

TOBACCO

Tobacco Icebreaker

Icebreaker: Tobacco People Hunt

Time Needed

10–20 minutes

National Standards

- Students will comprehend concepts related to health promotion and disease prevention to enhance health.
- Students will demonstrate the ability to use interpersonal communication skills to enhance health and avoid or reduce health risks.

Objectives

1. Students will initiate discussion regarding the use of tobacco products and their effect on health.
2. Students will interview classmates regarding their personal opinions, attitudes, and experiences with tobacco products.

Materials & Preparation

1. Duplicate the Tobacco People Hunt worksheet, one copy per student.
2. The teacher should make sure he or she knows the answers to the boxes in the

People Hunt game.

3. Arrange the desks around the perimeter of the classroom so there is space in the middle of the room to circulate.

Procedures

1. Explain to the class that they are going to begin a unit on *tobacco*. The first activity of the unit will be to play a game called Tobacco People Hunt!

2. Hand out the Tobacco People Hunt worksheets.

3. Advise students to write their name on top of their worksheet so that they do not lose it in the shuffle.

4. Tell students to read over the statements on the worksheet. The object of the game is to obtain as many signatures as they can before time runs out.

5. Students can sign only if they can answer or they fall into the category indicated. NO CHEATING!

6. No person may sign more than once on a page. Students may not sign anything on their own worksheet.

7. Tell students that they will circulate around the room and greet their classmates. Tell students to find out whether the students they speak to can sign anything on their worksheet, or vice versa. Remind students not to forget to find out the answer to what their classmates sign. The first student to get all their signatures wins! If no one has all the statements signed within the time allotted, the student with the most signatures wins.

8. Tell the students to start collecting signatures. You may want to consider telling them that they cannot obtain their first signatures from people sitting next to them. This will encourage them to get up out of their seats and circulate.

9. Continue the activity until the first student yells "Finished!" At this point all students should sit down. The winner must read off the statements that were signed, point out who signed them, and share the answers.

10. The teacher should go through the other statements and have students take turns sharing what they learned from their classmates. Discussion should separate myth from fact, clarify terms and definitions, and be fun!

11. Teachers can modify questions so they can be up-to-date and developmentally appropriate to their students' grade level.

Teacher Background Information: Suggested Answers to Tobacco People Hunt

Since answers and personal experience with tobacco will vary greatly from class to class, it is possible, and even likely, that some boxes will be left blank.

• Snuff is finely ground tobacco that may be snorted up the nose or placed in the mouth.

• Nicotine constricts blood vessels.

• The Surgeon General is the chief medical officer of the United States, appointed by the president and approved by Congress. The present Surgeon General (2006) is Dr. Richard H. Carmona.

- Cigarette ads were banned from television and radio in 1971.
- Four different warnings.
- Three main chemicals in smoke are tar, nicotine, and carbon monoxide.
- COPD stands for chronic obstructive pulmonary disease.
- A lit cigarette may burn anywhere from 6 to 12 minutes, depending on how it is smoked.
- Alveoli are microscopic air sacs in the lungs where the exchange of oxygen and carbon dioxide occurs.
- Mainstream smoke is the smoke inhaled directly into the mouth. Side stream smoke is the smoke that enters the environment from burning tobacco.
- A Group A carcinogen is a chemical that has been scientifically proven to cause cancer.
- The only industry that spends more money on advertising is the automobile industry.
- 85 to 90 percent of all regular smokers begin before the age of 18.

Conclude by telling the class that the topics that they discussed today were a preview of some of the tobacco-related topics the class will be discussing in more detail over the rest of the unit.

Assessment

- Participation in the Tobacco People Hunt activity.

Tobacco People Hunt

Instructions

Walk around the room and try to find a person who *can provide the answer* in the *spaces* below. When you find someone, have them *print* their first name on that *line.* No individual may sign more than two *lines.* You may sign no more than two *lines* yourself. Your objective is to have as many *lines* filled in as possible within the time limit.

Find Someone Who . . .

Knows what snuff is _____

Knows what nicotine does to blood vessels _____

Has never smoked a cigarette _____

Is allergic to cigarette smoke _____

Is an ex-smoker _____

Knows who the Surgeon General is _____

Can remember when cigarette ads were on TV _____

Thinks it's sexy for a 16-year-old girl to smoke _____

Thinks it's cool for a 16-year-old boy to smoke _____

Knows the three main chemicals in cigarettes _____

Knows what one of the warnings on a pack of cigarettes says _____

Knows what "COPD" stands for _____

Would rather date a nonsmoker _____

Knows about how many minutes a lit cigarette will burn _____

Knows the difference between alveoli and ravioli _____

Knows the difference between mainstream and side-stream smoke _____

Knows what a Group A carcinogen is _____

Knows the only industry that spends more $ than tobacco companies on advertising _____

Knows what percentage of all smokers begin smoking before age 18 _____

Tools for Teaching Health. Copyright © 2007 by John Wiley & Sons, Inc. Reproduced by permission of Jossey-Bass. An Imprint of Wiley

Tobacco Lessons

Lesson 1: Tobacco Grab Bag

Time Needed

One 40–50 minute class period

National Standards

- Students will analyze the influence of culture, media, technology, and other factors on health.

Objectives

1. Students will brainstorm what they know about various tobacco-related products.
2. Students will differentiate myths from facts in regard to smoking and health.

Materials & Preparation

Large bag (for example, shopping, grocery, canvas) with tobacco-related products or props—enough for one per student. Suggested items include

- Cigarette pack
- Canadian cigarette pack (more obvious, explicit warnings—in French and English)
- Smokeless tobacco tin
- Tobacco advertisement from magazine
- Roofing tar
- Model of a healthy lung versus a cancerous lung
- Bubble gum or candy cigarettes
- "Free" logo items (camel hat, Marlboro T-shirt)
- A model of a heart
- Running shoe
- A used cigarette filter
- A photograph of stained teeth
- Blood pressure cuff
- "No smoking" sign
- Anti-tobacco poster
- Surgeon General's warning from side of pack
- A sign that reads "$2,190.00" (amount a pack-a-day smoker spends in one year—for example, $6.00 × 365—revise that amount if the price per pack is different in your local area)
- An article of clothing that smells strongly of smoke
- A cup used for "spit" tobacco

- Cough drops
- Breath spray
- Toothpaste for smokers
- Model of an embryo
- Nicotine patch or gum
- Sign that says "Third Thursday in November" (National Smoke out Day)
- Picture of an older woman with "wrinkles."

Procedures

1. Ask the group whether they have ever heard the expression "a bag of goodies?" Tell them, "Well, today, I've brought along a Bag of Baddies, because many of the items in this bag are not very good for your health."

2. Explain that you will ask each student to come up and reach in the bag and pull out an item. You would then like them to tell the class what they know about the item and how it relates to the topic of Tobacco and Health.

3. If a student is stumped, ask if anyone else in the class has an idea about what the object has to do with the topic.

4. The teacher should facilitate discussion, clarify information, and give "hints" for some of the more abstract items.

5. Proceed with the activity until all the objects have been utilized.

6. Conclude by asking students to think of all the products that were discussed today. Point out that most or all of the items discussed were in some way related to the negative effects that tobacco has on physical mental, social, spiritual and intellectual health.

Assessment

- Participation in the Grab Bag activity
- Participation in class discussion

Lesson 2: Demonstration of Tobacco's Harmful Effects

Time Needed

One 40–50 minute class period

National Standards

- Students will comprehend concepts related to health promotion and disease prevention to enhance health.

Objectives

1. Students will list many harmful effects of tobacco smoke.
2. Students will describe several negative effects of tobacco smoke.
3. Students will discuss the dangers of secondhand smoke.

Materials & Preparation

1. One dry hard sponge, one damp moist sponge, one sheet of small packing bubbles.
2. A jar of dark molasses, a tall, thin clear glass cup (8 ounces or more).
3. One pack of cigarettes, one pouch of chewing tobacco, a cigar, a pipe, a tin of dip, and a tin of snuff.
4. Tell Me What You Know handout.

Procedures

1. Have students complete the Tell Me What You Know activity by writing down any information that they already know about tobacco smoke and second-hand smoke.
2. Review the assignment with the class.
3. Explain to students that they are about to take part in several activities that will give them a deeper understanding of the harmful effects of tobacco smoke.
4. Perform the Tobacco Demonstrations 1–4.
5. Conclude with a discussion in which students can share their responses to the activities that were performed.

Assessment

- Completion of the Tell Me What You Know worksheet.
- Participation in the Tobacco Demonstrations 1–4.

Demonstration #1: Nicotine Is a Stimulant

Time

7–10 minutes

Objectives

1. Students will practice taking their pulse.

2. Students will compare resting heart rate to a (simulated) heart rate after smoking a cigarette.

3. Students will discuss the relationship between increased heart rate and cardiovascular disease.

Procedures

1. Ask the students if they know what ingredient in tobacco is addictive *(nicotine)*.

2. Explain to students that nicotine is a drug that is called a stimulant. Like other stimulants *(caffeine, cocaine, crack)*, nicotine speeds up the body.

3. Show the students where and how to take their pulses *(radial, on the thumb side of the wrist, and carotid, on either side of the neck)*. Remind them that they cannot take their pulse with their thumb, because the thumb has its own pulse. They should feel for their pulse with their index and/or middle finger.

4. When all students have found their pulse, explain to the class that pulse is always counted in *beats per minute* (BPM). Explain to the students that they could count for 60 seconds, but there is an easier way to do it. Ask the students if they know the easier way *(some will have learned how to take their pulse in science)*. The easier way would be to count the pulse rate for 30 seconds and multiply the number by 2, or count for 20 seconds and multiply the number by 3, or count for 15 seconds and multiply the number by 4, or count for 10 seconds and multiply the number by 6, or, finally, count the pulse rate for 6 seconds and multiply the number by 10. Explain to the class that the way they are going to counts the BPM is to count how many pulses they feel in 30 seconds and multiply that number by 2.

5. Tell the class to make sure they have found their pulse and to start counting when you say "go." Start them counting and stop them after 30 seconds is up. Tell them to *write* the number down *(otherwise they will forget it)* and multiply it by 2.

6. Write the following categories on the board: *50 and under, 51–60, 61–70, 71–80, 81–90, 91–100, 101–110, 111–120, and 121+*. Ask the students for a show of hands and tally how many students had resting heart rates in each category.

7. Then tell the students that they are going to pretend that they have smoked a cigarette. Remind them that nicotine is a stimulant, and it speeds up the body. Ask them if they can think of a way to speed up their bodies *(exercise)*. Get the students up and lead them through jogging in place, jumping jacks, "Rocky" punches, and twists. Do this for 45–60 seconds, then tell the students to sit down and find their pulses. Once again, lead the students through a 30-second identification of their pulse rates and tally the rates on the board, in a second column next to where the resting heart rates were tallied *(it helps if you can do the tallies in different colored chalk for visual effect)*.

8. Students will be amazed that their pulse rates are so high the second time around. Tell them to imagine that this same thing would happen to their hearts

every time they smoked a cigarette. What might happen to their hearts *(get tired, wear out, heart attack)?*

9. Some students may then ask, "Well, isn't exercise good for you?" The answer to that question is that the heart is a muscle and exercise is a healthy way to strengthen that muscle, just as doing biceps curls strengthens the biceps muscle. Nicotine is an artificial, chemical product that speeds up the heart rate; it could be compared to steroids. It is not healthy. Also, when people exercise, they do it for 30–60 minutes a few times a week and the heart has a chance to rest in between. But the way that some people smoke, such as chain smokers, the heart never gets any rest.

10. Conclude by discussing how nicotine is a stimulant that artificially speeds up the heart rate. That is why people who smoke are at increased risk of heart disease and high blood pressure.

Demonstration #2: Simulated Emphysema

Time

5 minutes

Objectives

1. Students will see and feel the difference between a healthy lung and a tar-filled lung.

2. Students will hear and observe what happens to the alveoli when a person smokes.

Procedures

1. Show students the two sponges. Tell them that the damp, soft sponge is like healthy lung tissue. The dry hard sponge is like lung tissue that has been hardened by tar.

2. Allow students to compare the feel between the two sponges.

3. Tell students that alveoli are little air sacs in the lungs that hold the oxygen when we breathe.

4. Tell students that once the alveoli get hard, like in the dry sponge, they pop. This is called emphysema.

5. Hold the sheet of small packing bubbles up as a audiovisual effect. Slowly pop single air bubbles one by one. Tell students: *"The more a person smokes, the more alveoli they pop."* Continue popping the air bubbles. The more the alveoli pop, the worse a person's emphysema gets. Most of the time, the person knows that they are getting sicker and sicker, but they still won't quit smoking. They are that addicted to the nicotine.

6. Ask students if they know what happens when alveoli pop (it gets harder to breathe). A person is breathing in oxygen, but there are fewer places for it to go because the alveoli are popped and they don't grow back.

7. Conclude by discussing how alveoli function as air sacs in the lungs. If a person smokes, the nice soft lung tissue becomes hard and dry. When this happens

the alveoli can pop, making it harder to breathe. When a person's alveoli pop, he or she gets a disease called emphysema.

Demonstration #3: A Year's Worth of Tar

Time Needed

2–5 minutes

Objectives

1. Students will observe how much tar passes through the lungs of a pack-a-day smoker.

2. Students will visualize what tar from cigarettes looks like in the lungs.

Procedures

1. Hold up the jar of molasses and allow the students to look at the dark, sticky fluid.

2. Tell students that this is what tar looks like, the tar that is in cigarettes. *(Students may comment that the molasses looks like the tar on their driveways. Agree.)*

3. Show students the clear glass. Ask them whether they can guess how much tar would be in the lungs if a person smoked a pack of cigarettes a day.

4. Pour a little molasses in the glass. Ask them, "Is that enough?"

5. Continue pouring in a little molasses at a time until the glass contains 8 ounces.

6. Tell students that this is how much tar would pass through a person's lungs if they smoked a pack a day, according to the American Cancer Society. That is why a person's lungs turn black when they smoke—the tar makes them black.

7. Conclude by discussing how smoking cigarettes places the lungs at risk. Tar collects in the lungs and makes them turn black. The body tries to get rid of the tar, but usually the person is smoking faster than the body can get rid of the tar. The good news is that once a person stops smoking, the tar starts being processed out of the body. Eventually, if the person doesn't start smoking again, the tar will be completely gone after a year or two (but alveoli can't repair themselves).

Demonstration #4: Cigarettes, Cigars, Pipes, Chewing Tobacco, and Snuff

Time Needed

7–10 minutes

Objectives

1. Students will compare the different types of tobacco products.

Procedures

1. Begin by showing the students the pack of cigarettes. Take out a cigarette and walk around the room so the students can examine it.

2. Point out that if you hold it "upside down" the tobacco doesn't fall out. Point out that there are chemicals put in the cigarette so that the tobacco won't fall out, the cigarette will feel nice and smooth, and the tobacco won't rot on the shelves.

3. Ask the students what the filter (the white spongy pad at the lip-side of a cigarette) is and which side of the cigarette it is on (the white side). Ask what the point of the filter is (to filter out some of the chemicals). Ask the students whether the filter is perfect (no, it only filters out some of the chemicals, not all). Explain to the students that the filter is designed so that some of the chemicals get caught in it. Point out that some cigarettes are made without filters because people don't want them; that if you roll your own cigarette (which is possible to do), it probably wouldn't have a filter in it; and that there have been some health problems with little pieces of the filter being breathed in and getting caught in people's lungs.

4. Next show the students the pouch of chewing tobacco. Walk around the room and let the students smell the putrid smell. *(Warning: don't let them take too big a whiff, they may become nauseated.)* Pinch a few pieces of the tobacco and hold it up for the students to see. Note that chewing tobacco is merely the dried up tobacco leaves with chemicals in it.

5. Tell the students that people will put this in the side of their mouth between their cheek and their gums and suck on it. They don't chew it. They don't swallow it; that can make you throw up. Instead they spit out their saliva, which turns brown. This is what they see the baseball players using, although some chew gum or seeds now. (Ask whether any remember the movie *The Sandlot*, in which some kids get sick from chewing tobacco.) The students will ask, *"Why do people use it?"* Tell them that there is a "high," a "buzz" that people get from tobacco. Nicotine is a drug, so people are willing to do some disgusting things to get that feeling.

6. Next show the students the chewing tobacco in the circular container. Point out that this is the same stuff as in the pouch, but it is just chopped up a little finer.

7. Then show the snuff. Pinch some and hold it up and let it fall back into the container like sand or dirt. Walk around the room and do this so that all the students can see. Ask the class what the difference between chewing tobacco and snuff is (snuff is finer). Ask whether anyone knows why snuff is ground so finely (so you can sniff it like cocaine). You sniff snuff, although in this country, people don't really do that anymore. They used to, in "Paul Revere" days. They still sniff snuff quite a bit in Europe. It's just a different way to experience the effects of nicotine.

8. Show the students what the pipe and cigar look like. They are just different ways to use tobacco products.

9. Finally, alternately hold the products up and ask students from the back of the room to read what they can off the different sides of the products. Invariably, they will be able to see the symbols, and maybe the brand name, but never the Surgeon General's Warning. Discuss that they do this on purpose. If the tobacco companies didn't have to put the warning on the package, they wouldn't. As it is, they make it as small as possible.

10. Conclude by discussing how companies that sell tobacco products try to manipulate young people to encourage them to smoke.

NAME _____ DATE _____

Tell Me What You Know About Tobacco

Lesson 3: Tobacco No-No

Time Needed

One to two 40–50 minute class periods

National Standards

- Students will demonstrate the ability to use interpersonal communication skills to enhance health and avoid or reduce health risks.
- Students will demonstrate the ability to practice health-enhancing behaviors and avoid or reduce risks.

Objectives

1. Students will define assertive communication.
2. Students will practice Refusal Skills related to tobacco use.

Materials & Preparation

1. Duplicate the Refusal Skills handout—one copy per student.
2. Props for scenarios (cigarettes, tobacco tin, and so forth).
3. Cut apart the 7 role-play scenarios
4. Write or tape a big sign on chalkboard entitled "We all have special reasons not to use tobacco."

Procedures

1. Ask students to think of times that they let someone talk them into doing something they didn't want to do. Ask the following questions:
   - How did you feel about what you did?
   - Do you have any regrets?
   - Since then, have you given any more thought to how you could have avoided that situation?
   - What would you do differently, if you could?
2. Discuss peer pressure and give examples. Conclude that peer pressure can have positive or negative consequences. If people consider consequences and risks, they can choose to accept or reject encouragement (pressure) from others.
3. Pass out the Refusal Skills worksheet and instruct students to look over the Ways to Say No. Discuss various methods. (Many students have had some exposure to these skills in their elementary school. This can be a reinforcement for them.) Tell them that it is important to plan for situations in which tobacco may be in use. Using Refusal Skills can help them avoid getting involved in something that they might regret, like picking up the smoking habit.
4. Break the class up into seven groups and assign each group one of the following scenarios to act out, using the Refusal Skills just reviewed. Allow 3–5 minutes for groups to assign roles and practice. After each, have the class evaluate

how they resisted (for example, which Refusal Skill they used).

5. Point to the big sign on chalkboard: "We Have Special Reasons Not to Use Tobacco."

6. Then tell students:

   - "If you are an athlete or exercise regularly, please come up and stand under the sign."

   - "If you play a brass or wind instrument, stand under the sign."

   - "If you, or anyone in your family, has allergies, asthma, problems breathing, chronic colds, or coughs, please come up."

   - "If you have a younger brother or sister and you don't want them to smoke, please come up."

   - "If you think that someday you may become a parent, please come up."

   - "If you want to live a full, healthy life and lower your risk of cancer, lung disease, or heart attacks, please come up."

   - "If you like having white teeth, nice breath, and clean-smelling hair, skin, and clothes, please come up."

   - "If you are not a millionaire and don't want to waste your money on cigarettes, please come up."

7. Finally, join the group yourself, and close by pointing out that everyone has special reasons for not using tobacco.

Assessment

- Participation in the refusal skill role play.
- Participation in class discussion.

Extension Activity

- Scenarios can be videotaped and played back to students and parents at Open House.

Ways to Say No

1. Broken record—say no and say no over and over.

   When someone pressures you, simply say no and turn away.

2. Keep saying no (broken record).

   If the pressure continues, repeat the word no. Don't offer excuses or explanations.

3. Give a reason.

   Explain why you choose to refuse.

4. Make an excuse.

   "I have an allergy" or "I tried it once and got sick."

5. Leave the situation.

   As soon as you feel pressured, leave. Don't wait a minute longer.

6. Suggest something else to do.

   "How about shooting a few baskets?" or "I'm on my way to the library."

7. Ignore the problem.

   Change the subject or pretend you didn't hear.

8. Make a joke of it.

   "If I want to hang around smoke, I'll join the fire department."

Tools for Teaching Health. Copyright © 2007 by John Wiley & Sons, Inc. Reproduced by permission of Jossey-Bass, An Imprint of Wiley

NAME   DATE

Refusal Skill Scenarios

1. Your best friend's dad got two free hats from a cigarette company by sending in two thousand labels. Your friend wants to give you one. You think it's ugly and don't want to be a walking advertisement for cigarettes.

2. The captain of your baseball team takes out a little round tin and sticks a wad of "dip" tobacco in his mouth. You never knew this person was a tobacco user and you think it is gross. He offers some to you, saying, "A lot of baseball players use it." He says it will relax you and you'll play better.

3. You are with some friends after school. Sam, an older kid, takes out a pack of cigarettes and offers some to the group. Everyone takes one but you. Sam offers it to you again, saying, "What are you, a wimp?"

4. You are in a restaurant in a no-smoking section. The person at the next table lights up a cigarette.

5. Your favorite aunt just found out she is pregnant for the first time. She is a heavy smoker. She reaches for a cigarette and begins to light it up.

6. Your older sister just started smoking. She says she wants to lose weight and look like the models in the cigarette ads.

7. Your friend's dad has agreed to drive you and two other kids to a soccer tournament 50 miles away. After five minutes on the road, he lights up a cigar. It is cold out and all the windows are closed. You are allergic to tobacco smoke.

Lesson 4: Tobacco Decision Making

Time Needed

One 40–50 minute class period

National Standards

- Students will demonstrate the ability to use decision-making skills to enhance health.

Objectives

1. Students will define the word *risk.*

2. Students will apply the G.R.E.A.T. decision-making model to common problems that kids their age face.

Materials & Preparation

1. G.R.E.A.T. handout (Handout 1.4)

2. Scenario handout (Handout 1.3)

Procedures

1. As students enter the class, the teacher will instruct them to begin the Do Now question written on the board: "What kinds of decisions have you made today?"

2. Students will take out notebooks and begin "Do Now" immediately.

3. After students complete the "Do Now," the teacher will ask students at random one decision they have made today.

4. After each student has gone at least once, the teacher will ask the students some discussion questions leading toward activity.

5. Ask students:

   - What is a risk?

   - Is it OK to take a risk? Why or why not?

   - Why might people take risks?

   - What kinds of risks are worth taking?

6. The teacher will hand out the G.R.E.A.T. decision-making handout (Handout 1.4).

7. The teacher will review the G.R.E.A.T. model with students.

   - G: Give thought to the decision and problem.

   - R: Review all options.

   - E: Evaluate outcomes and each option.

   - A: Assess and choose the best option.

   - T: Think it over afterward. Would you make the same decision next time?

8. Pass out the worksheet and break the students up into dyads or triads to complete it.

9. Allow students 8–10 minutes to work together to complete the assignment.

10. Bring the class together and review student responses.

11. Conclude the lesson by asking the following questions:
    - What have you learned from this lesson?
    - Do you think it is worth it to take the risk to smoke cigarettes or do drugs? Why or why not?
    - Do you think G.R.E.A.T. could help you in the future?

Assessment

- Completion of the G.R.E.A.T. decision-making model worksheet.
- Participation in class discussion.

G.R.E.A.T. Decision-Making Model

Give thought to the decision or problem

Review all your options

Evaluate outcomes and each option

Assess and choose the best option

Think it over afterwards—would you make the same decision next time?

Tools for Teaching Health. Copyright © 2007 by John Wiley & Sons, Inc. Reproduced by permission of Jossey-Bass, An Imprint of Wiley

WORKSHEET 1.2

NAME _____   DATE _____

Practicing G.R.E.A.T. Decisions

Apply the G.R.E.A.T. Decision-Making model to the following scenario:

You are a high school junior. While going to class, you walk behind the building and find two of your friends and someone you have been wanting to ask out for a while smoking. They offer you a cigarette. You've tried it a few times and didn't like it. Another concern, if you get caught, is the loss of your parking privileges.

Give thought to the decision or problem. What is the problem?

_____

_____

Review all options. List them below.

_____

_____

Evaluate the outcome of each option. What are the consequences of each option?

_____

_____

Assess and choose the best option. What is it and why?

_____

_____

Think it over afterward. Would you make the same decision next time?

_____

_____

Lesson 5: Tobacco Talk Show

Time Needed

One 40–50 minute class period

National Standards

- Students will comprehend concepts related to health promotion and disease prevention to enhance health.

Objectives

1. Students will analyze a multitude of physical, social, and economic factors associated with smoking and tobacco use.
2. Students will synthesize their knowledge of tobacco and related concepts through an interactive role-play exercise.
3. Students will practice critical thinking skills in question-answer format.
4. Students will review the effects of tobacco products on lung and mouth cancer, prenatal development, and other health problems.

Materials & Preparation

Fake wireless microphone, and large name cards and props to identify characters:

- Danny Dip (baseball player who uses chewing tobacco)—baseball hat, spittoon or cup, black licorice
- Mr. Phil Mypockets (tobacco company executive)—dress shirt and tie
- Dr. I. C. Cancer (cancer doctor)—white lab coat, glasses
- Barbie Beautiful (cigarette ad model)—sunglasses and pearls
- Mrs. M. Bryo (pregnant mother who smokes)—extra large shirt, pillow to look pregnant, and a baby doll
- Chris Kidd (sixth grader)—school jacket, shirt, or sweatshirt

Procedures

1. Tell the students that today they will be simulating a TV talk show. Explain the format for the talk show. The teacher will be the talk show host, or the moderator, and the class will be the audience. Volunteers are needed to serve as talk show panelists.
2. Obtain six volunteers to play the parts and bring them into the hall. Assign the volunteers their roles and provide them with the background information and props necessary to get "in character."
3 While the panelists are getting ready, tell the audience what and who the panelists are. While the audience is waiting for the panelists to get into their costumes, tell them to prepare at least one question for each of the panelists so the audience is prepared to ask questions right away when the panelists begin.

4. When the panelists have their roles ready and costumes on, escort them into the room and introduce them. The panelists should sit in front of the room at desks with their characters' name-tag visible to the audience.

5. Tell the audience that the topic for today's show is, "Should Tobacco Be Banned in the United States?"

6. Explain that Chris Kidd is undecided about choosing whether to smoke or not. He (or she) was invited to the show to help him make a decision about whether to smoke or not.

7. The teacher should facilitate the lesson, allowing the audience to ask questions and the panelists to answer them. The teacher should attempt to evenly spread out the questions among the panelists. As moderator, the teacher can guide the discussion, acting as devil's advocate, throwing fuel on the fire. Allow the discussion to go on as long as it continues to be productive. The teacher can also "plant" some questions in the audience to generate discussion and stay on track.

8. With one or two minutes left in the "show," bring closure by asking Chris Kidd what he thinks about tobacco now that he has heard all the panelists. Will Chris start using tobacco or not?

9. Thank the panelists for playing their roles. This serves as a subtle reminder that panelists were merely playing a part and that they do not necessarily believe what they said in character. This is important, especially if the discussion becomes heated.

10. Conclude by asking students what the point of this exercise was. Was it a good review? Why or why not?

Assessment

- Participation in the Talk Show as a panelist or audience member.
- Participation in class discussion.

Follow-up Activities

Arrange to have the "show" videotaped or performed before a larger audience in the auditorium. Segments can be used at Open House for parents.

Tobacco Home–School Connection

Home–School Connection: Smoking Interview

Time Needed to Complete

3–5 days

Time Needed to Present

20 minutes during one class period

National Standards

- Students will comprehend concepts related to health promotion and disease prevention to enhance health.
- Students will demonstrate the ability to use interpersonal communication skills to enhance health and avoid or reduce health risks.

Objectives

1. Students will interview a family member about tobacco use.
2. Students will document responses to interview questions.

Materials & Preparation

1. Duplicate the Where There's Smoke worksheet—one copy per student.

Procedures

1. Explain to the class that they are going to have an assignment to complete with a family member. This should not be a sibling—unless the sibling is more than 10 years older than the student. The interview should be completed in person, if possible.
2. Distribute the Where There's Smoke worksheet and review.
3. Assign the due date for the assignment.
4. On the day that the assignment is due, students can share the results of their interview. This can take as much or as little time as is available.
5. Following are some process questions that can be asked to facilitate discussion:
   - Prior to completing this activity, did anyone ever have a conversation with their family member about smoking?
   - Which family member did you choose to speak to? How many of you spoke to more than one at the same time? Did anyone speak to someone other than a parent? Who?
   - What was it like talking to family members about this topic?
   - What did you find out? Does anyone want to share?

- Did anything surprise you during your conversation?
- Did any other issues come up during your conversation?
- What did you learn from this activity? What did your family member(s) learn?
- Are there any other comments or questions?

Assessment

Submission of the completed smoking interview.

NAME

DATE

Where There's Smoke: Smoking Interview

Due Date: _____

Directions

1. Choose a family member (or neighbor if you must) to interview.

2. Create ten or more questions to ask the relative about smoking.

   (a) If the relative smokes, ask questions such as, "How and why did you start smoking? Do you have any suggestions for people my age about smoking?". . .

   (b) If the relative has quit smoking, ask questions such as, "How did you quit? Why did you quit?". . .

   (c) If the relative has never smoked, ask questions such as, "Why did you never smoke?". . .

3. All of the questions should be open-ended questions. In other words, the person has to describe an answer. No questions should be close-ended. Close-ended questions are when the person can answer either "yes" or "no."

4. Write or type out the questions and answers. Make sure you write your name and the name and relationship of the person you interviewed on the interview paper before you turn it in.

5. At the end of the interview, have the person you interviewed write a short paragraph about what they feel is important for you to know about smoking. Attach this paragraph to your interview when you submit it.

Tools for Teaching Health. Copyright © 2007 by John Wiley & Sons, Inc. Reproduced by permission of Jossey-Bass, An Imprint of Wiley

Tobacco Project

Project: Multiple Intelligence Tobacco Project

Time Needed to Complete

3–7 days

Time Needed to Present

20 minutes during one class period

National Standards

1. Students will demonstrate the ability to advocate for personal, family, and community health.

Objective

1. Students will create a project that advertises the negative effects of tobacco use.

Materials & Preparation

1. Duplicate the Tobacco Prevention Experts student handout—one copy per student.
2. Duplicate the Tobacco Prevention Experts rubric—one copy per student.

Procedures

1. Begin the lesson by asking students whether they have ever seen advertisements to purchase tobacco. Where? Can anyone describe any of the ads?
2. Ask students whether they have seen advertisements for tobacco in places other than magazines. (For example, on T-shirts, shopping carts, baseball hats.)
3. Explain to students that they are going to create their own advertisements—but their advertisements will be advertising against tobacco. Their advertisements can take the form of a song, a letter, a poster, or any of the other options listed on the directions sheet.
4. Distribute and review the Tobacco Prevention Experts student handout and the corresponding rubric.
5. Once students understand what is expected of them, give the due date for the assignment and have students write the due date on their project handout.
6. On the day the assignment is due have students share their project with the class.
7. Use the following process questions to lead discussion:
   - Would anyone like to share his or her project with the class?
   - What did you learn from completing the project?

- Do you think your project would prevent others from using tobacco? Why or why not?

8. Conclude by pointing out that if students believe tobacco is unhealthy, they should be more vocal in speaking out against it. Teens are more likely to listen to other teens than they are to listen to adults. The only thing better than not using tobacco is to convince others not to use it either!

Assessment

- Completion of tobacco prevention project. See attached rubric.

Tobacco Prevention Experts!

Due Date: _____

Choose one of the following projects to complete.

- Write a letter encouraging a loved one to quit smoking. Make sure you include how you will support him or her through the effort and acknowledge that you are aware of how difficult it can be to break an addiction.

- Write a letter to a loved one congratulating him or her for quitting smoking. Make sure to include how that decision benefited both himself or herself and the friends and families.

- Create an advertisement to counteract the tobacco company advertisements.

- Write a letter about a tobacco issue you feel strongly about to a politician and voice your concerns.

- Make a poster that illustrates the dangers of tobacco use.

- Write a song, using a popular tune, about tobacco. Convey your message about tobacco prevention.

- Write a poem or series of poems about the consequences of using tobacco or dip.

- Create a bumper sticker, a game, or an educational video. Be creative! You may choose any project you wish as long as the outcome is based on one or more of the issues discussed in class. If you are opting to do a unique assignment, please check with the teacher before you begin to make sure your idea is acceptable.

Project Guidelines

The following guidelines apply to all types of projects:

- The project must contain at least seven facts about tobacco.

- The project must aim to convince others not to use tobacco.

- The project must be eye-catching and attractive to look at.

- The project must be free from spelling errors and be grammatically correct.

Tobacco Prevention Experts Rubric

	EXCELLENT 19–20 points	GOOD 16–18 points	FAIR 11–15 points	POOR 10 points or less	TOTAL SCORE
KNOWLEDGE	Project contains 7 or more facts about tobacco use.	Project contains 5–6 facts about tobacco use.	Project contains 3–4 facts about tobacco use.	Project contains 0–2 facts about tobacco use.	
APPEARANCE	Project is very neat—there are no obvious mistakes or corrections made on it. If applicable, the project uses a lot of color and arts-and-crafts items. People will stop to look at it or read it!	Project is neat—there are no obvious mistakes or corrections made on it. If applicable, the project uses some color and arts-and-crafts items. Most people will stop to look at it or read it!	Project is somewhat neat—there are some mistakes or corrections made on it. People may stop to look at it or read it.	Project is sloppy. People will not stop to look at it—except in disbelief.	
CREATIVITY	Project is entirely unique and creative.	Project shows a lot of thought and creativity.	Project is somewhat creative.	Project is not creative at all.	
CONVINCING	Project is very convincing! After reading or observing your project no one would ever, ever use tobacco again!	Project is convincing! After reading or observing your project most people would never use tobacco again!	Project is somewhat convincing! After reading or observing your project some people would never use tobacco again!	Project is not convincing. People would continue to use tobacco after reading or observing your project.	
SPELLING & GRAMMAR	There are no spelling or grammar errors in project.	There is 1 spelling or grammar error.	There are 2–3 spelling or grammar errors.	There are many spelling and grammar errors throughout project.	

Final Score: _____

Tools for Teaching Health. Copyright © 2007 by John Wiley & Sons, Inc. Reproduced by permission of Jossey-Bass, An Imprint of Wiley

Tobacco Assessment

Assessment: Functional Knowledge and Skills Exam

Time Needed

One 40–50 minute class period

National Standards

- Students will comprehend concepts related to health promotion and disease prevention to enhance health.
- Students will analyze the influence of family, peers, culture, media, technology, and other factors on health behaviors.
- Students will demonstrate the ability to use interpersonal communication skills to enhance health and avoid or reduce health risks.

Objectives

1. Students demonstrate knowledge and skills related to tobacco prevention.

Materials & Preparation

1. Duplicate the Functional Knowledge and Skills Exam—one copy per student.
2. Arrange the desks as needed for exam format.

Procedures

1. As students enter the room, advise them to take their seats, put their books and notebooks under their chairs, and place a pen or pencil on their desk.
2. Explain the test-taking rules to the class. Following are some suggestions:
   - No talking.
   - No "borrowing" answers from a neighbor—if caught cheating, students will receive a zero and a phone call to home.
   - If students have a question, they should raise their hand. The teacher will come to them, not the other way around.
   - When students are done, they should pass in their test and work quietly on a different assignment or read a book while waiting for the rest of the class to finish.
3. Students take varying amounts of time to complete exams. It may be advisable to have some type of activity for quick test takers to work on while they are waiting for slower test takers to finish.
4. Be prepared with an activity for the entire class in case all students finish the test prior to the end of the period. The *Kids Book of Questions* by Gregory Stock provides wonderful questions to spark class discussion on topics related to self-esteem, mental health and other health-related issues. Students enjoy talking about answers to the questions and it may be a relaxing way to conclude an otherwise stressful class period for them.

Assessment

Score on the exam

Answers to Multiple-Choice Questions

1. D
2. C
3. B
4. B
5. B
6. A
7. A
8. B
9. A
10. A
11. D
12. B
13. A
14. D
15. B
16. C
17. D
18. B
19. C
20. C

Constructed Response Question

Evaluate the role of advertising and the media on personal and family health.

Possible Answers: Content

Success, sex appeal, or romance (all are young and have white teeth); adventure (guys hiking up a mountain, but are not short of breath); health ("ours has less tar"); humor (everyone in the ad is smiling or having fun); catchy slogan or jingle; everyone is doing it; special promotions (hats, shirts, buy one get one free).

Possible Answers: Skills (Influence of Media)

Internal: curiosity, likes-dislikes, self-esteem, desire to fit in, lose weight, look like models.

External: peers, family, media, free stuff, norm in your school (do most kids smoke?).

NAME   DATE

Directions

This exam consists of twenty multiple-choice questions and two constructed-response (essay) questions. Please answer all questions.

Multiple Choice

Please circle the correct answer.

1. Tobacco advertisements are designed to make smoking appear . . .
   a. fun
   b. pleasurable and enjoyable
   c. romantic or sexy
   d. all of these

2. At a nationwide average cost of $5.00 per pack, how much money does the *average* smoker spend a year on cigarettes?
   a. $725
   b. $1,095
   c. $1,825
   d. $3,004

3. The main health risk of smokeless tobacco is . . .
   a. lung cancer
   b. oral cancer
   c. emphysema
   d. osteoporosis

4. Which of the following is true?
   a. Doctors can now cure all forms of cancer.
   b. Lung cancer is now the number one cause of cancer death for women.
   c. There is no scientific evidence that smoking increases the risk of lung cancer.
   d. Lung cancer is one of the deadliest forms of the disease.

5. A serious smoking-related disease in which the air sacs (alveoli) become damaged and lose their elasticity is called . . .
   a. atherosclerosis
   b. emphysema
   c. chronic erythrothrombosis
   d. carcinogenesis

(Continued)

Tools for Teaching Health. Copyright © 2007 by John Wiley & Sons, Inc. Reproduced by permission of Jossey-Bass, An Imprint of Wiley

NAME   DATE

6. What group of Americans makes up the largest percentage of new smokers?

   a. young teens

   b. the poor

   c. minorities

   d. people over the age of 30

7. If someone has been a regular smoker for a couple of years and then quits . . .

   a. lung tissue begins to repair itself

   b. emphysema can be reversed

   c. lung cancer will get better

   d. he or she will have an increase in carbon monoxide in the bloodstream

8. Curiosity is an example of . . .

   a. parental influence

   b. an internal influence

   c. an external influence

   d. a societal influence

9. Lung cancer deaths today, compared to fifty years ago, have . . .

   a. increased greatly

   b. decreased greatly

   c. stayed the same

   d. none of these

10. Premature aging and increased facial wrinkles of smokers is a result of . . .

   a. reduced blood flow to facial capillaries

   b. the fact that smokers use tanning booths more often than do nonsmokers

   c. a buildup of tar in the blood vessels

   d. a buildup of formaldehyde in the epidermal layer of the skin

11. The main ingredient in the "patch" used to help people quit smoking is . . .

   a. carbon monoxide

   b. cocaine

   c. lidocaine

   d. nicotine

12. Peer pressure is an example of . . .

   a. an internal influence

   b. an external influence

   c. a physiological influence

   d. heredity

NAME _____ DATE

13. Smoking even one cigarette . . .

    a. speeds up the heart

    b. slows down the heart

    c. decreases reaction time

    d. none of these

14. Cigarettes are not allowed to be advertised on any of these except . . .

    a. television

    b. billboards

    c. radio

    d. race cars

15. If someone has asthma, they must be careful around secondhand smoke because . . .

    a. it opens up the trachea

    b. it irritates the bronchial lining

    c. it decreases blood pressure

    d. the carbon dioxide causes a decrease in the air flow, especially in enclosed spaces

16. According to life insurance company statistics, a heavy smoker . . .

    a. has about the same life expectancy as a nonsmoker

    b. lives about 1–2 years more than a nonsmoker

    c. lives about 7–8 years less than a nonsmoker

    d. lives about 12–15 years less than a nonsmoker

17. If a woman quits smoking before becoming pregnant . . .

    a. she still runs a high risk of having a low-birth-weight baby

    b. she still runs a moderate risk of having a premature birth

    c. she has a higher chance of having a baby with respiratory problems

    d. she is more likely to have a normal weight baby

18. What is the first step in the decision-making model?

    a. List your choices.

    b. Give thought to the decision or problem.

    c. Look at the positive and negative consequences of your choices.

    d. Think it over and consider if you would make the same decision next time.

(Continued)

19. Miranda lights up a cigarette and the smoke really bothers Ramon. What would be an effective assertiveness statement that Ramon could use to reduce the risk of getting into a conflict with Miranda?

   a. "Miranda, your breath really stinks. Put out that butt!"

   b. "Miranda, can I have a puff of your cigarette?" Then put it out when she hands it to him.

   c. "Miranda, I get really nauseous around cigarette smoke. I would really appreciate it if you didn't smoke around me."

   d. "Miranda, you are going to get cancer, and emphysema, and all kinds of other horrible diseases if you don't put out that cigarette right now!"

20. Many teens, especially girls, mistakenly believe that cigarette smoking . . .

   a. makes your skin smooth

   B. causes pimples

   C. controls weight

   D. makes your breath smell attractive to others

Constructed Response Questions

Please write your answer in the space provided. Use the back of this test if you do not have enough room to complete your answer.

21. You have learned of several ways that advertisers attempt to get people to buy their products. This is especially true of ads for tobacco. To try to get people to begin to smoke, or to continue to smoke, advertisers often give a very one-sided or unrealistic picture of the people who smoke.

   Describe three (3) examples in which magazine or newspaper ads portray smoking unrealistically. For each example, explain why it is unrealistic or "false" advertising.

   _____

   _____

   _____

   _____

   _____

   _____

   _____

   _____

   _____

   _____

Tools for Teaching Health. Copyright © 2007 by John Wiley & Sons, Inc. Reproduced by permission of Jossey-Bass, An Imprint of Wiley

NAME _____ DATE

_____

_____

_____

_____

_____

22. In the space below, design your own ad using one of the examples listed above to *discourage* people from smoking. Your ad can be written in the form of a radio commercial, or you may draw an ad on your answer sheet with words or slogans written in.

In your ad, you should describe one (1) internal and one (1) external factor that may influence a teenager's decision about whether to use tobacco. Include in your response two (2) possible short-term effects and two (2) possible long-term effects of tobacco on your health.

_____

_____

_____

_____

_____

_____

_____

_____

_____

_____

_____

_____

_____

_____

CHAPTER 2

ALCOHOL

Alcohol Icebreaker

Icebreaker: Concentric Circles

Time Needed

10–20 minutes

National Standards

- Student will demonstrate the ability to use interpersonal communication skills to enhance health.

Objectives

1. Students will discuss issues related to alcohol with several classmates.
2. Students will compare and contrast their personal and family values related to alcohol.

Materials & Preparation

1. Instructor list of "Concentric Circle Questions."
2. Large open area, big enough for the group to form two concentric circles facing each other.

Procedures

1. Explain to the group that today they will be starting discussions on alcohol. In order to facilitate an atmosphere conducive to honest sharing of information and ideas, they will be taking part in an "Icebreaker" related to alcohol.

2. Ask the group to stand and form one large circle. Then ask them to count off out loud, starting with the student closest to the instructor.

3. Once this has been done, have all the even-numbered students take one step forward. Then have them turn around and take one step to the right. If they have followed your instructions, they should now be facing an odd-numbered student, in effect creating two concentric circles facing each other. (*Note:* if there is an extra student without a partner, the instructor should step in and "play" the game along with the group.)

4. Have students shake hands and greet their partner. Explain that you will be giving them some questions and you would like them to share their answers with their partner. For each question, the inside-circle partner answers first. Partners will have 30 seconds to complete their answer. Then they will switch roles, and the outside circle partners will share their responses with the inside circle for 30 seconds.

5. The activity will continue for about 5–7 minutes. At that point, the activity will conclude and students are to take their seats.

6. Begin by having the inside circle partners talk for 30 seconds to their partner in the outside circle *about their own personal experience with alcohol.* After 30 seconds, say, "Inside circle, stop talking. Now outside circle, talk to your partner about your own personal experience with alcohol."

7. After the first topic has been discussed by both inner and outer circles, switch partners by having the inside circle move two places to the right. Tell the students to shake hands and introduce themselves to their new partner. Now have the inside circle talk to the outside circle *about their parents' policy about alcohol.* After 30 seconds, switch. After the outside circle talks, the inside circle should move again two places to the right.

8. This time the conversation should be about a time the partners saw someone who was drunk. As before, both partners should take a turn discussing the topic.

9. Switch partners and talk about *parties that participants have attended where alcohol was served.* As before, both partners should take a turn discussing the topic.

10. Switch partners and *talk about a movie or TV show participants have seen where alcohol was being used by teens.* As previously, both partners should take a turn discussing the topic.

11. Switch partners and talk about participants' *opinions regarding the legal drinking age being 21.* As before, both partners should take a turn discussing the topic.

12. Switch partners and talk about feelings or *opinions related to drinking and driving.* As before, both partners should take a turn discussing the topic.

13. Send the students back to their seats and process the activity with the following questions:

    • What did you learn about any of your partners today?

    • Were you surprised about any of the responses you got?

- Is alcohol a problem in this school? Why or why not?
- Do your family values, rules, and traditions related to alcohol have an effect on *your* alcohol use?
- What percentage of kids your age drink? Get drunk? How often?
- Did anyone know someone who drank and drove?

14. Conclude by pointing out that many people consider alcohol to be the most commonly abused drug in the United States. For some teens, alcohol can become a major problem, affecting their grades, their health, and, in some cases, their life.

Assessment

- Participation in concentric circles activity.

Alcohol Lessons

Lesson 1: Alcohol Concept Splash

Time Needed

One 40–50 minute class period

National Standards

- Students will comprehend concepts related to health promotion and disease prevention.

Objectives

1. Students will share knowledge and work together to complete the activity.
2. Students will write sentences that demonstrate their understanding of "concept splash" words.

Materials & Preparation

- Butcher block paper
- Colored markers
- Tape
- The following terms written on the board or a large piece of newsprint or easel paper:

beer	party	police
tolerance	parents	blackouts
quit	peer	decision
liver	drive	ACOA
addiction	depressant	refusal
older	media	legal
customs	cool	shower
shots	communication	overdose
religion	toxic	calories
wine	self-esteem	AA

Procecdures

1. Explain to the class that they will be playing a game called Concept Splash. The object of the game is to write sentences using the concept splash words on the board.
2. Students will work in teams and will use the butcher block paper and markers provided by the teacher.
3. Explain the rules of the game:

- Students cannot use their book or notes to write the sentences, nor can they ask the teacher to explain or describe the terms. They just have to try their best to think of sentences with what they already know.

- The sentences must be compound sentences that describe the knowledge of the terms. The teacher is the judge of what sentences are the best.

- Each correct sentence wins a point for the team. No points are taken away for incorrect sentences.

- More than two concept splash words can be used in a sentence, but they will not be worth more points.

- Students must underline the splash word in the sentences.

- If the entire class earns thirty or more unique sentences, the entire class gets five extra credit points on their next exam.

- The writer must try to write in large letters so the rest of the class can see the sentences from their seats at the end of the game.

4. Students will be allowed 10–12 minutes to create sentences. When time is up, students will tape their papers to the wall.

5. Explain to the class that when you divide them into teams, they should pick one person to be the reporter, one person to be the recorder, one person to be the splash checker, and one person to be the facilitator.

6. Divide the class up into groups of 3–4, pass out the paper and markers, and start the timer.

7. Walk around the room to make sure students are on task. Pass out extra paper if necessary.

8. When time is up, tell students to tape their paper up on the wall and have the reporters stand next to their papers. One by one have each reporter read the group's sentences. Alternatively, have each group rotate, sharing one sentence at a time, until all the sentences are shared. Ask reporters to write an "X" over incorrect sentences and put a check mark next to the correct sentences.

9. Keep a master tally of how many check marks or points the class has received.

10. Move from group to group. As the reporters finish their tasks, they may sit down. If a group repeats the essentials of what another group has already won a point for, they will not get another point.

11. As the sentences are read, clear up any misconceptions the class seems to have, and encourage the class to take notes on important concepts.

12. If the class earns a total of thirty or more points, award the extra credit points.

13. Explain to the class that this was a taste of what they will be learning in the next unit. If they have any questions or would like to discuss any issues that were raised in class, they should feel free to discuss them with you.

Assessment

- Writing sentences in small groups.
- Participation in class discussion.

Sample Concept Splash Sentences

1. When people drink alcohol, they can develop a *tolerance,* so they have to drink more and more to get drunk.

2. Some people think they can *quit* drugs whenever they want, but before they realize it, they are addicted.

3. The *liver* is the primary organ affected by alcohol use and abuse.

Lesson 2: Alcohol Simulation Stations

Note to the Teacher

This lesson takes extensive preparation but is an excellent, student-centered way to teach important cognitive information related to alcohol use. It is strongly suggested that the teacher practice the activities at each station. This will make it easier to explain the directions to the students prior to the start of the lesson.

Time Needed

One to two 40–50 minute class periods

National Standards

- Students will comprehend concepts related to health promotion and disease prevention to enhance health.

Objectives

1. Students will participate in activities that simulate the short-term effects of alcohol.
2. Students will discuss the dangers associated with the short-term effects of alcohol.

Materials & Preparation

1. Prepare signs that identify each station and directions for completing each activity.
2. Clear desks and tables and set up stations around the room using the materials around the room. Make sure the materials are evenly spaced around the room to prevent classroom management issues.
3. Bag of marshmallows.
4. Vaseline.
5. Three to four pairs of old sunglasses or reading glasses with Vaseline smeared on the lenses.
6. Three to four spools of thread.
7. Three to four sewing needles.
8. Two rulers.
9. Cooler of ice.
10. Roll of tape to tape a line on the floor.
11. Rubber gloves.
12. Bag of Hershey's Kisses.
13. Thirty to forty tennis balls with two containers large enough to hold them.
14. Permanent marker.
15. Six balloons blown up with the following phrases written on them, one phrase per balloon: "school," "family," "friends," "sports," "extracurricular activities," and "work"; and one larger balloon with "ALCOHOL" written on it.

16. One gallon of water mixed with a container or two of baking soda. Label the water but cover the label up with a piece of paper with "Solution A" written on it.

17. One gallon of vinegar. Label it but cover up the vinegar label with a piece of paper with "Solution B" written on it.

18. Dollar bill taped to the floor.

19. Roll of paper towels (to clean up wet hands or spills).

20. Prepare a signal for students to see or hear prior to switching stations (for example, lights switched off and on, music stopped and started, bell dinged, or whistle blown).

Procedures

1. As students enter the room, instruct them to go directly to their seats and tell them to not touch any of the materials in the room.

2. Quickly move from station to station, reviewing the directions and performing a quick demonstration of what is supposed to happen at each station. Check for understanding at each station. Make sure it is clear to students which direction they are supposed to rotate around the room. Make sure students know they are not allowed to rotate until they hear or see the signal from the teacher (lights switched off and on, music stopped and started, bell dinged, whistle blown).

3. Distribute a blank copy of Worksheet 2.1: Alcohol Simulation Stations to each student and explain to the class that at each station students should record what happened at the station, how they think it relates to the short-term effects of alcohol, and how it might be dangerous to a person when drinking.

4. Divide the class into groups of 2–4 and send each group to a station to begin the activities.

5. After 2–3 minutes make the pre-arranged signal to switch stations. Monitor students to make sure they switch and move in the designated direction. Periodically remind students to complete the boxes on their worksheet. Monitor the class for safety issues.

6. When all students have completed each station, tell students to return to their seats.

7. Review student responses for each of the boxes on their worksheet (use teacher key for suggested answers).

8. Conclude by reviewing the short-term effects of alcohol use and some of the dangers associated with its use.

Assessment

- Completed student worksheet.
- Participation in class discussion.

Marshmallow Station Directions

1. Student A will put a marshmallow in his mouth, *but will not chew it!*

2. Student B will then ask student A what his opinion is on the abolishment of a drinking age. In other words, anyone would be able to drink at any age and not have to wait anymore until age 21 to be legal.

3. Student A will respond and student B will try to decipher what is being said. After 30 seconds, student A will put a second marshmallow in his mouth and continue with giving his opinion.

4. After a minute, partners will switch roles.

Foggy Glasses Station Directions

1. Each student will try to thread the needle with the thread.

2. After completing this task, students will put on the glasses and try to thread the needle again.

3. Please carefully put needle and thread down before rotating, so the materials are not lost.

Dollar Bill Station Directions

1. The student will put her toes at the edge of the dollar bill taped to the floor.

2. The student will grab her toes.

3. The student will attempt to jump over the dollar bill *without letting go of her toes.*

Glaciers Station Directions

1. One student will prepare the stopwatch and get ready to turn it on.

2. Simultaneously, all students will take an ice cube and try to get it to melt in their hand.

3. The student who is timing the group should be participating while recording how long it takes for each student to melt his cube.

4. Students should record their time on their worksheet.

5. Please wipe up water before rotating to the next station.

Walk-the-Line Station Directions

1. Please be conscious of safety during this activity.

2. Student A will walk the line on the floor from beginning to end. Student B will observe.

3. Next, student A will place her palms together and raise her arms straight above her head and look up at her hands.

4. Student B will then spin student A around approximately 5 or 6 times. Immediately following this procedure, student B will guide student A to the line, and student A will once again walk the line. Student B will observe.

5. Partners will switch roles.

Kisses Station Directions

1. All students in the group will take a Hershey's Kiss and put it in front of them.
2. Then each person will unwrap the Kiss and eat it.
3. Next, all group members will put on a pair of rubber gloves, and once again, put a Hershey's Kiss in front of them.
4. Again, each person will unwrap the Hershey's Kiss and eat it.
5. Please throw away any wrappers before rotating to the next station.

Twisted Station Directions

1. Partner A should put both his arms straight out in front of the body with the palms facing each other.
2. Cross arms over each other with arms still straight out. Now turn the palms so they face each other again, and interlock fingers.
3. Now pull the hands in toward the body by going in a downward motion and then bring them up under the chin.
4. At this point, partner B will point (but not touch) to a finger, and partner A will try to move that finger.
5. Try this a few times, on a few different fingers, and then switch.

Tennis Balls Station Directions

1. Partner A will hand a tennis ball to Partner B, approximately 1 ball every 10 seconds.
2. Partner B will squeeze the tennis ball 10 times before putting it back in the basket.
3. After a few balls, partner A will start handing tennis balls to partner B once every 5 seconds, and after a few balls, once every 3 seconds.
4. Partner B must still squeeze each ball 10 times before putting it down.
5. Keep this going as long as possible, and then switch. Please put all the balls back in the basket before rotating.

One Plus One Station Directions

1. Both partners complete this station together.
2. Pour vinegar in one of the glasses so that it is one-third full.
3. Take a second glass and pour the "secret solution" in it, until it is also one-third full.
4. Put the third empty cup inside the plastic tub.
5. Take the cup with the vinegar and the cup with the secret solution and pour them simultaneously into the empty cup.
6. Observe the results.

Juggling Balloons Station Directions

1. Partner A holds all of the balloons except for the balloon marked "family." Partner B holds this balloon.

2. Partner B begins to constantly tap the "family" balloon up into the air.

3. One balloon at a time, Partner A tosses a new one to Partner B, who must juggle the new balloon as well as the old ones.

4. Partner A should toss the balloon labeled "ALCOHOL" last.

5. No matter what, Partner B is not allowed to let the "ALCOHOL" balloon hit the floor.

6. Partner A should be observing what is happening to Partner B.

7. After two minutes, the partners should switch roles.

Alcohol Simulation Stations

Station	What Did You Observe or Experience at This Station?	How Does This Relate to Alcohol Use or Abuse?	How Can These Effects Be Dangerous to a Drinker?
Marshmallows			
Foggy Glasses			
Glaciers			
Juggling Balloons			
Walk-the-Line			
Kisses			
One Plus One			
Tennis Balls			
Twisted			
Dollar Bill			

Tools for Teaching Health. Copyright © 2007 by John Wiley & Sons, Inc. Reproduced by permission of Jossey-Bass, An Imprint of Wiley

Teacher Answer Key for Alcohol Stations Worksheet

Station	What Did You Observe or Experience at This Station?	How Does This Relate to Alcohol Use or Abuse?	How Can These Effects Be Dangerous to a Drinker?
Marshmallows	Hard to talk with the marshmallows in your mouth	Can't talk properly when you drink	Can't communicate, safety issue, can't ask for medical help, can't say no to sex
Foggy Glasses	Hard to thread the needle with the foggy glasses on	Can't see properly when you drink	May trip and fall and hurt yourself, fall down the stairs, can't see things when you are driving
Glaciers	Different people had the ice cubes melt at different times	Different people process alcohol at different rates	Alcohol is metabolized at different rates depending on how much you weigh and whether you ate before you drank
Juggling Balloons	It was hard to keep all the balloons up when you had to keep the alcohol balloon up	Can't juggle all the aspects of your life when you are focused or addicted to drinking	Your family suffers, you may lose your job, your grades drop, you may get kicked off an athletic team
Walk-the-Line	It was harder to walk the line after being spun	Balance is affected by drinking	You may hurt yourself by tripping and falling when you are drinking.
Kisses	It was harder to open the kisses with the rubber gloves on	Motor coordination is affected by drinking	Hard to perform simple tasks like opening the door or using first aid supplies; might not be able to open and use a condom correctly

(Continued)

Station	What Did You Observe or Experience at This Station?	How Does This Relate to Alcohol Use or Abuse?	How Can These Effects Be Dangerous to a Drinker?
One Plus One	The combination of the two liquids overflowed the cup	Mixing two drugs does not equal the effects of one drug plus the effects of the other	You could overdose or have other serious consequences, like getting really sick or much higher than you wanted
Tennis Balls	The faster the tennis balls were passed, the harder it became to keep up with the squeezing	When you drink a lot your liver becomes overloaded with alcohol	You could pass out, overdose, or throw up.
Twisted	I thought I knew which finger to lift, but I didn't lift the right one	When you drink, you think you are doing something properly but you aren't	You make stupid decisions: you think you are OK to drive but you aren't; you think you can dive into the pool OK, but you hit your head
Dollar Bill	Person trying to jump over a dollar bill unsuccessful because they have to keep their hands on their toes	Thought process is distorted by drinking	You think some tasks are very easy, including driving, putting a condom on, or opening a door, whereas they are much more difficult than you thought

Tools for Teaching Health. Copyright © 2007 by John Wiley & Sons, Inc. Reproduced by permission of Jossey-Bass, An Imprint of Wiley

Lesson 3: Drinking and Driving Timeline

Time Needed

One 40–50 minute class period

National Standards

- Students will demonstrate the ability to use goal-setting skills to enhance health.
- Students will demonstrate the ability to practice health-enhancing behaviors and avoid or reduce risks.

Objectives

1. Students will identify goals and life events they are looking forward to.
2. Students will describe high-risk activities that have the potential to end or alter life.
3. Students will identify the consequences associated with drinking or driving or riding with a drunk driver.

Materials & Preparation

1. Construction paper, masking tape, and a marker for each member of the class.
2. Prior to the class, cut construction paper into strips that are approximately 2 by 8 inches long. There should be enough strips so each student can have two strips.
3. Hold the strips vertically (lengthwise) and draw a black line that separates the bottom fifth (1.5 to 2 inches) of the strip from the rest of the strip. With a dark magic marker write random numbers below the line you just drew. The numbers should range from birth to 90 and represent various ages throughout a person's lifetime. Be sure to include ages that are milestones (such as 13, 16, 18, 21, 40, 50, 65, etc.) and that represent all stages of growth.
4. Make an additional strip with the number 17 on the bottom (or the age closest to the students with whom you are working). Set this strip aside and do not distribute this strip to any student. Above the age line write "Party."
5. String (optional).

Procedures

1. At the beginning of the lesson, place a long piece (10–12 feet) of masking tape on the board or on a wall to create a timeline (or string a piece of string from wall to wall and secure it to create a 3-D timeline), and give each student two small pieces of tape.
2. Randomly distribute two strips of paper to each student. The teacher should save the paper with the number 17 on it for himself or herself.
3. Explain that on the bottom of each strip is a number representing an age in someone's lifetime. Tell the class to write one goal, major decision, accomplishment, or other event that might occur to someone at that age in the upper

portion of each strip of paper. Advise the class that they can be creative with their ideas, but they should attempt to correlate the life event to the age on the bottom of their strip of paper. For example, for age 24 months they might write "toilet trained," for age 16 they might write "driver's license," or for age 65 they might write "retire."

Stress that students should write about a milestone in their past or event *that they look forward to* in their future.

5. Once the students have completed writing on their strips, explain that the line of tape (or string) represents time. Using the left side of the tape to represent someone's life, have students come up in groups of 3–4 and tape their events to this line. Ask them to place their strips in chronological order. Continue this process until all students have contributed to the timeline.

6. Using the events that the students have created, tell the class a story about a fictional character, Chris. Go through the timeline and the events experienced by this character. Try to develop the character as though you know him or her very well. Describe the good things in great detail and speak frankly and real-istically about the events that are learning experiences. For example, maybe this person was married at 18, and again at 22, and again at 30. Describe how this could possibly happen. The success of this activity is your ability to cre-ate a realistic character.

7. When you get to the end of the timeline, get very quiet. Explain to the class that unfortunately, this character did not have the opportunity to experience the full life that we have portrayed in the timeline. At this point, add the final strip to the timeline "Age 17/Party."

8. Explain that when Chris was 17, she was at a party. Chris had a good time at the party. Listening to music, laughing, dancing, and drinking. Chris didn't usu-ally drink, didn't even like the taste of beer that much, but well, you know how it is. Everyone else was doing it . . .

9. Explain that what happened the rest of the evening isn't very clear, but one thing is for certain: the decision to drink and drive meant that Chris never made it to her eighteenth birthday.

10. Slowly start to remove the strips toward the end of the timeline. Tell the class that Chris never got to buy a new sports car, that big house, become a famous lawyer (or whatever the students have indicated on their strips) because of her deci-sion to get in that car with her friends the night of the party when she was 17.

11. Begin a class discussion about the activity:

   • How did it feel when you found out that Chris died in a drinking-and-driving accident?

   • What was the point of this activity?

   • What were some options Chris had besides trying to drive home drunk?

   • What are some other consequences of driving drunk, other than death?

   • What other decisions do kids make that place their life in jeopardy?

- What other goals do you have for your future?
- How does it feel when you think about choices in terms of how you are risking your goals?

12. Conclude by pointing out that many times students make risky choices without thinking about how those choices will affect their goals for the future.

Assessment

- Participation in the activity and class discussion.

Follow-up Activities

1. Invite a local police officer or district attorney to your classroom to discuss laws pertaining to alcohol-related accidents.

2. Create a mock trial of a teen convicted of drinking and driving. Assign roles to students, such as defense attorney, prosecuting attorney, defendant, judge, court reporter, and press.

Lesson 4: Dysfunctional Families—An Alcohol Story

Note to the Teacher

The teacher may want to consider alerting a drug and alcohol counselor about the topic under discussion. The counselor may want to attend class to briefly discuss options available to students living with an alcoholic family member or may simply want to observe student reactions to the activity and be available in case a student needs someone to talk to.

The topic of dysfunctional families and children of alcoholics is being introduced using a teaching technique called jigsaw. A jigsaw is a cooperative learning technique that groups and regroups students to share information. The class is divided into "Home Groups." Within the Home Groups, each student has a particular assignment. The students with the same assignment come together to read, discuss, and complete their task. They come to a consensus on what information is the most important and should be shared with all of the students. These are the "Expert Groups." Next, all students return to their Home Groups and take turns sharing the information from their Expert Groups. In this way the teacher creates positive interdependence among group members.

Time Needed

One to two 40–50 minute class periods

National Standards

- Students will comprehend concepts related to health promotion and disease prevention to enhance health.
- Students will demonstrate the ability to access valid information and products and services to enhance health.

Objectives

1. Students will become an "expert" on one of the roles in an alcoholic family.
2. Students will write a story that illustrates the primary roles that family members adopt in an alcoholic family.
3. Students will discuss community resources for children of alcoholics.

Materials & Preparation

1. Duplicate each of the five roles described later in this chapter—chief enabler, mascot, family hero, lost child, and scapegoat. Make enough copies so that each student gets a role and each group has five students in it. If there are an odd number of students, arrange the groups so that some have only four roles to play.
2. The teacher should precode the roles in a way to facilitate dividing into home groups. For example, you may use stickers of different colors: one handout for each role can have a red sticker affixed to it, one handout from each role can have a yellow sticker affixed to it, and so forth. In organizing students into

home groups, the teacher can simply say, "Find the people with the same sticker." In organizing students into expert groups, the teacher can simply say, "Find the people with the same role as you."

Procedures

1. Write the letters COA on the board and ask the class whether anyone knows what the letters stand for. Solicit student responses.

2. If no one knows, explain that COA stands for children of alcoholics. Explain to the class that today's lesson deals with dysfunctional families and roles that children of alcoholics adopt within a family to survive the dysfunction.

3. Tell students that this may be a difficult subject to discuss, particularly for those students who have alcoholics in their family. Tell students that you are available at any time to talk, and that the school's guidance counselor or drug and alcohol counselor is also available to talk.

4. Explain to the class that you will be dividing the class into groups of five. Each group will form a "home group." Each member of the home group will be assigned a role.

5. Distribute the handouts that have been divided between "home" and "expert" groups (as shown in preparation section). Instruct students to find their "home" group members and introduce themselves.

Jigsaw Group Scheme

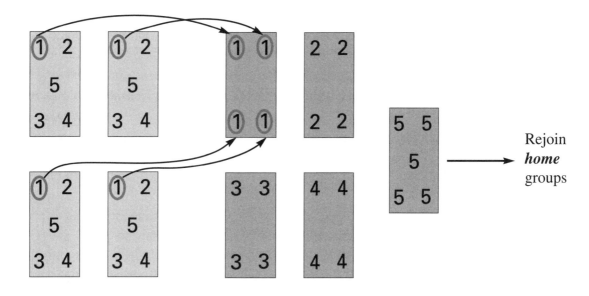

Four *home* groups, with five members each

Five new *expert* groups with one representative from each *home* group

From Aronson et al. (1978). *The Jigsaw Classroom.* Beverly Hills, CA: Sage.

6. Once students find their "home" groups, explain that the students are now going to form expert groups. This means, for example, that every student with the family hero role will form a group, and so forth. It is in the expert group that students learn the most about their role.

7. Allow students to form their expert groups. The members of the expert group may read alone, pair up, or read all together. Explain that it is the responsibility of the expert group members to work together to identify key points in their handout so that when they return to their home group each expert can teach the home group members about his or her topic.

8. Allow expert groups 5–10 minutes to learn their roles and determine how they will explain their role to their home group. Send the experts back to their home groups to teach their group members about the assigned roles.

9. Allow some time for experts to teach home group members about the different roles in a dysfunctional family.

10. Next tell students that each home group is going to have a chance to write a story and apply what they learned as experts to create the story.

11. Distribute copies of Worksheet 2.3: An Alcohol Story and have each home group read it and quickly review.

12. Allow home groups time to complete the story. Walk around the room to check on home groups to make sure they are engaged and on task.

13. Once home groups have completed their stories, ask for volunteers to read the stories out loud and have students identify which story characters are playing each role.

14. Conclude the lesson by asking students whether they know where to go for help if they come from an alcoholic family. Ask students what they think they should do if they find out a friend belongs to an alcoholic family. Solicit student responses.

15. Write the words *Al-Anon* and *Alateen* on the board with the organizations' URL and telephone number: http://www.al-anon.alateen.org (phone: 1–888–4Al-Anon).

16. Point out that these programs are nationally recognized as organizations that can help people whose family members are alcoholics. Discuss some other school and community resources for children whose family members are or may be alcoholics.

17. Reiterate that alcoholic families develop many strategies to deal with alcoholism and the guilt, hopelessness, or anxiety that alcoholism can cause. The most common strategy is denial. All COA characteristics are learned coping strategies to promote survival but not growth. Although these behaviors help children survive with an alcoholic parent, such survival strategies often become problems when the children become adults. For example, a young child of an alcoholic may survive by denying his emotions, but an adult who does the same will be unable to form intimate relationships.

18. Conclude by pointing out that COAs don't have to follow their old behavior patterns. They have a choice. The first step is awareness; the next step is seeking help. You hope that today's lesson addressed both those issues and provided

students with a credible, safe place to seek guidance in dealing with alcoholic family members.

Assessment

- Completed alcohol story and participation in class discussion.

Follow-Up Activities

1. Have students act out their stories in front of the class.
2. Invite a guest speaker from Alateen to come and talk to the class.

Chief Enabler

The chief enabler allows the family to continue to function and gives the appearance that everything is OK. The spouse, parent, or older child of the alcoholic generally fills the enabler role. This person takes on the responsibilities, duties, and obligations of the alcoholic family member. As the alcoholic gradually loses control, the chief enabler makes more choices to compensate for the alcoholic's lack of power. This person is called an "enabler" because by taking on more responsibility, the chief enabler actually makes it easier for the alcoholic to behave irresponsibly.

The Family Hero

The family hero is often an overachiever. The family hero does well in school, is a leader, and outwardly appears to be mature and in control. In order to prove to the world that everything is normal at home, the family hero becomes super responsible. Taking responsibility allows these children to displace all their mixed feelings and energy into success, caretaking, school, or sports. In addition to making himself or herself feel more in control, the hero also tries to make the family look good by taking attention off the alcoholic. Unfortunately, the hero never feels good for long; although he or she might succeed at sports or school, he or she can't fix the family's problems. The family hero is usually the oldest child in the family.

The Scapegoat

Children may also express their pain and frustration with family alcoholism by acting out, becoming trouble-makers, or even delinquents. They may run away, use alcohol or other drugs, get pregnant, or just act rebellious, angry, stubborn, and withdrawn. They tend to do poorly in school. These children are called the scapegoats, because the disruptions they cause distract other family members from the real problem of alcoholism. The scapegoat takes the blame and shame for the actions of the alcoholic by being the most visibly dysfunctional. Although the scapegoat puts on a "tough act," underneath he or she feels like a misfit—lonely, guilty, and hurt.

The Lost Child

Lost children cope with alcoholism in the family by withdrawing or isolating themselves. They deny their feelings, pulling inward, convincing themselves that their problems don't exist and that they themselves are invisible. The lost child has learned not to make connections within the family or community. He or she has few or no close friends, is often shy, and spends much time alone. The lost child remains in the background and is quiet and undemanding, adopting whatever behavior will allow him or her to remain behind the scenes within the family, at school, or in a relationship. The lost child has learned that this is a safe role, one that is unlikely to cause trouble. Most people fail to notice the lost child, because he or she tries not to be a bother. Middle children often fill this role.

The Mascot

The mascot is often a younger child who uses humor or other distracting behavior to take some of the focus off the alcoholic and to inject humor and fun into a stressful situation. If the parent is violently drunk, the mascot may take the abuse to "save" the rest of the family, or may be able to crack a joke at the necessary moment to take everyone's mind off the pain of their reality. In school, the mascot may be labeled as the class clown. Mascots are often cute, fun to be around, and able to use humor to survive in their painful family system. While outwardly mascots appear happy-go-lucky, underneath they often feel fearful, anxious, confused, and unsure. They mask inner feelings with humor, wit, or even cynicism.

WORKSHEET 2.3

An Alcohol Story

Group Members: _____ _____ _____

_____ _____ _____

Instructions

Use the knowledge you gained in your expert and home groups to complete the story below. Following are the characters in the story:

Dad

Mom

Ryan, 17 years old

Kate, 15 years old

Courtney, 12 years old

Jake, 10 years old

- In your group, determine which characters are going to play which role of family members of alcoholics (chief enabler, family hero, scapegoat, lost child, and mascot). Each person in the group should contribute his or her expertise and ideas to assist in developing character roles and storylines.

- You can use your imagination and creativity, but you must include at least three accurate, identifiable characteristics about each role somewhere in your story. These characteristics can be demonstrated by the characters' actions or words.

- In addition, your story should be at least long enough to fill the lines on this side of the paper. If you need more room, continue on the back of this paper.

The Story

Kate comes home from soccer practice at 5:15 pm. She walks in the door and . . .

_____

_____

_____

_____

_____

_____

_____

Lesson 5: Pick-and-Choose Refusal Skills

Time Needed

One 40–50 minute class period

National Standards

- Students will demonstrate the ability to use interpersonal communication skills to enhance health and avoid or reduce health risks.
- Students will demonstrate the ability to practice health-enhancing behaviors and avoid or reduce risks.

Objectives

1. Students will discuss ways to refuse alcohol if it is offered to them.
2. Students will develop a role play related to alcohol refusal skills.
3. Students will evaluate classmates' role plays to assess the effectiveness of refusal techniques.

Materials & Preparation

1. Using Handout 2.1: Pick-and-Choose Refusal Skills, cut apart and, if you wish, laminate the selection slips of paper for these four categories: The Place Where the Incident Occurs, The Person Offering Alcohol, The Type of Refusal Used, and Character Names. Place the slips of paper for each category in four containers. The containers should be large enough for students to reach in and take one piece of paper from each category.
2. Chalkboard and chalk or newsprint and marker.
3. Duplicate the Role Play Evaluation worksheet (Worksheet 2.4), one per student.

Procedures

1. Begin the class by telling the students that you have been thinking about a project for them to work on, and you've decided that you are going to assign a twenty-five-page paper, to be due next week.
2. Allow students to complain and give you a million reasons why they don't think this project is a good idea. If your students are shocked into silence or too polite to complain, solicit some reasons from them as to why they think the paper is a bad idea.
3. Point out that many of them have been using refusal skills to try and get out of the assignment. Use the board or a piece of newsprint paper to identify the categories of responses that they used. Use the categories in Table 2.1 to help identify the types of refusals.
4. If students have not thought up ideas on how to refuse doing the paper in all of the categories in Table 2.1, share the missing categories with the students and then think of what they might have said as an excuse in that category. When all is said and done, the list of refusal techniques should be up on the board or on newsprint, and students should all understand what the techniques mean.

Table 2.1. Types of Refusal Skills.

Refusal Technique Category	Example
Give a reason	I can't do a 25-page paper in a week, I have soccer practice every afternoon!
Make an excuse	I am going to my grandparents' house this weekend—I can't possibly finish a 25-page paper in a week!
Make a joke out of it	What are we, college students?
Broken record	There is no way, are you kidding me? Forget about it!
Blame someone else	I can't do a 25-page paper—my mom grounded me and I can't use the computer.
Make an alternative suggestion	Why does the paper have to be 25 pages, can't it be shorter—like 2 pages?
Change the subject	Hey, did you see what was on the news last night? *(Probably wouldn't happen in this example!)*
Cold shoulder	Students ignore the teacher and talk among each other. *(Probably wouldn't happen in this example!)*
Strength in numbers	All students complain together.
Convince them out of it	You don't want us to do a 25-page paper—then you'd have to grade them!
Leave the situation	Walk out of the room. *(Probably wouldn't happen in this example!)*

5. Explain to the class that they really don't have to write a twenty-five-page paper—you were just pretending! Point out that now they know the refusal techniques. Explain that they are going to create a role play about refusing alcohol, by using a refusal technique discussed in class.

6. Divide the class into dyads or triads.

7. Show the class the four containers with the pick-and-choose papers in them. Tell them one container holds slips of paper with different places written on them—these are the places where the pressure to drink alcohol occurs. One container holds slips of paper with the name of the person who applies the pressure on it, such as friend or sibling. One container holds the type of refusal technique to be used, and the other container holds the names of characters for the role play.

8. One person from each group will come to the front of the room and select a slip of paper from each container. These slips of paper will help the partners or small groups develop their role play. The number of slips selected from the character-names container will depend on the number of people in each group. The number of characters will equal the number of students in the small group—this is how many slips of paper should be selected for the names container.

9. Once students understand what is expected of them, allow one representative from each group to come to the front of the class to select a slip of paper. Once they have selected their paper, the students should return to their group to help write the role play.

10. Allow students enough time to develop ideas, write the role-play script, and practice acting it out.

11. Prior to having the students act the role plays out in front of the class, distribute the role-play evaluation worksheet to every student. Explain that each student will evaluate his or her classmates as they are acting out the role play.

12. Allow students to begin acting out their role plays. As the role plays are being acted out, have the class complete their evaluation sheet. At the end of each role play have the class members share their responses on the evaluation worksheet.

13. After all the role plays have been completed, conclude the lesson by pointing out that today students had the opportunity to practice refusing alcohol. There may be times in the future when students are really pressured to use alcohol. You hope that today's activity will help them know how to say "No" in a real-life situation. You have two other tips to help students refuse alcohol. (1) Know ahead of time how you feel about using alcohol and that you intend to be abstinent. (2) Avoid settings in which the pressure to use alcohol is more likely to occur.

Assessment

- Acting in the role-play scenario.
- Completion of the role-play evaluation worksheet.

Role Play Evaluation Worksheet

Student Name: _____

Name of Class Members	What Was the Scenario About?	What Type of Refusal Was Used?	Was the Refusal Effective? Did Body Language and Tone of Voice Match the Refusal?

Pick-and-Choose Refusal Skills

The Place Where the Incident Occurs

At a football game	At a sleepover at your house; your parents are upstairs sleeping	At a party at someone else's house; their parents are home but bought the alcohol for everyone
At a party at a friend's house whose parents are away for the weekend	In the cafeteria	At the movies
While at a park over the summer	While at a family party	At a barbeque
At a basketball game	At the senior prom	The night of graduation
At a school dance	When you are cutting class during the school day	Before the class play
Before class	During band practice	At the beach
In the bathroom between periods	During class when there is a substitute	On the school bus

Tools for Teaching Health. Copyright © 2007 by John Wiley & Sons, Inc. Reproduced by permission of Jossey-Bass, An Imprint of Wiley

NAME   DATE

On the way home from an extracurricular event	On an overnight school trip	In the car in the parking lot of the school
On a snow day	On a teacher conference day	When you are babysitting
In the school library	On a college visit	Under the stairwell in school

The Way You Say No

Give a reason	Give a reason	Give a reason
Make an excuse	Make an excuse	Make an excuse
Make a joke out of it	Make a joke out of it	Make a joke out of it
Broken record	Broken record	Broken record
Blame someone else	Blame someone else	Blame someone else
Make an alternative suggestion	Make an alternative suggestion	Make an alternative suggestion
Change the subject	Change the subject	Change the subject
Cold shoulder	Cold shoulder	Cold shoulder
Strength in numbers	Strength in numbers	Strength in numbers
Convince them out of it	Convince them out of it	Convince them out of it
Leave the situation	Leave the situation	Leave the situation

(Continued)

Who Is Offering You Alcohol

Your best friend	Your older brother	Your older sister
Your team captain	Someone you want to be friends with	Someone you want to date
A classmate	Someone on your team	A friend
An upper classman	A jock	A college student
A cousin	A next-door neighbor	The newspaper editor
The "most popular" guy at your school	The "most popular" girl at your school	The "coolest" guy at your school
The "coolest" girl at your school	Someone you know from camp	Someone you know from your job
A childhood friend	Someone who graduated from your school 2 years ago	Someone you look up to
A club president	The president of the student body	The valedictorian
Your boss at your night job	A student from a different school	A stranger

Character Names

Shannon	Nicki	Marissa
Patricia	Beth	Ryan
Derek	Christine	Emma
Amy	Mike	Russ
Brian	Mark	Jamison

NAME   DATE

Avery	Maura	Brittany
Jesse	Phoenix	Tanya
Stephen	Erica	Lacey
Gina	Justin	Cindy
Kara	Laura	Stephanie
Melissa	Timothy	Luke
Will	Debra	Felix
Ebony	Dakota	Odyssey
Phoebe	Courtney	Michelle
Toby	Max	Ashley
Dan	Adam	Sean
Ben	Kevin	Scott
Jonathan	Ray	Kyle
Peter	Andrew	Mitchell
Margaret	Evan	Andrea
Cari	Amanda	Jamie
Rod	Tyler	Tony
Hakim	Zach	Becky
Maria	Leslie	Emily
Jerry	Robby	Errol
Jennifer	Jeff	Lisa
Jerome	Brandon	Brendan
Joe	Donna	Tracey
Andre	Jacob	Aaron
Lee	Nick	Wesley

Alcohol Home–School Connection

Home–School Connection: Contract for Life

Time Needed to Complete

1–3 days

Time Needed to Present

20 minutes during one class period

National Standards

- Students will demonstrate the ability to practice health-enhancing behaviors and avoid or reduce risks.
- Students will demonstrate the ability to advocate for personal, family, and community health.

Objectives

1. Students will sign a contract agreeing that they will not drink or drive.
2. Students will discuss underage drinking with their family members.

Materials & Preparation

1. Duplicate the Contract for Life worksheet, one copy per student.

Procedures

1. Explain to the class that they are going to have an assignment to complete with a family member. This should not be a sibling—unless the sibling is more than 10 years older.
2. Distribute the Contract for Life worksheet and review.
3. Assign the due date for the assignment.
4. On the day the assignment is due, students can share the results of their discussion with their family members. This can take as much or as little time as is available.
5. Following are some process questions that can be asked to facilitate discussion:
   - Prior to completing this activity, did anyone ever have a conversation with his or her family member about alcohol use?
   - Which family member did you choose to speak to? How many of you spoke to both parents or guardians at the same time? Did anyone speak to someone other than a parent or guardian?
   - What was it like talking to family members about alcohol use?
   - How many of you signed the contract with your family members?

- How many of you chose not to sign the contract? Whose choice was it to not sign? What were the reasons?
- Did anything surprise you during your conversation?
- Did any other issues come up during your conversation?
- What did you learn from this activity?
- Are there any other comments or questions?

Assessment

- Submission of the completed Contract for Life.

Home-School Connection: Contract for Life

All the statistics reveal that the best prevention of underage alcohol abuse is communication between parent and child. To assist in developing this line of communication, review the following:

Directions

Dear Family Member: Please read, discuss, and sign the following contract with your child to establish a safe option and assistance in case of an emergency situation. Please use this document to begin an important discussion about underage alcohol use and the dangers associated with drinking and driving.

Teenager

I agree to call you for advice and transportation at any hour, from any place, if I am ever in a situation in which I have been drinking or the person driving has been drinking.

Signature _____   *Date* _____

Family Member

I agree to come and get you at any hour, any place, no questions asked, and no argument at that time, or I will pay for a taxi to bring you home safely. I expect we would discuss this issue at a later time.

I agree to seek safe, sober transportation home if I am ever in a situation where I have had too much to drink or where the person driving has had too much to drink.

Signature _____   *Date* _____

We choose to sign or not to sign the contract for the following reasons:

_____

_____

_____

_____

_____

Tools for Teaching Health. Copyright © 2007 by John Wiley & Sons, Inc. Reproduced by permission of Jossey-Bass, An Imprint of Wiley

Alcohol Project

Project: Show Us the Money! Alcohol Grant Writing

Time Needed to Complete

7–14 days

Time Needed to Present

20 minutes during one class period

National Standards

- Students will demonstrate the ability to access valid information and products and services to enhance health.
- Students will demonstrate the ability to use interpersonal communication skills to enhance health and avoid or reduce health risks.

Objective

1. Students will write a grant proposal to decrease underage alcohol use.

Materials & Preparation

1. Duplicate the Show Us the Money! student handout, one copy per student.
2. Duplicate the Show Us the Money! rubric, one copy per student.

Procedures

1. Begin the lesson by asking students whether they know of anything being done in their community to combat the problem of underage drinking. Can anyone describe any initiatives or actions the community has undertaken? Drinking age laws? Advertising regulations? Drinking and driving penalties?
2. Explain to students that they are going to work together to create a proposal to combat underage drinking in their community.
3. Distribute and review the Show Us the Money! student handout and the corresponding rubric.
4. Once students understand what is expected of them, give the due date for the assignment and have students write the due date on their project handout.
5. On the day the assignment is due have students share their project with the class.
6. Use the following process questions to lead the discussion:
   - Would anyone like to be the first to share his or her project with the class?
   - What did you learn from completing the project?
   - Do you think your projects would prevent underage alcohol use? Why or why not?
   - What were some of the best ideas?

7. Conclude by pointing out that if students believe in their ideas, they should write a local politician to share the idea. Teens may have better ideas than any adults have thought of!

Assessment

- Completion of alcohol prevention grant. See the attached Show Us the Money! rubric.

Show Us The Money! Alcohol Grant Writing

Project Due Date: _____

Group Members: _____

_____

_____

_____

Background

The town of Clarksville (population 25,000) has been noticing a large increase of underage alcohol problems: More arrests have been made by the Clarksville police for

a. youth violence

b. vandalism

c. underage drinking parties

d. counterfeit IDs

e. suspensions in school due to alcohol abuse

The school district decided to survey the middle school and high school students anonymously in grades eight and ten to develop a better picture of this dilemma. The results were the following:

1. 24.5 percent of eighth-graders use beer monthly.

2. 38.3 percent of tenth-graders use beer monthly.

3. How easy is it to get beer in our community?

   a. eighth-graders: 67.6 percent "easy."

   b. tenth-graders: 82.6 percent "easy."

4. When do you use beer?

   a. eighth-graders: 22.6 percent weekend (of the 24.5 percent that use)

   b. tenth-graders: 35.7 percent weekend (of the 38.3 percent that use)

5. Clarksville compared to national statistics for drinking:

   Grade 8   National: 19.1 percent   Clarksville: 24.5 percent

   Grade 10   National: 27.6 percent   Clarksville: 38.3 percent

(Continued)

> Now that you have all of the background information, you can begin writing your proposal for a government grant for $100,000. Be specific on how you would spend the $100,000 to combat the above problem.

Requirements for Proposal *(minimum 5 pages)*

1. *Title page.* Include the name of project and the group members.

2. *Review of literature.* Research and discuss existing successful programs presently being used to reduce underage drinking.

3. *Goals of the project.* What will this project try to accomplish in one year? Be specific—give at least three goals. How will you measure your accomplishment? Be specific.

4. *Personnel.* Who will be the staff members? What are their job titles and credentials? Who will be the coordinators of the grant? How much school, home, and community involvement will there be?

5. *Budget.* How will the money be used? Be very specific. All monies must be used to answer the objective "to decrease underage alcohol abuse."

6. *Implementation.* Present plans for implementing the proposal. Create a one-year time line.

Show Us The Money! Alcohol Grant Writing Rubric

	Superior 10–11 Points	Good 7–9 Points	Needs Improvement 6 or Fewer Points
Title Page	Title page is present and contains title, author, students' names, and appropriate graphics.	Title page is present but lacks complete information	No title page
Review of Literature	Three or more resources used. Clearly reviews existing programs in place for prevention of underage drinking. Bibliography page included.	Two resources used. Reviews existing programs in place for prevention of underage drinking. Bibliography page included.	Only one resource used or no bibliography page included. Does a poor job reviewing existing programs related to prevention of underage drinking.
Goals of the Project	The goals of the project are well thought out and discussed in detail. Three or more goals are identified. Goals all relate to the aim of decreasing underage alcohol use.	For the most part, the goals of the project are well thought out and discussed, although not in as much detail as possible. Two–three goals are identified. Goals all relate to the aim of decreasing underage alcohol use.	The goals of the project are not well planned or articulated. Only 1–2 goals are identified and/or goals do not all relate to the aim of decreasing underage alcohol use.
Personnel	The coordinators of the grant are identified and discussed. Ten or more group members are identified by title and discussed. The relationship among the school, home, and community is discussed in detail.	The coordinators of the grant are identified. Seven to ten group members are identified by title and discussed. The relationship among the school, home, and community is discussed.	The coordinators of the grant are not identified or discussed. Six or fewer group members are identified and discussed. The relationship among the school, home, and community is not discussed or not discussed in detail.

(Continued)

NAME _____   DATE

	Superior 10–11 Points	Good 7–9 Points	Needs Improvement 6 or Fewer Points
Budget	Budget is detailed and matches goals and implementation. Budget is correctly computed. The product of the proposed project justifies the cost. The budget does not exceed $100,000 but comes close to the full amount.	Budget is detailed and matches goals and implementation. Budget is correctly computed. The product of the proposed project justifies the cost. The budget does not exceed $100,000 but may be less than $75,000.	Budget is detailed and matches goals and implementation. Budget is correctly computed. The product of the proposed project justifies the cost. The budget exceeds $100,000 or spends less than $50,000.
Implementation	Presents plans for implementing the proposal in great detail. Creates a professional looking one-year timeline. Plans are creative yet realistic.	Presents plans for implementing the proposal in great detail. Creates a one-year timeline. Plans are creative but not very realistic.	Presents plans for implementing the proposal, but the plans are poorly outlined. Does not create a timeline or the timeline is not well planned out. Plans are neither creative nor realistic.
Writing Style	Project is well-written: Written in own words in interesting style. Focused and on-topic. Good sentence structure.	Parts of project are difficult to understand. Some evidence of copying. Writing is not completely focused on topic. Difficult to follow because of sentence and paragraph structure.	Project is poorly written and difficult to understand. Much evidence of copying. Writing is unfocused and off topic.
Editing	Project is neatly done; creative and organized, great deal of attention is paid to detail, writing or word processing is neatly done. Evidence of proofreading and editing. Legible; neatly typed (12 or 14 point size, double spaced). Good grammar, spelling and punctuation.	Project is somewhat neatly done. Some attention is paid to detail, some white-out cross-outs. Some evidence of proofreading and editing. Somewhat legible; typed (12 or 14 point size, double spaced). Some mistakes in grammar, spelling and punctuation	Project is done in messy and careless manner: no attention is paid to detail, too many white-out cross-outs. Little evidence of proofreading and editing. Illegible; not neatly typed. Many grammar, spelling, and punctuation errors.
Timeliness	Project is on time.	Project is one day late.	Project is more than two days late.

Tools for Teaching Health. Copyright © 2007 by John Wiley & Sons, Inc. Reproduced by permission of Jossey-Bass, An Imprint of Wiley

78

Alcohol Assessment

Assessment: Functional Knowledge and Skills Exam

Time Needed

One 40–50 minute class period

National Standards

- Students will comprehend concepts related to health promotion and disease prevention.
- Students will analyze the influence of family, peers, culture, media, technology, and other factors on health behaviors.
- Students will demonstrate the ability to use interpersonal communication skills to enhance health and avoid or reduce health risks.
- Students will demonstrate the ability to use goal-setting skills to enhance health.

Objectives

1. Students demonstrate knowledge and skills related to alcohol prevention.

Materials & Preparation

1. Duplicate the Functional Knowledge and Skills Exam, one per student.
2. Arrange the desks as needed for exam format.

Note to the Teacher

The teacher may want to consider having a number of health-related challenge activities or extra credit assignments available for students who complete their exam prior to the end of the class period.

Procedures

1. As students enter the room, advise them to take their seats, put their books and notebooks under their chairs, and place a pen or pencil on their desk.
2. Explain the test-taking rules to the class. Following are some suggestions:
   - No talking!
   - No "borrowing" answers from a neighbor—if caught cheating, students will receive a zero and a phone call home.
   - If students have a question, they should raise their hand. The teacher will come to them, not the other way around.
   - When students are done, they should pass in their test and work quietly on a different assignment or read a book while waiting for the rest of the class to finish.
3. Be prepared with an activity for the entire class in case all students finish the test prior to the end of the period. The *Kids Book of Questions* by Gregory Stock provides wonderful questions to spark class discussion on topics related

to self-esteem, mental health, and other health-related issues. Students enjoy talking about answers to the questions, and it may be a relaxing way to conclude an otherwise stressful class period for them.

Assessment

Answers to Multiple Choice and Essay Questions (Worksheet 2.7).

Answers to Multiple Choice Questions

1. D
2. B
3. B
4. D
5. A
6. D
7. D
8. B
9. B
10. D
11. B
12. C
13. C
14. C
15. B
16. D
17. C
18. A
19. C
20. A

Possible Answers: Content

Short-term effects on driving ability include

- Impaired vision, coordination
- Reaction time
- Delayed judgment
- Difficulty judging speed and safe following distance
- Depressant effect of alcohol may increase the likelihood of falling asleep
- Short attention span
- Increased risk of "night blindness"

Possible Answers: Skills

- No, let's leave the car here and get a ride home with someone else.
- No, let's call our parents to come pick us up.
- No, let's call a taxi to come pick us up.
- No, let's call a friend to come pick us up.
- No, we live right down the street—let's leave the car here and walk home (may be unsafe depending on the neighborhood and the level of intoxication).

WORKSHEET 2.7

NAME DATE

Directions

This exam consists of twenty multiple choice questions and one constructed response (essay) question. Please complete all questions.

Multiple Choice

Please circle the correct answer.

1. In the United States, there is a warning label on every container of beer, wine, or liquor. What does the warning say?

   a. "Alcoholism is a serious health problem."

   b. "Women should not drink alcoholic beverages during pregnancy because of the risk of birth defects."

   c. "Consumption of alcohol impairs the ability to drive a car or operate machinery, and may cause health problems."

   d. b and c only.

2. Most wine coolers

   a. have no alcohol

   b. have a lot less alcohol than beer

   c. have about the same percentage of alcohol as beer

   d. can be legally purchased by minors

3. Which of the following is a possible long-term effect of alcohol abuse?

   a. intoxication

   b. cirrhosis of the liver

   c. loss of hearing

   d. sudden infant death syndrome

4. Which of the following are illegal in most states?

   a. driving with an open container of alcohol in the vehicle

   b. purchasing alcohol for a minor

   c. using false identification to purchase alcohol

   d. all of these

5. When a person has a high blood alcohol concentration (0.08 percent or higher), they are considered to be

   a. intoxicated

   b. alcoholic

   c. addicted to alcohol

   d. all right to drive

Tools for Teaching Health. Copyright © 2007 by John Wiley & Sons, Inc. Reproduced by permission of Jossey-Bass, An Imprint of Wiley

NAME   DATE

6. Sal's seventh-grade friends ask him to have a beer at a party. All of the following would be good refusal techniques except

   a. just saying "No"

   b. saying "No" and giving a reason

   c. saying "No" and walking away

   d. taking one gulp, then holding the can without drinking for the rest of the party

7. Which of the following can influence how a person reacts to alcohol?

   a. body weight

   b. food in the stomach

   c. how fast you drink

   d. all of these

8. Which of the following groups is designed to help children of alcoholics?

   a. Alcoholics Anonymous

   b. Alateen or a COA group

   c. Al-Anon

   d. AAA

9. Which of the following drugs would be the *most* dangerous to mix with alcohol?

   a. Stimulants

   b. Depressants

   c. Marijuana

   d. Steroids

10. If an intoxicated driver is convicted of causing the death of someone, he or she

   a. can be sued by the deceased person's family

   b. can go to jail for manslaughter

   c. can have his or her license revoked

   d. all of these

11. Which of the following does not affect a person's blood alcohol concentration (BAC)?

   a. the person's gender

   b. the person's socioeconomic status

   c. the amount they drink

   d. if they take a BAC test immediately after drinking or if several hours have passed since their last drink

12. Advertisements for alcohol usually do all of the following except

   a. make it look like people are having fun

   b. make it seem like "everyone" drinks

   c. show alcohol-related car accidents

   d. use humor or a catchy phrase to help you remember the ad

(Continued)

13. A person with a BAC of 0.38 is likely to

    a. be slightly drunk

    b. be able to drive effectively

    c. be severely intoxicated and in need of immediate medical assistance

    d. be telling jokes and enjoying the social occasion with friends

14. A disease characterized by physical and psychological dependence on alcohol is referred to as

    a. intoxication

    b. drunkenness

    c. alcoholism

    d. multi-drug habituation

15. In an alcoholic family where the father is the problem drinker, who usually plays the role of the enabler?

    a. oldest child

    b. spouse

    c. youngest child

    d. the grandchild

16. Alcoholism plays a major role in

    a. domestic violence

    b. spousal and child abuse

    c. suicide

    d. all of these

17. When teens regularly abuse alcohol, they are more likely to

    a. be abstinent

    b. do well in school

    c. have unprotected sex

    d. become better drivers

18. George and Rick stop by Jim's house. They ask him if he wants to go "driving around" with them. They have open cans of beer in the car and have obviously been drinking. Jim says, "I don't feel like going with you guys because you seem to be drunk. I want you to get out of the car and hang out at my house for a while until you sober up." This is an example of

    a. an assertive response

    b. a passive response

    c. an aggressive response

    d. using an excuse to say no

19. A period of time when an intoxicated person is awake but cannot remember what has happened is called

   a. tolerance

   b. synergism

   c. an alcoholic blackout

   d. coma

20. Compared to most regular beers, "lite" beer is lower in

   a. calories

   b. alcohol content

   c. fiber content

   d. protein

Constructed Response Question

Please write your answer in the space provided. Use the back of this test if you do not have enough room to complete your answer.

Scenario

Anna and her boyfriend Brian are both going into their senior year of high school. It is August and they have been invited to an "end of summer" party at the beach. Anna has tried beer before, but usually has had just one or two and has never had enough to be considered drunk. Brian, on the other hand, has difficulty stopping when he is drinking with his friends, and tonight is no exception. By the time the party winds down, Brian tells Anna to get in the car so he can drive them home. Anna does not think that Brian is sober enough to drive, nor is she.

Create at least three statements Anna could say to Brian to refuse a ride home. Incorporate into your statements at least three (3) short-term effects of alcohol on driving ability, one per statement.

_____

_____

_____

_____

_____

_____

_____

_____

CHAPTER 3

DRUGS

Drugs Icebreaker

Icebreaker: Raise Your Hand If You Take Drugs

Time Needed

10–20 minutes

National Health Education Standards

- Students will comprehend concepts related to health promotion and disease prevention to enhance health.

Objectives

1. Students will analyze the pervasive nature of drugs in society.
2. Students will discuss and debate the concept of "good" and "bad" drugs.

Materials Needed

1. "Mystery drug" (a nondescript vitamin, aspirin, or supplement in pill or tablet form).

Activities

1. Inform students today's lesson will introduce the topic of drugs.
2. Without clarifying, ask students: "Raise your hand if you take drugs."
3. Almost always, you will have students look around the room to see who might be crazy or foolish enough to admit that they take drugs. Often, you will have

to repeat the statement. "Maybe you didn't understand me. I said, 'Raise your hand if you take drugs.'"

4. At this point, the "light bulb" will go off and one or two students will raise their hand, generally with a smile on their face! Other students will soon catch on and begin to raise their hand until eventually everyone, or almost everyone, will have their hand up.

5. Ask one of the first volunteers whether they wouldn't mind telling the class one of the "drugs" that they have taken. Tylenol, Advil, or aspirin are very common answers.

6. Ask other students if they can tell the class other drugs that they have taken. Cold medicine, allergy medicine, caffeine, cough syrup, antibiotics, and other over-the-counter and prescription medications are commonly mentioned. The class should then conclude that with very rare exceptions, everyone takes drugs at one time or another.

7. Next, pick up the pill or tablet that you have available for the second part of the activity. Ask for a volunteer to come to the front of the room.

8. Offer the student the "mystery drug" by holding out your hand and showing it to him. Ask him if he would take it and swallow it. Most students will say "No." When asked why, they generally say that they want to know what's in it. You might then say that it is a "secret formula," but assure him that it will make him feel "really good."

9. Most students will again refuse, saying that they don't know what's in it or where it came from. If a student accepts the "mystery drug," ask class members whether they think the student volunteer made a wise choice.

10. This is a good time to make the analogy that many illegal drugs, like marijuana, ecstasy, and cocaine, come from unknown sources and are of unknown quality, yet millions of people take that risk every day!

11. Ask the class to come up with a definition of a "drug." Elicit enough responses so that you can put together a simple definition, such as

   • "A drug is a chemical substance that has an effect (change) on the mind or body."

12. Explain that one of the reasons drugs are so popular is that they generally do what people expect them to do. If someone took a drug and it did absolutely nothing, it wouldn't be a very popular drug.

13. Conclude the activity by pointing out that drugs can be used medicinally or they can be abused. When people hear the word *drug*, they often think of substances like alcohol or marijuana. However, over-the-counter and prescription drugs can improve the quality of many people's lives dramatically and in some cases help keep them alive. Unfortunately, medicinal drugs have a downside when they are abused. The misuse and abuse of alcohol, tobacco, and other drugs is a very big problem in our society. By learning more about some of the dangers and negative health effects of commonly abused drugs, students will be able to make informed decisions about the role that chemical substances will play in their lives.

Drugs Lessons

Lesson 1: Paper Plate Pharmacology

Time Needed

One 40–50 minute class period

National Standards

- Students will comprehend concepts related to health promotion and disease prevention to enhance health.

Objective

1. Students will match common legal and illegal drugs with slang names and classifications.

Materials & Preparation

Thirty paper plates, each one labeled with a drug name, slang term, drug category, or other drug-related term. Following are sample terms that might be used:

Alcohol	Heroin	Addict
Wine	Ecstasy	Withdrawal
Powder	Designer drug	Tobacco
Cocaine	Opium	Nicotine
Narcotic	Morphine	Glue
Inhalant	LSD	Downers
OTC	Acid	Caffeine
Aspirin	Marijuana	Stimulant
Prescription	THC	Legal
Ritalin	Depressant	Illegal

Procedures

1. Explain to the class that they are going to play a game called Paper Plate Pharmacology.

2. Explain that each student is going to receive a paper plate with a term on it. The term may be a category of drug, a slang name for a drug, a type of drug, or other drug-related term.

3. Students should hold their plate in front of them, word facing out, and walk around the room until they find someone that they can match up with.

   There are many ways to make a match. For instance, similar drugs may match, drugs within a category may match, or a slang name and a proper name for a drug may match:

- Tobacco: nicotine
- Glue: inhalant
- Legal: aspirin

4. Once students understand the rules of the game, allow them to get up and walk around the room to find a "match."

5. When all students have been paired, instruct them to discuss for one minute why they are paired up. This will allow them to exchange information about what they know or don't know about the drugs or other terms on their plates.

6. Then go around the room and have all the students explain what they know about the word on their plate and why they are paired up with their partner. This serves as a good informational activity for a drug unit, since it generates a broad, though brief description of many legal and illegal drugs.

7. Note: Each time the activity is attempted, the pairings may be slightly different. More than one "match" is possible for many of the cards. If students are having difficulty, ask other students to assist them with pairings. You may also have to intervene on occasion to form some pairings.

8. Conclude the activity by telling students that over the course of the unit they will be studying many of these drugs in greater depth. If at any time students have questions, they should feel free to ask them.

Assessment

- Participation in the paper plate activity.
- Participation in class discussion.

Lesson 2: Refusal Skills and Marijuana

Time Needed

One 40–50 minute class period

National Standards

- Students will comprehend concepts related to health promotion and disease prevention to enhance health.
- Students will demonstrate the ability to use interpersonal communication skills to enhance health and avoid or reduce health risks.
- Students will demonstrate the ability to practice health-enhancing behaviors and avoid or reduce risks.

Objectives

1. Students will identify Myths and Facts related to marijuana.
2. Students will discuss the importance of refusal skills and the ability to say no to drugs.

Materials & Preparation

1. The Pot Party: Separating Myths from Facts worksheet (Worksheet 3.1), one for each student.
2. Dear Abby handout (Handout 3.1), one for each student.

Procedures

1. Inform students that this will be a short quiz to determine their knowledge about marijuana. The quiz is in the form of an imaginary story. Each of the underlined, numbered statements should be read as a separate statement that is either a true Fact about marijuana or a false Myth about marijuana. On their separate answer sheet, students should write the numbers 1 through 20 and simply write the word Fact or Myth for each statement.
2. When students have completed this, collect papers and review and discuss the correct answers.
3. Next, inform students that they are going to play a game called the Right Choice Activity.
4. Have the class stand in a circle.
5. Choose one person to be in the middle of the circle.
6. Explain that the game is played just like the traditional Rocks, Paper, Scissors.
7. Have everyone in the circle turn around and face out of the circle.
8. Count: one, two, three, go!
9. At the word "Go!" everyone in the circle turns and does one of the hand signals.
10. The person in the middle also chooses one of the three hand signals.

11. Everyone in the circle checks to see how they did against the person in the middle.

12. Play a few rounds just to get the feel of the game.

13. After each round or two, change the person in the middle.

14. For the second part of the activity, change the rules slightly.

15. If you are beaten by the person in the middle, you have to sit down.

16. If you have the same hand sign as the person in the middle, nothing happens.

17. Play a few rounds until most people are sitting.

18. Repeat the activity as many times as you wish.

19. Repeat again with one more change.

20. Get everyone back into the circle, except for one person in the middle.

21. This time have the person in the middle announce what hand motion they're going to do before you start counting.

22. You will probably need to do this part of the activity only once to show that when you know which hand signal to anticipate, your own hand signal choice is easy to make.

23. Discussion questions:
    - Did you always use the same hand signal for each round? Why or why not?
    - How hard was the game when you knew what the person in the middle was going to do?
    - Do different situations in which you are being pressured to do drugs require different types of responses?
    - What would happen if you used the same response in all situations?
    - How would you tell your best friend "no"?
    - How would you tell a stranger "no"?
    - How would you tell someone you sort of knew "no"?
    - Would the situation you are in determine how you say "no"?
    - Give some examples of what you would say to successfully refuse drugs.
    - If you knew in advance what the situation might be and planned ahead, would it be easier to say "no"?

24. If time allows, pass out the Dear Abby worksheet and have the students complete it in class. If there is not enough time to complete this activity it can be sent home as a homework assignment.

25. Conclude by pointing out that one of the best ways to refuse marijuana is to know how you feel about using it in the first place and then practicing ways to say "no" before being asked to use it. Practice make perfect!

Assessment

- Completion of The Pot Party worksheet.
- Participation in the Rocks, Paper, Scissors activity.
- Participation in class discussion.

The Pot Party: Separating Myths from Facts

Instructions

In the story that follows, each underlined, numbered statement should be taken as a separate myth (false) or fact (true) statement. On your answer sheet, simply write whether you believe the statement is a myth or a fact.

Chris, age sixteen, arrived at the party about 9 p.m. He saw some of his friends in a corner of the room and went over and said, "Hey, wassup?"

"Just chillin," said Kate, as she took a toke on a joint. "Your turn," she said, as she handed him the marijuana cigarette.

"Nah, not right now," he said. "I'm on my good behavior tonight. Football season, you know. I'm not really into pot, but thanks anyway."

"It's only pot, man," said Phil, the starting halfback. "It's not like it's gonna kill you or anything."

"I just don't feel like it, OK? We *do* have a game tomorrow you know!" said Chris.

"So what?" replied Phil. "It's not like we're gonna have a hangover or anything." (1) Pot doesn't have anything in it that can hurt you.

Chris decided to just take one hit. He had heard that (2) smoking marijuana isn't as bad as smoking tobacco. (3) Marijuana is a natural herb and has no tar or nicotine or other cancer-causing chemicals in it. (4) Besides, Phil got it from his best friend, Ryan, so he was positive that it wasn't "laced" with anything. (5) Smoking one joint would cause a lot less lung irritation than smoking one tobacco cigarette. He remembered hearing in health class that (6) the main ingredient that gets you high from pot is called PCP. He also learned that (7) marijuana comes from the opium poppy and (8) in New York State, it is legal to have a small amount of marijuana for personal use. He also seemed to recall hearing that (9) marijuana is used in medicine to help cure cancer. (10) It is also sometimes prescribed to people living with AIDS to help stimulate their appetite.

Chris's father told him that (11) the pot around now is a lot more potent than the pot that was around 20 or 30 years ago. His dad also told him that (12) marijuana can cause a psychological addiction and that (13) some people can also develop a physical addiction to marijuana.

(Continued)

(14) Marijuana can also make your heart beat faster, (15) dilate the capillaries in your eyes, and (16) make your eyebrows fall off.

In his defensive driving course, Chris remembered the instructor saying that (17) teenagers who drive while under the influence of marijuana actually drive better because they are more cautious. Unlike alcohol, (18) marijuana does not distort your judgment.

Chris decided that he would only have one hit and then his friends would get off his case. But just then, someone else in the group offered him a (19) blunt, which is a sliced open cigar stuffed with marijuana. He didn't smoke, so when he tried to inhale he started coughing and his eyes got all red. He felt stupid in front of his fellow senior. Statistics showed that (20) over 90 percent of high school seniors around the country smoke pot regularly. He knew some seniors went to class stoned. They usually just sleep during the boring lectures. Even if they were awake, they probably wouldn't remember much because (21) marijuana affects your short-term memory.

Chris decided that he had had enough. Why do something he didn't really want to do? He heard that some coaches were giving their players drug tests and that (22) marijuana can be detected for up to several weeks after smoking. (23) Most teenagers who smoke pot do not go on to other "harder" drugs. But he knew that (24) using marijuana increases the chance that he would be more likely to be around people who might use and/or sell other drugs. (25) Marijuana is considered a "gateway" drug. Although he had experimented, he was glad that he never really got into smoking tobacco. He also had a beer now and then, but he thought it was pretty dumb when his buddies would get really drunk and get sick and act like jerks.

He was hoping to get a football scholarship next year. (26) Getting arrested for possession of marijuana could affect his ability to get into a good college.

"I'm outta here," he said. "I'm gonna be ready for the game tomorrow. I sure hope you guys will be ready too."

Tools for Teaching Health. Copyright © 2007 by John Wiley & Sons, Inc. Reproduced by permission of Jossey-Bass, An Imprint of Wiley

Answers to the Pot Party Worksheet

1. *Myth*
2. *Myth*
3. *Myth*
4. *Myth*
5. *Myth*
6. *Myth*
7. *Myth*
8. *Fact*
9. *Myth*
10. *Fact*
11. *Fact*
12. *Fact*
13. *Fact*
14. *Fact*
15. *Fact*
16. *Myth*
17. *Myth*
18. *Myth*
19. *Fact*
20. *Myth*
21. *Fact*
22. *Fact*
23. *Myth*
24. *Fact*
25. *Fact*
26. *Fact*

NAME   DATE

Dear Abby: Marijuana

Dear Abby,

   I am very concerned about my friend Sue. She told me that she smoked weed with her older brother. First of all, what is weed? Is it legal? What are the effects? What should I do if she asks me to try it with her? I am very upset. Please tell me everything I need to know.

Your Friend,

Upset

Tools for Teaching Health. Copyright © 2007 by John Wiley & Sons, Inc. Reproduced by permission of Jossey-Bass, An Imprint of Wiley

Lesson 3: How Social Is Norm? Using Social Norms to Assess Current Student Knowledge, Beliefs, and Attitudes

Note to the Teacher

Current research suggests that when students believe that most or almost all of their peers are engaging in a risky behavior, *they are more likely to do so themselves.* Conversely, when students believe that they are in the majority with respect to positive health beliefs, attitudes, and behaviors, *they will continue to engage in those health-enhancing ways.*

Very often however, adolescents overestimate the norm (that is, "Everyone smokes," or "Everyone gets drunk on weekends") or underestimate the norm ("10 percent of the seniors are abstinent"). Activities related to social norm theory seek to correct such mistaken beliefs so that students can see that in many cases, *positive, healthy behaviors are the norm.*

The statistics in this lesson are from the *2003 YRBS Survey,* administered by the Centers for Disease Control (CDC). If the statistics become out of date, simply change the statements to reflect the current statistics. They can be found at the following URL: http://www.cdc.gov/HealthyYouth/yrbs/index.htm

Time Needed

One 40–50 minute class period

National Standards

- Students will comprehend concepts related to health promotion and disease prevention to enhance health.

- Students will analyze the influence of family, peers, culture, media, technology, and other factors on health behaviors.

Objectives

1. Students will analyze how the perceptions of norms influence healthy and unhealthy behaviors.

2. Students will predict, estimate, infer, and evaluate data from the Youth Risk Behavior Survey.

3. Students will analyze personal susceptibility to injury, illness, or death if engaging in unhealthy behaviors.

Materials

Three large signs in different places around the room:

Agree	Disagree	Not Sure

Procedures

1. Point to the Agree, Not Sure, and Disagree signs around the room. Explain to the class that you will be reading *ten* statements related to drug use in the

United States. The statements are based on the results of the latest (2003) National Youth Risk Behavior Survey, conducted every two years by the Centers for Disease Control. These are the actual results of anonymous and random responses from teenagers all over the country.

2. Tell the students that when you read a statement, you want students to stand under one of the signs. Tell the students to try to take the position Agree or Disagree, but if they are really torn between supporting or opposing a statement, they should stand under the Not Sure sign.

3. Read the first statement to the class:

The percentage of teenagers who smoke cigarettes (have had one or more in last 30 days) has *decreased* in the last 6 years.

4. Prompt the class to stand up and move toward the sign that best represents what they think about that statement. Once all students have situated themselves under a sign, share the answer with the class.

The correct answer would be AGREE. *Teen smoking has shown a fairly big decrease in the last 6 years (decreased from 36 percent in 1997 to 22 percent in 2003).*

5. Can anyone think of some reason that it has gone down? (*Possible answers: enforcement of laws selling to minors, cost, not "cool" to smoke.*)

6. Using the same procedures as the first question above, read the following questions to the class (leave time between each for discussion):

The percentage of students who have ever tried marijuana has *increased* in the last 6 years.
DISAGREE (*gone down—47 percent in 1997 versus 40 percent in 2003*).
The percentage of students who have had an alcoholic beverage in the last 30 days has *increased* in the last 6 years
DISAGREE (*51 percent to 45 percent*).
The percentage of students who have ever sniffed glue, breathed the contents of aerosol spray cans, or inhaled any paints or sprays to get high has *stayed about the same* since 1995.
DISAGREE (*gone down from 20 percent to 12 percent*).
Since 1993, the percentage of students who have used any form of cocaine has *decreased.*
DISAGREE (*gone up from 5 percent to almost 9 percent*).
Since 1993, the percentage of students who have taken illegal steroids has *increased.*
AGREE (*from 2 percent in 1993 to 6 percent in 2003*).
When it comes to binge drinking (five or more drinks in a row within a couple of hours), male binge drinking is almost twice as high as female binge drinking.

DISAGREE (almost the same: males 29 percent, females 28.3 percent).

According to the 2003 survey, approximately 52 percent of students have been offered, sold, or given an illegal drug on school property by someone in the last 12 months.

DISAGREE (about 29 percent).

The percentage of students who tried marijuana for the first time before age 13 was 3 percent.

DISAGREE (about 10 percent).

In virtually all surveys, males had a higher involvement with drugs than females.

AGREE.

The percentage of all students who have ever used ecstasy in 2003 was 29 percent.

DISAGREE (about 11 percent).

7. After all the questions have been read, use the following further questions to process the activity:

   • Which questions did many of you *overestimate* the percentage of students engaged in the health risk behaviors? Which did you underestimate? Why do you think many of you tended to believe that a higher percentage of students were engaged in unhealthy behavior than actually were? (For example, peer influences; idea that "everybody is doing it"; the media seems to make it seem like everyone is drinking, smoking, having unprotected sex; thinking it's cool to do.)

   • Of the above influences, which one has the greatest influence on your age group? Why?

   • Do you think that parents and other caregivers can influence teenagers to make healthy choices and behaviors? How? What "advice" have you gotten from adults related to any of these issues? Is it easy to talk to parents and other caregivers about these issues? Why or why not?

   • What *generalizations* can you make about the results of the Youth Risk Behavior Survey? Which answers were you least surprised about? Which answers were you most surprised about?

   • The statistics in this activity were taken from the National Youth Risk Behavior Survey. How do you think your *state* compares with the national statistics? Why do you feel this way?

   • Do you think the youth in the United States are getting *healthier* or *unhealthier?* Why? What can be done to improve the health of our nation's young people?

   • Do you think that health classes can make a difference in improving the health of students? Why or why not? If so, how can they best accomplish this?

8. Conclude the class by reiterating that young people are actually more healthy than many people are led to believe.

Extension Activities

1. In small groups, students can create products (posters, brochures, PowerPoint presentations) to encourage students to engage in healthier behaviors. Results from the Youth Risk Behavior Survey can be incorporated into the project.

2. Students can present information to younger students, advocating for healthy lifestyles, especially when it comes to drugs. They can write letters to school administration, board of education, and legislators to advocate for more health or P.E. class time, healthier snacks in vending machines, and so forth.

Lesson 4: The "I's" Have It—
Assertiveness Role Playing Activities

Time Needed

Two 40–50 minute class periods

National Standards

- Students will demonstrate the ability to use interpersonal communication skills to enhance health and avoid or reduce health risks.
- Students will demonstrate the ability to practice health-enhancing behaviors and avoid or reduce risks.

Objectives

1. Students will design skits demonstrating an Assertive, Aggressive, or Passive response related to drug use.
2. Students will practice "I" messages and assertiveness skills.
3. Students will demonstrate strategies to prevent or resolve conflicts without physical or emotional harm to self or others.
4. Students will demonstrate healthy ways to express needs, wants, and feelings.
5. Students will apply effective verbal and nonverbal communication skills into real-life situations involving the use and misuse of chemical substances.

Materials & Preparation

1. Three large signs with Assertive, Passive, and Aggressive written in bold print.
2. Communication Styles Student Handout, one copy per student.
3. Sample scenarios for student skits and role plays.
4. Assertiveness Skills: Role-Play Rubric, one copy per student or group.
5. Tape.

Procedures

Day 1

1. Introduce the concept of conflict and ask students to give examples of conflicts they observe in school or at home.
2. Lead students in a discussion about how people respond to these conflicts and what the consequences might be.
3. Hold up the Passive sign. Walk to one end of the room and explain that passive people do not like confrontation, let things that bother them go without responding, and have trouble standing up for themselves. They will sometimes do things they do not want to do because *they have trouble saying "No."* Tape the Passive sign on the wall.

4. Hold up the Aggressive sign and stand on the extreme opposite end of the classroom. Explain that *aggressive people are bossy and may always seek to get their own way.* They may appear rude, loud, and at times threatening. Tape the Aggressive sign on the wall.

5. Finally, hold up the Assertive sign and stand in the middle of the room. Explain that *assertive people can stand up for themselves without having to hurt or use others.* They can be honest about how they feel but can also be sensitive to someone else's feelings. Very often they are willing to compromise to achieve a win-win situation. Tape the Assertive sign on the wall.

6. Explain to students that from time to time we all use each of these communication styles. Depending on the situation, any one of these styles might be appropriate. Occasionally, being Passive may be the most appropriate behavior (if a mugger has a gun and asks for your wallet). Some situations may require an Aggressive response (someone is attempting to abduct your child from the playground). But research on conflict indicates that knowing how to be Assertive can be a very important skill to have in your personal and professional lives.

7. At this point, the teacher should provide an example of a situation illustrating each of the types of communication styles. The following scenario is a common one that students can relate to.

Situation: You are in a restaurant. You order a hamburger well-done. When it comes, it is very rare. The teacher can play the part of the waiter. Ask for students to play the role of customer.

The three responses should go something like this:

PASSIVE RESPONSE	AGGRESSIVE RESPONSE	ASSERTIVE RESPONSE
"I don't like my food cooked this rare, but I feel uncomfortable saying anything. I'll just try to eat it."	"Hey waiter, this burger is so rare I can hear it Moo! Get me the manager right now!"	"Excuse me, but I am afraid that this is just too rare. May I please have this more well done?"

8. Distribute the Communication Styles handout (Handout 3.3) about passive, assertive, and aggressive communication.

9. Explain to the class that communication can be an important skill in their personal or professional relationships.

10. Explain that I-messages are statements that can be used in a variety of situations but most often are used to honestly express feelings and needs about something that's going on that is bothering someone or making them feel uncomfortable.

11. Explain that there are many forms of I-messages, but they all have the same basic ideas in common. I-messages focus on

   • A particular behavior or statement

- The effect that behavior is having on you
- The feelings that result from that behavior and why you feel that way
- What you want or need from the other person to do or *stop* doing

12. Have students look at the descriptions of passive, assertive, and aggressive behavior outlined in the boxes of Handout 3.3. Ask students to recall some situations in which they witnessed or experienced any of these types of behaviors (no personal names please!!).

13. Discuss the I-message format.

14. Point out that I-messages are extremely useful when attempting to solve a conflict in an assertive fashion.

15. As a class or individually, have the students work through the I-message example given.

16. Explain to students that they are going to be involved in an activity that tries to illustrate the different types of communication styles. All of the scenarios will deal with alcohol or other drugs.

17. Pair off students (some scenarios may be a small group of three or four to even out the number of students in your class). Assign each group a scenario from suggested list.

18. Distribute the role play rubrics, either one rubric per student or one rubric per pair or small group. Tell students to use the rubric to help them develop their skit. Explain that you will be using the rubric to assess the skits.

19. Allow students 5–10 minutes to work out a brief (30 second to 1 minute) skit that deals with the situation in a Passive, Assertive, or Aggressive manner—whichever manner they deem to be the most appropriate given the particular situation. Every student must have a speaking part in the skit.

20. Remind students that there is to be no actual physical contact or inappropriate language in the skit—even if they chose to role play the aggressive communication style.

Day 2: Presentation of Skits

1. Allow pairs or small groups a minute to review the skit that they put together the previous day.

2. One by one, call on student groups come up to the front of the class and act out their skit.

3. Class members are to observe their classmates' skit and determine which method of communication was exhibited in the skit. Tell class members to use the rubrics distributed the previous day to assess their classmates during the role play. Remind the class that you will be doing the same.

4. After each skit, have a class discussion about the following:

   - How the drug use in the scenario might have resulted in their health or the health of others being harmed.
   - The possible short- or long-term effects of their decision to ignore or deal with the situation, including effects on friendships and relationships.

- Which communication style was used—was it the most effective way to promote health?
- If the skit involved Aggressive or Passive behavior, ask students whether they thought the behavior was helpful or appropriate for the particular situation. If not, how could an Assertive response have been better? Very often characters in the scenarios will exhibit more than one behavior that the class can pick out. (For Example: Parent was Aggressive and son or daughter was Passive.)
- What score would you assign to the pair or small group and why?

5. After all students have acted out their skits, use the following questions to conclude the lesson:
   - What are some problems associated with being too passive? Overly aggressive?
   - Why is assertiveness a good skill to have?
   - How can assertiveness help prevent drug use and abuse?

Variation

1. Students may be assigned to work in groups to develop their own role play related to healthy or unhealthy behaviors.
2. The teacher may want to give them the additional task of incorporating accurate, factual information into the skit. (For example: five accurate facts about the health risks of using drugs.) In this variation, the rubric can be expanded to assess not only the skills involved but also students' understanding and illustration of accurate information that may influence their behaviors.

Assessment

- Participation in the role play. See attached rubric.
- Participation in class discussion.

HANDOUT 3.2

NAME   DATE

Suggested Group Scenarios:
Passive, Aggressive, or Assertive Behavior

Most scenarios involve only two people. Others may involve three or more.

1. Your ride home from a party has been smoking marijuana. You don't feel safe riding with him.

2. Your boyfriend, who is usually very nice, acts like a jerk when he drinks.

3. A long-time friend of yours has started hanging out with a different group of kids. You know that most of these kids smoke pot every day after school. You totally disagree with what your friend is getting into. One day, she invites you to join them.

4. You are invited to your friend's house for dinner. You are both fourteen. His family recently moved to the United States from Europe, and they serve wine with the evening meal. Your friend gets poured a glass of wine by his father. His father asks if you would like some.

5. You've been invited to a party. You know that no parents will be home and many kids take ecstasy and other drugs.

6. You are at a party. A girl comes up to you and puts her arm around you and starts to try to make out with you. You do not even know her. She is very high.

7. Your football team has strict rules about drinking or doing drugs during the football season. You are hanging out at the park on the night before a game. You see the captain of the team smoking pot with some of his friends.

8. Your eighteen-year-old son asks you if he can have a graduation party in your backyard. He wants to have a keg of beer, claiming that none of his friends will come if there is no alcohol.

9. You have been babysitting a three-year-old for neighbors who live about a half-mile from your home. When the couple returns, you realize that the mother has been drinking and doesn't seem to be OK to drive. She tells you to get your coat and she'll take you home.

10. Your twenty-year-old sister is four months pregnant. You are all at a wedding and you've noticed that she is taking medication.

11. You find a "stash" of marijuana in your eleven-year-old brother's dresser drawer.

12. Someone at your gym offers you steroids.

13. You are invited to a "friend of a friend's" house to listen to music and hang out. When you get there, several people are doing "lines" of cocaine.

14. You and your roommate in college both have a big exam tomorrow. You see him taking some pills. When you ask what they are, he says that he gets them from a friend who has attention deficit hyperactivity disorder (ADHD). He claims that it helps him stay up all night to study. He offers you some.

Communication Styles

Passive	Aggressive	Assertive
Feeling one way, but acting in the opposite way	Ignoring or making light of the other person's feelings	Trying to understand the other person's feelings
Hoping the other person can "read your mind"	Using "you" messages to put the blame on the other person	Using "I- messages" to explain your feelings
Listening but rarely talking; voice is quiet; shy, looking away	Doing most of the talking, not listening, loud	Actively listening to the person, making eye contact, not interrupting
Getting taken advantage of, not standing up for yourself	Always wanting your way, not willing to compromise, getting what you want through bullying	Willing to compromise, looking for a "win-win" solution
Being easily swayed, having trouble saying "no," weak or defensive body language	Having trouble taking "no" for an answer, using threatening body language, refusing to speak, using physical force	Being respectful but firm in your beliefs

The Basic Format for an I-Message Is . . .

1. I . . . (feel, think, believe). *Always start with "I," not "You." "I" puts the focus on your feelings, wants, and needs.*

2. When . . . (simply state the situation as you see it).

3. Because . . . (tell the person why you feel that way).

4. I . . . (want, need you to, would appreciate it if [tell them what you want]).

Example of an I-Message

1. I feel taken for granted. . .

2. When you say you are going to call me at a certain time and you don't. . .

3. Because I wait around for the phone to ring all afternoon when I could be doing something else. . .

4. I want you to remember to call me the next time you say you will.

Tools for Teaching Health. Copyright © 2007 by John Wiley & Sons, Inc. Reproduced by permission of Jossey-Bass, An Imprint of Wiley

Assertiveness Skills: Role-Play Rubric

Scoring Criteria	Excellent (4 Points)	Good (3 Points)	Fair (2 Points)	Needs Much Improvement (1 Point)	Points Earned
Accuracy of Information	The content is superior to meeting the requirements of the task. Provides accurate, detailed, up-to-date information related to functional knowledge area	The speakers provide adequate, accurate content to meet the requirements of the task	The speakers do not provide enough content to meet the requirements of the task. Some content may be inaccurate or out of date	Little if any content is presented in the scenario, may wander off topic. Content presented may be irrelevant to the task	
Communication Skills	Delivery emphasizes the true meaning of the message, uses "I" messages, repeated demonstration of the skills, health-promoting behavior encouraged, suggests positive alternatives	Skills are demonstrated but not articulated in a manner that makes them so clearly evident to the audience	Some evidence of demonstrating the health skill is present, but the main steps involved in the skill may be irrelevant or out of sequence	Shows little or no evidence of demonstrating the appropriate health skill, does a poor job of communicating its intended message, disorganized	

(Continued)

NAME   DATE

Scoring Criteria	Excellent (4 Points)	Good (3 Points)	Fair (2 Points)	Needs Much Improvement (1 Point)	Points Earned
Speech and Body Language	Speakers deliver the lines in a lively, enthusiastic fashion. Gestures, facial expressions match spoken words, all students actively engaged and respond with appropriate cues	Generally clear and interesting to audience, generally good eye contact with some variation in tone and volume pattern that adds to the overall effect	Poor articulation, still able to convey most of the message to the audience, body language may be inconsistent with message	Volume, rate of speech, and enunciation make the message difficult to understand, students show little or no involvement with what is happening in the scenario	
Promotes Positive Health Message or Behavior	Health message is very clear in communicating the effects of choosing certain behaviors, promotes practicing positive health behaviors or illustrates effects of negative/ risky behaviors	Some difficulty understanding sequence of events, but overall message promotes positive health practices or shows risks of negative behaviors	Health message is missing some key ingredients, disorganized, does not clearly show the effects of practicing healthy or risky behaviors	Health message is unclear or missing, roles do not demonstrate the consequences of positive or negative decisions/ behaviors on health	

Total points: _____

Tools for Teaching Health. Copyright © 2007 by John Wiley & Sons, Inc. Reproduced by permission of Jossey-Bass, An Imprint of Wiley

Lesson 5: Up Close and Personal

Note to the Teacher

Up Close and Personal provides the opportunity for students to talk while others actively listen. Students develop the ability to clarify their feelings and develop a heightened self-awareness.

By sharing their thoughts in a safe environment, without the threat of being "wrong," students can learn skills that will enable them to become responsible for their own health and behavior. This can be an excellent culminating activity to a unit on drugs and substance abuse.

Time Needed

One 40–50 minute class period

National Standards

- Students will demonstrate the ability to use interpersonal communication skills to enhance health.

Objectives

1. Students will share personal feelings and opinions related to drugs and drug-related issues.
2. Students will discuss drugs and drug-related issues with their classmates.

Materials & Preparation

1. Following are some suggestions for facilitating an Up Close and Personal session:
   - Facilitation is a skill, and you will get better with practice.
   - Silence is not always a bad thing. Often, it indicates that higher-level thinking is taking place.
   - Some classes may get through three incomplete sentences while other classes may get through seven to eight. The point of the lesson is not to plow through each incomplete sentence. Different classes respond in different ways, depending on the number of students in the class and the class culture. The point is to allow thoughtful, reflective dialogue to occur among classmates.
   - Unacceptable behavior should be stopped the moment it is recognized. Stop and point out the offense to the individual. For example, if someone uses a derogatory term toward someone in the circle, stop and say: "That's a put-down (or personal name) and that's not allowed in the circle discussion. Please don't do that again." or "Please don't talk to your neighbor when you should be listening to the one person who is supposed to be talking."
   - If a student persists in breaking the rules, talk to him or her one-to-one after class. Let the student know that if the behavior continues, he or she may not be able to participate in the future. This almost always stops the offensive behavior.
2. Small lamp (optional, but it helps set the mood).
3. Relaxation music and music player (optional, but it helps set the mood).

Procedures

1. Students will form a circle with their chairs.

2. Turn off overhead lights and turn on the lamp to make the environment more conducive to informal discussion (optional). Turn on relaxation music (optional).

3. Introduce the activity by stating: "Today we are going to do an activity called Up Close and Personal. It is very simple to do, but in order for it to go smoothly, there are some rules that will be strictly enforced."

4. Review the following rules of the activity with the class:

   - This is not group therapy. It is just an opportunity for you to talk about how you feel about yourself, relationships, likes, dislikes, things that have come up in class, memories, and life in general.

   - I will read an unfinished sentence. You will think about how you would finish the sentence.

   - Someone in the circle will raise his or her hand and start us off by saying how he or she would complete the sentence. That person will then determine which way around the circle we will go by pointing to their left or right.

   - When we are taking turns speaking around the circle there is absolutely no talking by anyone else. If something is said that you want to respond to or comment on, you must wait until we have gone all the way around the circle. If you cannot think of anything to say or choose not to respond, you may simply say "Pass" when it comes around to you.

   - No personal names should be used at any time during the activity. "I know someone who . . . " is a better alternative.

   - Confidentiality. What is said here stays here. Do not share anything that is too personal or that makes you uncomfortable. Remind students that there are three things that teachers *must* report if shared: (a) if they are going to hurt themselves, (b) if they are going to hurt others, or (c) if they are being abused.

   - When we have gone around the entire circle, I will ask those who "Passed" whether they would like to respond at this time. Then I will ask: "Are there any questions or comments about anything that was said when we were going around the circle?"

5. Once all students understand how the activity will proceed, read the first unfinished sentence. After all students have commented on the statement, open the discussion about the statement. If no one has a question or comment, the facilitator should try to get some discussion going by asking some questions or commenting on something that was said. Stay on that topic for as long as it is viable, and then move on to the next unfinished sentence.

6. Proceed with the rest of the statements using the above procedures.

7. Conclude the Up Close and Personal session with a final unfinished sentence or two, such as

- "Today I learned . . . "
- "I learned that I . . . "
- "Right now I feel . . . "
- "Something I want to say to one of my classmates is . . . "

8. Thank the class for following the rules and sharing their thoughts and say: "That ends our Up Close and Personal session for today."

Suggested Incomplete Sentences for Drugs, Alcohol, and Tobacco

1. Right now, I feel . . .
2. When I feel bad and I want to feel better, I . . .
3. Drugs are . . .
4. When it comes to marijuana, the attitude of most kids in this school is . . .
5. Most kids our age get involved with drugs because . . .
6. One thing that I've learned in school about drugs is . . .
7. The best reason to *not* get involved with drugs is . . .
8. When I get to high school (college), I'm looking forward to . . .
9. One thing my parents and I have talked about when it comes to drugs is . . .
10. If my parents caught me smoking pot, they would . . .
11. One drug I would never try is . . . because . . .
12. If I had a 13-year-old son or daughter, the advice I would give them about drugs would be . . .
13. A big decision I'm going to have to make in the next few years is . . .
14. One thing I learned today is . . .

Drugs Home–School Connection

Home–School Connection: Talking About Marijuana

Time Needed to Complete

1–3 days

Time Needed to Present

20 minutes during one class period

National Standards

- Students will demonstrate the ability to practice health-enhancing behaviors and avoid or reduce risks.
- Students will demonstrate the ability to advocate for personal, family, and community health.

Objectives

1. Students will take a quiz about marijuana with a family member.
2. Students will discuss marijuana with a parent or guardian.

Materials & Preparation

1. Duplicate the Talking About Marijuana worksheet, one copy per student.

Procedures

1. Explain to the class that they are going to have an assignment to complete with a family member. This should not be a sibling, unless the sibling is more than ten years older.
2. Distribute the Talking About Marijuana worksheet (Worksheet 3.3) and review.
3. Assign the due date for the assignment.
4. On the day the assignment is due, students can share the results of their discussion with their family members. This can take as much or as little time as is available.
5. Following are some process questions that can be asked to facilitate discussion:
   - Prior to completing this activity, did anyone ever have a conversation with his or her family member about marijuana or other drug use?
   - Which family member did you choose to take the quiz with? How many of you spoke to many family members at the same time?
   - What was it like talking to family members about marijuana and drug use?
   - Did anything surprise you during your conversation?

- Did any other issues come up during your conversation?
- What did you learn from this activity?
- Are there any other comments or questions?

Assessment

- Submission of the completed Talking About Marijuana worksheet.

Home–School Connection: Talking About Marijuana

Due Date: _____

Instructions

The following questions should be discussed with a family member or other adult. Under the heading Student, the student should write whether they believe the statement is true or false. In the Adult answer column, the adult should write whether they believe the statement is true or false. This home–school connection activity is designed to share not only your knowledge about marijuana but also your opinions and values about the drug. When completed, it should be signed by both parties, and the adult should write a brief response to the question on the bottom of the page for the student to receive extra credit for the assignment.

Student	Adult	True or False?
		Marijuana smoke is safer than tobacco smoke.
		The chemicals in marijuana stay in the body for only a short time after it is smoked.
		Today's marijuana is stronger than varieties grown in the 1960s.
		Marijuana affects many skills required for safe driving, such as alertness, coordination, and reaction time.
		Chronic marijuana smokers have many of the same respiratory problems that tobacco smokers have.
		Marijuana is the most commonly used illegal drug in the United States.
		In national surveys, over 50 percent of tenth graders report that they have used marijuana in the last month.
		Scientific research has indicated that marijuana can help cure several different types of diseases.
		Getting arrested for possession of marijuana can affect your ability to get a job or get into a college.
		You can't get addicted to marijuana.

NAME _____ DATE _____

Parent/Adult Question: What *message* do you want your son/daughter to get from you about marijuana?

_____

_____

_____

_____

_____

_____

_____

_____

_____   _____
Student Signature   Adult Signature

Drugs Project

Project: What's Up in Health?

Time Needed to Complete

Three to seven days

Time Needed to Present

20 minutes during one class period

National Standards

- Students will demonstrate the ability to use interpersonal communication skills to enhance health and avoid or reduce health risks.

Objectives

1. Students will use technology to obtain current health information.
2. Students will analyze and synthesize current health information.
3. Students will use technology to complete a written summary of a drug-related article.

Materials & Preparation

1. Duplicate and pass out the What's Up in Health? handout (Handout 3.4) and the corresponding rubric (Handout 3.5) to students prior to the Show and Tell presentation date. (Enough time should be allowed for students to prepare the assignment.)

Procedures

1. Students will bring in the completed assignment on the presentation day.
2. Students will take turns sharing what they learned with other students in the class.
3. Depending on how many students are in the class, students may take approximately 3–7 minutes for their presentation.
4. Time should be allowed for questions and answers.
5. Conclude by pointing out that health information changes daily. New research reports and studies are constantly released. New laws are constantly created. The ability to access and analyze current health information is an important skill to learn to help a person remain healthy.

Assessment

- Completion of the What's Up in Health project. See rubric in this section.

HANDOUT 3.4

NAME _____   DATE _____

Drugs Project: What's Up in Health?

Directions

1. Use the Internet to find an article about alcohol, tobacco, or other drugs (ATOD).

2. The article should be no more than one year old, should come from a reputable source, and should be at least two pages in length.

3. Read the entire article and type a summary of its main points. Your summary should be at least 150 words in length.

4. As part of your summary, type two (2) or more "I learned . . . " statements

5. As part of your summary, type two (2) or more reaction statements ("I feel . . . ," "In my opinion . . . ")

6. Attach the article to the back of the summary before you turn it in to the teacher.

7. Be prepared to share your findings in class.

8. Use the suggestions below to give you ideas about what kind of articles would be appropriate. You are not restricted to the topics below. Any article related to ATOD is acceptable.

9. Use the attached rubric to help you complete the assignment and to determine what your grade will be.

Alcohol and accidents	Addiction	Advertising and alcohol or tobacco
Al-Anon	Alateen	Alcoholism
Alcohol & law	AA	Alcohol & college
Alcohol recovery	Angel dust	Alcohol and violence
Breathalyzer	COAs	Caffeine
Chewing tobacco	Crack	Cocaine
Date rape drugs	Drug testing	Drinking age law
Drunk driving	Ecstasy	Dysfunctional families
Hangovers	Hashish	Fetal alcohol syndrome
Inhalants	LSD	MADD
Marijuana	SADD	Narcotics Anonymous
Nonsmokers rights	Peer pressure	Steroids
Nicotine	Uppers	Tobacco legislation
Downers	PCP	LSD
Ritalin	OTC drugs	Drugs and safety

Rubric for What's Up in Health?

Current Events Assignment

	Excellent Work 10–12 points	Good Work 7–9 points	Passing Work 4–6 points	Poor Work 3 or fewer points
Summary	Clearly understands the article. Writes about the topic in his or her own voice. Summarizes the entire article and not just parts of the article.	For the most part, understands the article. Writes about the topic in his or her own voice. For the most part, summarizes the entire article and not just parts of the article.	For the most part, understands the article, but copies phrases right out of the article. Doesn't do a good job of summarizing the entire article.	Doesn't demonstrate that he or she understands the article. Copies phrases right out of the article. Only summarizes part of the article and not the whole article.
I Learned Statements	Writes 3 or more "I learned" statements as part of the summary.	Writes 2 "I learned" statements as part of the summary.	Only writes 1 "I learned" statement as part of the summary.	Does not write any "I learned" statements.
Reaction Statements	Writes 3 or more reaction statements as part of the summary.	Writes 2 reaction statements as part of the summary.	Only writes 1 reaction statement as part of the summary.	Does not write any reaction statements.
Depth of Discussion	In-depth discussion and elaboration in the paper.	For the most part, in-depth discussion and elaboration in the paper.	Brief discussion in the paper.	Cursory discussion in the paper.

Tools for Teaching Health. Copyright © 2007 by John Wiley & Sons, Inc. Reproduced by permission of Jossey-Bass, An Imprint of Wiley.

	Excellent Work 10–12 points	Good Work 7–9 points	Passing Work 4–6 points	Poor Work 3 or fewer points
Article	More than 2 pages long.	2 pages long.	1–1.5 pages long.	1 page long or less than one page long.
Issue	The health issue in the article clearly relates to drugs, alcohol, and/or tobacco.	For the most part, the health issue in the article clearly relates to drugs, alcohol, or tobacco.	The health issue in the article relates to drugs, alcohol, or tobacco in a secondary, rather than primary, way.	The health issue of the article does not relate to drugs, alcohol and/or tobacco.
Spelling and Grammar	No spelling or grammar mistakes.	Minimal spelling or grammar mistakes.	Noticeable spelling & grammar mistakes.	Unacceptable number of spelling and/or grammar mistakes.
Appearance	Clean, neat, and well organized. Standard format, typeset, and font. Extra effort taken to look professional.	Clean, neat, and well organized. Standard font, typeset, and format.	Different fonts, typesets, and formats throughout the paper. Somewhat tattered and tired looking.	Unorganized, different fonts, unprofessional looking, spelling corrections written in or changed.

Drugs Assessment

Asssessment: Functional Knowledge and Skills Exam

Time Needed

One 40–50 minute class period

National Standards

- Students will comprehend concepts related to health promotion and disease prevention.

- Students will analyze the influence of family, peers, culture, media, technology, and other factors on health behaviors.

- Students will demonstrate the ability to use interpersonal communication skills to enhance health and avoid or reduce health risks.

Objective

1. Students demonstrate knowledge and skills related to drug prevention.

Materials & Preparation

1. Duplicate the Functional Knowledge and Skills Exam, one per student.

2. Arrange the desks as needed for exam format.

Procedures

1. As students enter the room, advise them to take their seats, put their books and notebooks under their chairs, and place a pen or pencil on their desk.

2. Explain the test-taking rules to the class. Following are some suggestions:

   - No talking!

   - No "borrowing" answers from a neighbor—if caught cheating, students will receive a zero and a phone call to home.

   - If students have a question, they should raise their hand. The teacher will come to them, not the other way around.

   - When students are done, they should hand in their test and work quietly on a different assignment or read a book while waiting for the rest of the class to finish.

3. Be prepared with an activity for the entire class in case all students finish the test prior to the end of the period. The *Kids' Book of Questions* by Gregory Stock provides wonderful questions to spark class discussion on topics related to self-esteem, mental health, and other health-related issues. Students enjoy talking about answers to the questions, and it may be a relaxing way to conclude an otherwise stressful class period for them.

Assessment

Score on the exam.

Answers to Multiple Choice Questions

1. A
2. C
3. B
4. C
5. D
6. C
7. A
8. B
9. D
10. B
11. C
12. B
13. C
14. C
15. D
16. B
17. D
18. B
19. D
20. C

Possible Answers: Content

Memory loss; lack of motivation; increased heart rate; decreased ability to drive or perform other tasks; burning in mouth and throat, coughing, dilated pupils; distorted sense of time, judgment; trouble with parents, against the law; increased risk of respiratory problems with chronic use; possible psychological or physical addiction.

Possible Answers: Skills

Use a firm tone of voice and strong body language. Use refusal skills to avoid marijuana use and possibly convince Jessica to avoid use as well. When all else fails, walk away from the situation.

WORKSHEET 3.4

Drug Prevention: Functional Knowledge and Skills Exam

Directions

This exam consists of twenty multiple choice questions and one constructed response (essay) question. Please complete all questions.

Multiple Choice

Please circle the correct answer.

1. Narcotics are drugs that
   a. relieve pain
   b. reduce fatigue
   c. promote alertness
   d. produce hallucinations

2. Which of the following is an illegal narcotic?
   a. percodan
   b. morphine
   c. heroin
   d. MDMA

3. Anabolic steroids can be taken orally and can also be
   a. inhaled
   b. injected
   c. smoked
   d. sprinkled on food and eaten

4. The first step toward recovery from substance abuse is
   a. see a psychiatrist
   b. throw all your drugs away
   c. admit you have a problem
   d. check into rehab

5. Abusing inhalants may cause
   a. dizziness
   b. headaches
   c. sudden sniffing death
   d. all of these

6. Which of the following would be most dangerous to consume while barbiturates are in one's system?

   a. marijuana

   b. amphetamines

   c. alcohol

   d. LSD

7. The scientific name for the hemp plant from which marijuana comes is *cannabis sativa*

   a. coca

   b. GHB

   c. creatine

8. Tylenol is an example of a(n)

   a. prescription drug

   b. over-the-counter drug

   c. antibiotic

   d. narcotic

9. Abusing drugs can increase individuals' risk for

   a. suicide

   b. accidents

   c. unwanted sexual activity

   d. all of these

10. The most common abusers of inhalant drugs are

    a. elementary students

    b. middle school students

    c. high school students

    d. college students

11. Drug tolerance occurs when

    a. a person gets sick and goes into withdrawal

    b. a person starts getting side effects

    c. a person needs to increase the dose to get the same effect

    d. a person needs to decrease the dose to get the same effect

12. Marissa's ride home from a party has had too much to drink. She tells him, "I feel uncomfortable going home with you because I don't think you're in any condition to drive. I want you to let me call a cab so that we can both get home safely." This is an example of

    a. a passive response

    b. an assertive response

    c. an aggressive response

    d. changing the subject

(Continued)

NAME   DATE

13. Which of the following Web sites is more likely to be an accurate, unbiased source of information about substance abuse?

   a. www.hightimes.com

   b. www.joesdrugsite.com

   c. www.NIDA.gov (National Institute on Drug Abuse)

   d. www.Ilegalsteroids.com

14. In most schools, who would be the better resource person to go to for help with a drug problem?

   a. principal

   b. custodian

   c. school counselor or social worker

   d. security guard

15. Which of the following can serve as an "alternative high" to smoking marijuana?

   a. athletics

   b. music

   c. dancing

   d. any of these

16. Timmy's best friend got kicked off the basketball team for getting caught using illegal supplements. Which of the following actions would reduce or eliminate the risk of this same situation happening to Timmy?

   a. only use supplements that other guys on the team are using

   b. only use supplements that are prescribed or recommended by a physician and the medical community

   c. only take supplements from guys who sell them behind the health club in town

   d. only take supplements that you can buy on line

17. Which of the following is considered a drug?

   a. soda with caffeine

   b. tobacco

   c. children's aspirin

   d. all of these

18. The marijuana around today is stronger than years ago because

   a. the weather is better

   b. it has a higher THC content

   c. it is more "natural" and organically grown

   d. it often has PCP mixed in with it

19. The best way to refuse illegal drugs if offered is

    a. say no

    b. say no repeatedly

    c. say no and walk away

    d. all of these

20. Research has indicated that the most effective drug education programs

    a. teach facts only

    b. show movies about the dangers of drugs

    c. teach facts along with skills such as decision-making and communication

    d. have ex-addicts as guest speakers

Constructed Response Question

Skill: Communication Styles

Please write your answer in the space provided. Use the back of this test if you do not have enough room to complete your answer.

Amanda is invited over to Jessica's house. It is after school and no one is home. Amanda and Jessica go back into the woods behind Jessica's house. Jessica offers to smoke a joint with Amanda. Amanda has never tried it before.

• What are three facts about marijuana that Amanda needs to know to make a healthy decision?

• How can Amanda communicate to Jessica in an assertive manner that she does not want to get involved with drugs?

_____

_____

_____

_____

_____

_____

_____

_____

CHAPTER 4

NUTRITION

Nutrition Icebreaker

Icebreaker: Toilet Paper Game

Note to the Teacher

If for some reason toilet paper is not available, the same activity can be played by passing around a bowl of pretzel nuggets, raisins, or other healthy food and having the students "take some" (but don't let them eat it until the activity is over!) or by having students randomly select a playing card stating the number of nutritious foods that correspond with the number on their card—face cards represent eleven foods, aces represent one food. This is also a good review activity for the end of a unit if students are asked to state one thing they learned during the course of the unit for each piece of toilet paper they have.

Time Needed

10–20 minutes

National Standard

- Students will comprehend concepts related to health promotion and disease prevention to enhance health.

Objective

1. Students will state one nutritious food they like to eat for each piece of toilet paper they take.

Materials & Preparation Needed

1. One roll of toilet paper, with pre-perforated sheets.

Procedures

1. Arrange the desks in a circle.

2. Hand a student the roll of toilet paper and tell them to "Take some," and pass the roll along. Inevitably students will ask, "How much do I take?" Simply respond, "As much as you want."

3. As the students are taking their toilet paper, the teacher should tell them to separate the perforated squares.

4. Once all the students have their toilet paper, the teacher will then announce that students have to state one nutritious food they like to eat for each square of toilet paper they have.

5. Tell the class that there is one rule—no student can repeat a food that another student has stated! If all healthy foods a student eats have been stated by the time it is his or her turn, the student is then given permission to state any other healthy food—not necessarily one that he or she likes to eat.

6. Once all students have had a chance to share, ask the following questions:
   - Was it hard to name nutritious foods?
   - Do you eat all the foods you named? Why or why not?
   - If there are so many different kinds of nutritious foods, why are people eating fast food?
   - What did you learn from this activity?

7. Conclude by pointing out that over the course of the unit students will be studying healthy and unhealthy foods and nutrition-related behaviors. It is important for people to eat a variety of foods in order to obtain all essential vitamins and minerals.

Assessment

- Ability to provide healthy foods for each piece of toilet paper they possess.

Nutrition Lessons

Lesson 1: Puzzling Pieces

Time Needed

One 40–50 minute class period

National Standards

- Students will comprehend concepts related to health promotion and disease prevention to enhance health.

Objectives

- Students will work in groups to assemble puzzle parts.
- Students will accurately fill in missing information on their worksheets from the completed puzzles.
- Students will discuss facts related to the six nutrients.

Materials & Preparation Needed

- Duplicate the attached puzzles on brightly colored paper. Laminate the paper and cut it into jigsaw pieces. Place each puzzle in a Ziploc bag.
- Duplicate the eight student worksheets, one per student.

Procedures

1. Place the puzzles in stations around the classroom.
2. Distribute one student worksheet to each student.
3. Explain to students that today's lesson is about the six nutrients: carbohydrates, protein, fat, water, vitamins, and minerals. Rather than lecturing to the class on the nutrients, you will be teaching them about the nutrients through puzzles.
4. Explain that students will be rotating from station to station putting the puzzles together. Once a puzzle is completed, students should use the puzzle to fill in the blanks on their worksheet.
5. Once all students understand the directions, divide the class into groups (one group per puzzle) and set each group up at a station.
6. Explain that you will be giving students a minute or two to complete the puzzle and fill in the blanks on their worksheets. You will then give a signal to rotate stations. Students will only rotate to the next puzzle on your signal.
7. Begin students on the first station and rotate the groups within a reasonable amount of time (about 2–4 minutes).
8. When students have rotated to each station, ask them to return to their original seats. Review the answers to all the worksheets with the class.

9. Use the following questions to lead a discussion:
   - What new information did you learn about carbohydrates? Fats? Proteins? Water? Vitamins? Minerals?
   - Why is it important to know about the six nutrients?
   - From what you learned, do you think you are consuming the right amount of nutrients in your diets? If not, what foods can you add to your diet to replace missing nutrients?
   - What can you tell others about nutrients after today?

10. Conclude by stating that although each person's diet is different, all diets comprise the same six nutrients—the ones that were discussed today. If a person's eating patterns do not contain the proper proportion of each of the nutrients, then their eating patterns are not healthy.

Assessment

Completion of the student worksheets.

- Participation in class discussion.

NAME DATE

Puzzling Pieces

Protein: On the Scene!

Even though it sounds like just one substance, *protein* is really a combination of many chemicals called *amino acids.* Scientists have found twenty different amino acids in protein, which can combine in lots of ways—in fact, they have joined together to make thousands of different proteins!

Some types of amino acids are made by you, right inside your body, without your ever thinking about it or doing anything special. These are called *nonessential amino acids,* and there are eleven of them. They *are* necessary—meaning you need them to keep your body in tip-top shape—but they are not essential as part of the food you eat. The *essential amino acids*—all nine of them—must come from food. Your body won't ever make essential amino acids. That's where eating foods with protein comes in—to give your body the amino acids it needs.

Protein is so important that your body needed it and used it even before you were born. Protein's *biggest* job is to build up, keep up, and replace the tissues in your body. Your muscles, your organs, even some of your hormones are made up mostly of protein. Making a big muscle? Taking a deep breath with your big lungs? Running down the street on your strong feet? You've got the power of protein!

Protein helps your body in other ways, too. It likes to make sure things get around by making *hemoglobin,* the part of red blood cells that carries oxygen to every part of your body. It even makes antibodies, the cells that fight off infection and disease. And the next time you fall off your bike and scrape your knee, call for protein to the rescue—it's what helps make your cuts and scrapes heal!

It's easy to get the protein your body needs. Protein is in tasty foods such as meat, chicken, fish, eggs, and nuts. Dairy products such as cheese, milk, and yogurt are good sources of protein. And don't forget your beans—your lentil beans or peas, that is! These guys are full of protein.

Puzzling Pieces

The Great Carbohydrate

Carbohydrates are sometimes also called carbs or carbos, and your body can make them. Carbs come in two different types: sugars and starches. Sugars are called *simple carbohydrates.* Starchy carbohydrates have their own name, too: *complex carbohydrates.*

Carbohydrates have an important job: giving all the cells in your body the energy they need! When you eat foods with carbohydrates in them, your body breaks them down into two different types of fuel. For energy that you'll use right away, your body takes those carbs and turns them into *glucose.* Glucose is carried in your blood to all the cells in your body and gives you energy. It powers every part of your body. Whatever you do, as long as you're using your body, you need the great power of glucose. Have you ever felt hungry and found it kind of hard to think? That's because you were running out of glucose, and your brain needed more fuel.

But your cells can only use so much glucose at one time. So when there is glucose left over that can't be used right away, your cells save it. But there's no sticking it in the refrigerator like regular leftovers—instead, this leftover glucose is stored in your liver and muscles, and it's called *glycogen.* The glycogen that doesn't fit into your liver and muscle cells is turned to fat.

Glycogen hangs out until it's needed and is then released for quick energy when you're exercising. Your body decides to release the power from either glycogen or fat depending on the type of sport or activity you're doing, and how long you're doing it. If you're sprinting or doing another quick exercise, your body calls on glycogen for energy. But if you are exercising for a long time, your body turns to its "reserve tank" of fuel for energy: fat.

NAME DATE

Puzzling Pieces

How Do We Get Carbohydrates?

Carbohydrates are in lots of foods, but carbs are very different from each other—and if you guessed that complex carbs are different from simple carbs, you're right! That's because *simple carbohydrates* are absorbed into your blood much faster, and although they provide some really quick energy, they can also often come with lots of fat and lack important vitamins that your body needs. So even though a can of soda or a candy bar every once in a while isn't too bad, you wouldn't want to make these simple carbohydrates a regular part of the food you eat.

Many fruits are a good source of simple carbs, so if you're looking for some quick energy and a healthy snack, these are the way to go! Apples, bananas, grapes, and raisins pull out in front of the simple carbs pack. And fruit cocktail, oranges, and pears will get carbs in there, too.

Complex carbohydrates are the slowpokes of the group: they give you energy more slowly. They take longer to be digested, so your body needs more time to release these carbs into your blood as glucose. Complex carbs are better when you are exercising or playing in a game, because you can count on them to give you energy that lasts through the ninth inning or the fourth quarter! Complex carbs also beat simple carbs because they usually come with lots of vitamins and minerals that your body needs.

It's easy to get the complex carbs your body likes to use as fuel—they are in bread, cereals, and pasta. Rice is a great source of complex carbs, just like oatmeal, pretzels, and even bagels. If you're a very veggie kind of kid, then you're in luck, because corn, potatoes, sweet potatoes, tomatoes, carrots, cucumbers, lettuce, and peppers are all great ways to get complex carbs.

HANDOUT 4.1 (Continued)

Puzzling Pieces

All That Fat

Fat is the body's major form of energy storage, and our bodies can make fat. Many fats that people eat are really a combination of two different types of substances: saturated fatty acids and unsaturated fatty acids. *Saturated fatty acids* come from animal foods such as meat, milk, cheese, and some oils that come from plants. *Unsaturated fatty acids* are different—they come from plants and fish. Together, these two substances are grouped and called the fat content in food.

Fat sometimes sounds like it's always a bad thing that people should not eat, but actually our bodies need some fat to work correctly. Fat insulates our bodies from the cold and provides some cushioning for our organs. Fat gives our bodies energy. Some fats help make up important hormones that we need to keep our bodies at the right temperature or keep our blood pressure at the right level. Fat helps you have healthy skin and hair. And fat is like your body's very own storage and moving service: it helps vitamins A, D, E, and K get transported through your bloodstream when your body needs them!

Even though our bodies need *some* fat to work properly, it's a good idea to avoid eating a lot of fat, because it can contribute to obesity and other illnesses that can occur when you're older, such as heart disease or adult onset diabetes.

But foods with lots of fat in them taste good—like cookies, chocolate, and fast-food hamburgers and French fries! It's OK to eat fatty foods *once in a while.* But the real trick is not to eat these kinds of foods all the time, or even most of the time. Instead, you should eat them in moderation—that means eating only a little bit at a time and not very often. Staying healthy and keeping your body in shape is easier when you go for foods and snacks that are lower in fat—and you'll feel better, too!

Tools for Teaching Health. Copyright © 2007 by John Wiley & Sons, Inc. Reproduced by permission of Jossey-Bass, An Imprint of Wiley

Puzzling Pieces

You're So Waterful

Water is the main ingredient in the fluids in your body systems. Fluids travel through your body, carrying nutrients and waste to and from all your cells and organs. Your heart, your eyes, your intestines, and even your big toe need water-based fluids to survive. So what is water's job in the body?

Water Keeps Things Lubricated

If you've ever heard a squeaky door or wheel, you know the sound of something that needs to be *lubricated.* Lubricating means making it easier for something to move by keeping the parts from rubbing together. In the case of a squeaky object, people usually put a little oil on the rubbing parts so they move more easily. But in the case of your body, it isn't anything in a hardware store that does the job: it's water! Water is in charge when it comes to keeping things moving freely because it's a big part of the fluid that lubricates the body's joints.

Water is also the biggest part of *mucus,* the slimy substance that's in your eyes, nose, throat, and many other parts of your body that you can't see, such as your stomach. Sometimes when you have a cold and your nose is running, you might wish you never even heard of mucus. But the truth is, you need it to keep things lubricated and running right in your body. The same goes for saliva, which is also known as spit. It is made mostly of water, and it keep things lubricated in your mouth and down into your digestive system.

Water Makes Things Move

As you digest food, the food moves through your intestines. At the end of the trip, the stuff your body doesn't need gets ready to leave your body as waste, which is called a bowel movement. And if you guessed that water is the ingredient that moves everything along, you're right!

Water Keeps Things Cool

People's bodies like to be at about 98.6 degrees Fahrenheit (37 degrees Celsius). But if you're out running around or exercising in warm weather, you can feel pretty hot. And sometimes you don't even need to be exercising—if the weather's warm enough, you can feel hot just sitting still. And that's where water comes in, by cooling you down with *sweat.* When your body generates a lot of heat, water comes up through your skin as sweat, and it evaporates into the air. (Evaporation happens when a liquid changes into a vapor—like when water boils and turns into steam.) As the sweat evaporates, it cools down your skin, which cools down your blood. When your blood is cooler, your insides become cooler, and your whole body cools down. It's like your body's own personal air conditioner!

NAME _____ DATE _____

Puzzling Pieces

Vitamins, Vitamins

If you're like most kids, you've probably heard at least one parent say, "Don't forget your vitamins!" "Eat your salad—it's packed with vitamins!" But what exactly are vitamins? *Vitamins* are substances that are found in foods we eat. Your body needs them to work properly, so you grow and develop just like you should.

When it comes to vitamins, each one has a special role to play. For example, there are two types of vitamins: *fat soluble* and *water soluble.* When you eat foods that contain *fat-soluble* vitamins, the vitamins are stored in the fat tissues in your body and in your liver. They wait around in your body fat until your body needs them. Fat-soluble vitamins are happy to stay stored in your body for awhile—some stay for a few days, some for up to 6 months! Then, when it's time for them to be used, special carriers in your body take them to where they're needed. Vitamins A, D, E, and K are all fat-soluble vitamins.

Water-soluble vitamins are different. When you eat foods that have water-soluble vitamins, the vitamins don't get stored as much in your body. Instead, they travel through your bloodstream. And whatever your body doesn't use comes out when you urinate. So these kinds of vitamins need to be replaced often because they don't like to stick around! This crowd of vitamins includes vitamin C and the big group of B vitamins— B1 (thiamin), B2 (riboflavin), niacin, B6 (pyridoxine), folic acid, B12, biotin, and pantothenic acid.

Your body is one powerful machine, capable of doing all sorts of things by itself. But one thing it can't do is make vitamins. That's where food comes in. Your body is able to get the vitamins it needs from the foods you eat because different foods contain different vitamins. Though some kids take a daily vitamin, most kids don't need one if they're eating healthy foods.

Puzzling Pieces

Vitamins from A to K

Vitamin A

Vitamin A plays a really big part in eyesight. It's great for night vision and helps you see in color, too, from the brightest yellow to the darkest purple. In addition, Vitamin A helps you grow properly and aids in healthy skin. Which foods are rich in vitamin A? Eggs, milk, apricots, nectarines, cantaloupe, carrots, sweet potatoes, and spinach.

The B Vitamins

There's more than one B vitamin. Here's the list: B1, B2, B6, B12, niacin, folic acid, biotin, and pantothenic acid. Whew—that's quite a group! The B vitamins are important in metabolic activity—this means that they help make energy and set it free when your body needs it. So the next time you're running to third base, thank those B vitamins. This group of vitamins is also involved in making red blood cells, which carry oxygen throughout your body. Which foods are rich in vitamin B? Whole grains, such as wheat and oats; fish and seafood; poultry and meats; eggs; dairy products, such as milk and yogurt; leafy green vegetables; beans and peas; and citrus fruits, such as oranges.

Vitamin C

Vitamin C is important for keeping body tissues in good shape. C is also key if you get a cut or wound, because it helps you heal. This vitamin also helps your body resist infection. Even though you can't always avoid getting sick, vitamin C makes it a little harder for your body to become infected with an illness. Which foods are rich in vitamin C? Citrus fruits, such as oranges, cantaloupe, strawberries, tomatoes, broccoli, and cabbage.

Vitamin D

No bones about it, vitamin D is the vitamin you need for strong bones and teeth! Vitamin D even lends a hand to an important mineral—it helps your body absorb the amount of calcium it needs. Which foods are rich in vitamin D? Milk and other dairy products fortified with vitamin D, fish, and egg yolk.

Vitamin E

Everybody needs E. This hard-working vitamin maintains a lot of your body's tissues, such as those in your eyes, skin, and liver. It protects your lungs from becoming damaged by polluted air. And it is important for the formation of red blood cells. The following foods are high in Vitamin E: whole grains, such as wheat and oats, wheat germ, leafy green vegetables, sardines, egg yolks, and nuts.

Vitamin K

Vitamin K is the clotmaster! Remember the last time you got a cut? Your blood did something special called clotting. This is when certain cells in your blood act like glue and stick together at the surface of the cut. Which foods are rich in vitamin K? Leafy green vegetables, liver, pork, and dairy products, such as milk and yogurt.

Puzzling Pieces

Mineral Me!

Just like vitamins, minerals help your body grow, develop, and stay healthy. The body uses minerals to perform many different functions—from building strong bones to transmitting nerve impulses. Some minerals are even used to make hormones or maintain a normal heartbeat. When people don't get enough of these important minerals, they can have health problems. Some kids may take mineral supplements, but most kids don't need them if they eat a nutritious diet. So eat those minerals and stay healthy!

Macro and Trace

There are two kinds of minerals: macrominerals and trace minerals. *Macro* means "large" in Greek (and your body needs larger amounts of macrominerals than trace minerals). The *macromineral* group is made up of calcium, phosphorus, magnesium, sodium, potassium, chloride, and sulfur. A trace of something means that there is only a little of it. So even though your body needs trace minerals, it needs just a tiny bit of each one. Scientists aren't even sure how much of these minerals you need each day. *Trace minerals* includes iron, manganese, copper, iodine, zinc, cobalt, fluoride, and selenium.

Calcium

Calcium is the top macromineral when it comes to building strong bones and teeth. Which foods are rich in calcium? Dairy products, such as milk, cheese, and yogurt, canned salmon and sardines with bones, leafy green vegetables, such as broccoli, and calcium-fortified foods—from orange juice to cereals and crackers.

Iron

The body needs iron to transport oxygen from your lungs to the rest of your body. Iron helps because it's important in the formation of hemoglobin, which is the part of your red blood cells that carries oxygen throughout the body. Which foods are rich in iron? Meat, especially red meat, such as beef, tuna and salmon, eggs, beans, baked potato with skins, dried fruits, like raisins, leafy green vegetables, such as broccoli, and whole and enriched grains, such as wheat or oats.

Potassium

Potassium keeps your muscles and nervous system working properly by making sure the amount of water is just right. Which foods are rich in potassium? Bananas, tomatoes, potatoes with skins, leafy green vegetables, such as broccoli, citrus fruits, such as oranges, dried fruits, and legumes, such as beans, peas, lentils, and peanuts.

Zinc

Zinc helps your immune system, which is your body's system for fighting off illnesses and infections. It also helps with cell growth and helps heal wounds, such as cuts. Which foods are rich in zinc? Beef, pork, lamb, and legumes, such as beans, peas, lentils, and peanuts.

Tools for Teaching Health. Copyright © 2007 by John Wiley & Sons, Inc. Reproduced by permission of Jossey-Bass, An Imprint of Wiley

NAME _____   DATE

Puzzling Pieces

Protein: On the Scene!

Even though it sounds like just one substance, *protein* is really a combination of many chemicals called _____ . Scientists have found _____ differ-ent amino acids in protein, which can combine in lots of ways—in fact, they have joined together to make _____ of different proteins!

Some types of amino acids are made by you, right _____, without your ever thinking about it or doing anything special. These are called _____ *amino acids,* and there are eleven of them. They *are* necessary—meaning you need them to keep your body in tip-top shape—but they are not essential as part of the food you eat. The _____ *amino acids*—all nine of them—must come from food. Your body won't ever make essential amino acids. That's where eating foods with protein comes in—to give your body the _____ it needs.

Protein is so important that your body _____ and used it even before you were born. Protein's *biggest* job is to build up, keep up, and replace the _____ in your body. Your muscles, your organs, even some of your _____ are made up mostly of protein. Making a big muscle? Taking a deep breath with your big lungs? You've got the power of protein!

Protein helps your body in other ways, too. It likes to make sure things get around by making _____, the part of red blood cells that carries _____, to every part of your body. It even makes antibodies, the cells that fight off infection and disease. And the next time you fall off your bike and scrape your knee, call for protein to the rescue—it's what helps make your _____ heal!

It's easy to get the protein your body needs. Protein is in tasty foods such as meat, _____, fish, eggs, and nuts. Dairy products such as cheese, milk, and yogurt are good sources of protein. And don't forget _____ or peas! These guys are full of protein.

Puzzling Pieces

The Great Carbohydrate

Carbohydrates are sometimes also called carbs or carbos, and your body can make them. Carbs come in two different types: sugars and starches. Sugars are called _____ *carbohydrates.* Starchy carbohydrates have their own name, too: _____ *carbohydrates.*

  Carbohydrates have an important job: giving all the cells in your body the _____ they need! When you eat foods with carbohydrates in them, your body breaks them down into two different types of fuel. For energy that you'll use right away, your body takes those carbs and turns them into _____. Glucose is carried in your blood to all the cells in your body and gives you energy. It powers every part of your body. Whatever you do, as long as you're using your body, you need the great power of glucose. Have you ever felt _____ and found it kind of hard to think? That's because you were running out of glucose, and your _____ needed more fuel.

(Continued)

  But your cells can only use so much glucose at one time. So when there is glucose left over that can't be used right away, your cells _____. But there's no sticking it in the refrigerator like regular leftovers—instead, this leftover glucose is stored in your _____ and muscles, and it's called *glycogen.* The glycogen that doesn't fit into your liver and muscle cells is turned to _____.

  Glycogen hangs out until it's needed and is then released for quick energy when you're _____. Your body decides to release the power from either glycogen or fat depending on the type of sport or activity you're doing, and how long you're doing it. If you're sprinting or doing another quick exercise, your body calls on _____ for energy. But if you are exercising for a long time, your body turns to its "reserve tank" of fuel for energy: _____.

Tools for Teaching Health. Copyright © 2007 by John Wiley & Sons, Inc. Reproduced by permission of Jossey-Bass, An Imprint of Wiley

Puzzling Pieces

How Do We Get Carbohydrates?

Carbohydrates are in lots of foods, but carbs are very different from each other—and if you guessed that complex carbs are different from simple carbs, you're right! That's because *simple carbohydrates* are absorbed into your blood much _____, and although they provide some really quick energy, they can also often come with lots of fat and lack important _____ that your body needs. So even though a can of soda or a candy bar every once in a while isn't too bad, you wouldn't want to make these simple carbohydrates a regular part of the food you eat.

   Many _____ are a good source of simple carbs, so if you're looking for some quick energy and a _____ snack, these are the way to go! Apples, bananas, grapes, and raisins pull out in front of the simple carbs pack. And fruit cocktail, _____, and pears will get carbs in there, too.

   Complex carbohydrates are the slowpokes of the group: they give you energy more _____. They take longer to be digested, so your body needs more time to release these carbs into your blood as _____. Complex carbs are better when you are _____ or playing in a game, because you can count on them to give you energy that lasts! Complex carbs also beat simple carbs because they usually come with lots of _____ and _____ that your body needs.

   It's easy to get the complex carbs your body likes to use as fuel—they are in bread, _____, and _____. Rice is a great source of complex carbs, just like oatmeal, pretzels, and even _____. If you're a very veggie kind of kid, then you're in luck, because corn, potatoes, sweet potatoes, _____, carrots, cucumbers, lettuce, and peppers are all great ways to get complex carbs.

Puzzling Pieces

All That Fat

Fat is the body's major form of energy _____, and our bodies can make fat. Many fats that people eat are really a combination of two different types of substances: _____ fatty acids and unsaturated _____. *Saturated fatty acids* come from animal foods such as meat, _____, cheese, and some oils that come from plants. *Unsaturated fatty acids* are different—they come from plants and _____. Together, these two substances are grouped and called the fat content in food.

Fat sometimes sounds like it's always a bad thing that people should not eat, but actually our bodies need some fat to _____. Fat _____ our bodies from the cold and provides some _____ for our organs. Fat gives our bodies energy. Some fats help make up important hormones that we need to keep our bodies at the right temperature or keep our _____ at the right level. Fat helps you have healthy _____ and hair. And fat is like your body's very own storage and moving service: it helps vitamins A, _____, E, and _____ get transported through your bloodstream when your body needs them!

Even though our bodies need *some* fat to work properly, it's a good idea to avoid eating a lot of fat, because it can contribute to _____ and other illnesses that can occur when you're older, such as heart disease or adult onset diabetes.

But foods with lots of fat in them taste good—like cookies, _____, and fast-food hamburgers and French fries! It's OK to eat fatty foods _____. But the real trick is not to eat these kinds of foods all the time, or even most of the time. Instead, you should eat them in _____—that means eating only a little bit at a time and not very often. Staying healthy and keeping your body in shape is _____ when you go for foods and snacks that are lower in fat—and you'll feel _____, too!

Tools for Teaching Health. Copyright © 2007 by John Wiley & Sons, Inc. Reproduced by permission of Jossey-Bass, An Imprint of Wiley

NAME _____   DATE

Puzzling Pieces

You're So Waterful

Water is the main ingredient in the fluids in your body systems. Fluids travel through your body, carrying _____ and _____ to and from all your cells and organs. Your heart, your eyes, your _____, and even your big toe need water-based fluids to survive. So what is water's job in the body?

Water Keeps Things Lubricated

If you've ever heard a squeaky door or wheel, you know the sound of something that needs to be *lubricated.* Lubricating means making it _____ for something to move by keeping the parts from rubbing together. In the case of a squeaky object, people usually put a little _____ on the rubbing parts so they move more easily. But in the case of your body, it isn't anything in a hardware store that does the job: it's _____! Water is in charge when it comes to keeping things moving _____ because it's a big part of the fluid that lubricates the body's joints.

Water is also the biggest part of _____, the slimy substance that's in your eyes, nose, throat, and many other parts of your body that you can't see, such as your stomach. Sometimes when you have a cold and your nose is running, you might wish you never even heard of mucus. But the truth is, you need it to keep things lubricated and running right in your body. The same goes for _____, which is also known as spit. It is made mostly of water, and it keep things lubricated in your mouth and down into your _____ system.

Water Makes Things Move

As you digest food, the food moves through your _____. At the end of the trip, the stuff your body doesn't need gets ready to leave your body as _____, which is called a bowel movement. And if you guessed that water is the _____ that moves everything along, you're right!

Water Keeps Things Cool

People's bodies like to be at about 98.6 degrees Fahrenheit (37 degrees Celsius). But if you're out _____ around or _____ in warm weather, you can feel pretty hot. And sometimes you don't even need to be exercising—if the weather's warm enough, you can feel hot just sitting still. And that's where water comes in, by cooling you down with _____. When your body generates a lot of heat, water comes up through your skin as sweat, and it _____ into the air. As the sweat evaporates, it cools down your _____, which cools down your blood. When your blood is cooler, your insides become cooler, and your whole body cools down. It's like your body's own personal _____!

Puzzling Pieces

Vitamins, Vitamins

If you're like most kids, you've probably heard at least one parent say, "Don't forget your vitamins!" "Eat your _____—it's packed with vitamins!" But what exactly are vitamins? *Vitamins* are substances that are found in foods we eat. Your body needs them to work properly, so you _____ and _____ just like you should.

   When it comes to vitamins, each one has a special role to play. There are two types of vitamins: *fat soluble* and *water soluble.* When you eat foods that contain _____ vitamins, the vitamins are stored in the fat tissues in your body and in your liver. They wait around in your body fat until your body needs them.

   Fat-soluble vitamins are happy to stay stored in your body for awhile—some stay for a few _____, some for up to 6 _____! Then, when it's time for them to be used, special carriers in your body take them to where they're needed. Vitamins _____, D, _____, and K are all fat-soluble vitamins.

   Water-soluble vitamins are different. When you eat foods that have water-soluble vitamins, the vitamins don't get _____ as much in your body. Instead, they travel through your _____. And whatever your body doesn't use comes out when you urinate. So these kinds of vitamins need to be _____ often because they don't like to stick around! This crowd of vitamins includes vitamin C and the big group of B vitamins—B1 (thiamin), B2 (riboflavin), niacin, B6 (pyridoxine), _____, B12, biotin, and pantothenic acid.

   Your body is one powerful _____, capable of doing all sorts of things by itself. But one thing it can't do is make vitamins. That's where food comes in. Your body is able to get the vitamins it needs from the foods you eat because different foods contain different vitamins. Though some kids take a daily vitamin, most kids don't need one if they're eating _____.

NAME _____ DATE

Puzzling Pieces

Vitamins—from A to K

Vitamin A

Vitamin A plays a really big part in eyesight. It's great for _____ and helps you see in color, too, from the brightest yellow to the darkest purple. In addition, Vitamin A helps you grow properly and aids in healthy _____. Which foods are rich in vitamin A? Eggs, milk, apricots, nectarines, cantaloupe, carrots, sweet potatoes, and _____.

The B Vitamins

There's more than one B vitamin. Here's the list: B1, B2, B6, B12, niacin, folic acid, biotin, and pantothenic acid. Whew—that's quite a group! The B vitamins are important in _____ activity—this means that they help make energy and set it free when your body needs it. So the next time you're running to third base, thank those B vitamins. This group of vitamins is also involved in making _____, which carry _____ throughout your body. Which foods are rich in vitamin B? Whole grains, such as wheat and oats; fish and seafood; _____ and meats; eggs; dairy products, such as milk and yogurt; leafy green vegetables; beans and peas; and _____, such as oranges.

Vitamin C

This vitamin is important for keeping body tissues in good shape. C is also key if you get a _____ because it helps you heal. This vitamin also helps your body resist _____. Even though you can't always avoid getting sick, vitamin C makes it a little harder for your body to become infected with an illness. Which foods are rich in vitamin C? Citrus fruits, such as oranges, cantaloupe, _____, tomatoes, _____, and cabbage.

Vitamin D

No bones about it, vitamin D is the vitamin you need for strong _____ and _____! Vitamin D even lends a hand to an important mineral—it helps your body absorb the amount of _____ it needs. Which foods are rich in vitamin D? Milk and other dairy products fortified with vitamin D, fish, and egg yolk.

Vitamin E

Everybody needs E. This hard-working vitamin maintains a lot of your body's tissues, such as those in your _____, skin, and _____. It protects your lungs from becoming damaged by _____. And it is important for the formation of red blood cells. The following foods are high in vitamin E: whole grains, such as wheat and oats, _____, leafy green vegetables, sardines, egg yolks, and _____.

Vitamin K

Vitamin K is the clotmaster! Remember the last time you got a cut? Your blood did something special called clotting. This is when certain cells in your blood act like glue and stick together at the surface of the cut. Which foods are rich in vitamin K? Leafy green vegetables, _____, pork, and _____, such as milk and yogurt.

Puzzling Pieces

Mineral Me!

Just like vitamins, minerals help your body grow, develop, and stay healthy. The body uses minerals to perform many different functions—from building strong bones to transmitting _____. Some minerals are even used to make hormones or maintain a normal _____. When people don't get enough of these important minerals, they can have health problems. Some kids may take mineral supplements, but most kids don't need them if they eat a _____ diet. So eat those minerals and stay healthy!

Macro and Trace

There are two kinds of minerals: macrominerals and trace minerals. *Macro* means "large" in Greek (and your body needs larger amounts of macrominerals than trace minerals). The *macromineral* group is made up of calcium, _____, magnesium, sodium, potassium, chloride, and _____. A trace of something means that there is only a little of it. So even though your body needs trace minerals, it needs just a tiny bit of each one. _____ aren't even sure how much of these minerals you need each day. *Trace minerals* includes iron, manganese, copper, _____, zinc, cobalt, _____, and selenium.

Calcium

Calcium is the top _____ when it comes to building strong bones and teeth. Which foods are rich in calcium? Dairy products, such as milk, cheese, and _____, canned salmon and sardines with bones, leafy green vegetables, such as broccoli, and calcium-fortified foods—from _____ juice to cereals and crackers.

Iron

The body needs iron to transport _____ from your lungs to the rest of your body. Iron helps because it's important in the formation of hemoglobin, which is the part of your _____ that carries oxygen throughout the body. Which foods are rich in iron? Meat, especially red meat, such as beef, _____ and salmon, eggs, beans, baked potato with skins, _____, like raisins, leafy green vegetables, such as broccoli, and whole and enriched grains, such as _____ or oats.

Potassium

Potassium keeps your muscles and _____ working properly by making sure the amount of water is just right. Which foods are rich in potassium? _____, _____, potatoes with skins, leafy green vegetables, such as broccoli, citrus fruits, such as oranges, dried fruits, and _____, such as beans, peas, lentils, and peanuts.

Zinc

Zinc helps your immune system, which is your body's system for fighting off _____ and infections. It also helps with _____ and helps heal wounds, such as cuts. Which foods are rich in zinc? Beef, pork, _____, and legumes, such as beans, peas, lentils, and peanuts.

Lesson 2: Did I Eat That? How to Read a Food Label

Time Needed

One to two 40–50 minute class period

National Standards

- Students will comprehend concepts related to health promotion and disease prevention to enhance health.
- Students will demonstrate the ability to access valid information and products and services to enhance health.

Objectives

- Students will read and calculate the information on a food label.
- Students will compare and contrast information provided on food labels.
- Students will line up consecutively in various orders based on different nutrition contents.

Materials & Preparation

- *(Optional.)* Duplicate any handout on how to read a food label, one per student.
- Bring in thirty snack food items or assorted food labels from snacks sold in convenience stores and vending machines (one for each student).
- Duplicate a Food Label Analysis Worksheet (Worksheet 4.2) for each student.

Procedures

1. Distribute and review the handout on how to read food labels.
2. Make sure students know how to do the following:
   - Identify the serving size and how many servings there are in the package.
   - Identify the total calories per serving.
   - Calculate the total calories per package.
   - Identify the total grams of fat.
   - Calculate the number of calories from fat.
   - Identify the total grams of saturated fat.
   - Identify the total grams of carbohydrates.
   - Calculate the number of calories from carbohydrates.
   - Identify the total grams of simple carbohydrates.
   - Identify the total grams of complex carbohydrates.
   - Identify the total grams of protein.
   - Calculate the number of calories from protein.
   - Identify the amount of sodium in the product.
   - Identify the three main ingredients in this product.

3. Pass out a snack food or a snack food label to each student.

4. Have students complete the Food Label Analysis Worksheet (Worksheet 4.2).

5. Briefly review some answers with students to make sure students comprehend the concepts.

6. Next explain to students that they will be forming a line continuum in the front of the room based on the information on their food labels.

7. The first line continuum should be based on the *Total Calories* in their packaged food item (if the student was to eat the entire package). The person with the least total calories should arrange themselves at the beginning of the line, the person with the most total calories will be at the end of the line, and everyone else will be somewhere in between.

8. The second line continuum should be based on the *Total Grams of Fat* in their packaged food item. The person with the least total grams of fat will be at the beginning of the line, the person with the most total grams of fat will be at the end of the line, and everyone else will be somewhere in between.

9. The third line continuum should be based on the *Total Milligrams of Sodium* in their packaged food item. The person with the least sodium will be at the beginning of the line, the person with the most sodium will be at the end of the line, and everyone else will be somewhere in between.

10. The fourth line continuum should be based on the *Total Grams of Simple Carbs* in their packaged food item. The person with the least total grams of simple carbs will be at the beginning of the line, the person with the most total grams of simple carbs will be at the end of the line, and everyone else will be somewhere in between.

11. Use the following process questions to lead a class discussion:
    - What did you learn about your snack?
    - Which snacks were the least healthy? Most healthy?
    - Does "Low Fat" or "Fat Free" mean low in calories?
    - What were some of the main ingredients in your products?
    - What would be a better choice for a snack? Why?
    - Why are many of these foods called "empty calorie" foods?

12. Conclude by pointing out that many of the snack foods students typically eat are high in calories and low in nutritional value. By learning how to read food labels, students will be able to select more nutritious foods in the future.

Assessment
- Participation in the junk food lineup.
- Participation in the class discussion.

WORKSHEET 4.2

Food Label Analysis Worksheet

Directions

Use the food item or label you were given to answer the following questions.

1. Identify the serving size and how many servings are in the package.

2. Identify the total calories per serving.

3. Calculate the total calories per package (calories per serving multiplied by number of servings per package).

4. Identify the total grams of fat per serving.

5. Calculate the number of calories from fat (grams of fat per serving multiplied by 9 calories per gram).

6. Identify the total grams of saturated fat (grams of saturated fat per serving multiplied by 9 calories per gram).

(Continued)

7. Identify the total grams of carbohydrate per serving.

8. Calculate the number of calories from carbohydrates (grams of carbohydrates per serving multiplied by 4 calories per gram).

9. Identify the total grams of simple carbohydrates per serving.

10. Identify the total grams of complex carbohydrates per serving.

11. Identify the total grams of protein per serving.

12. Calculate the number of calories from protein (grams of protein per serving multiplied by 4 calories per gram).

13. Identify the three main ingredients in this product.

Lesson 3: What's That?

Time Needed

One 40–50 minute class period

National Standards

- Students will comprehend concepts related to health promotion and disease prevention to enhance health.
- Students will demonstrate the ability to access valid information and products and services to enhance health.
- Students will demonstrate the ability to advocate for personal, family, and community health.

Objectives

- Students will guess the name of food products by reading the lists of ingredients.
- Students will discuss the difference between food products that are processed and those that are homemade.

Materials & Preparation

- The preparation for this lesson is extensive. The teacher must locate ten food products whose lists of ingredients are difficult to interpret; for example, bouillon cubes, baby formula, dog food, canned ravioli, and processed fruit snacks. The lists of ingredients should be cut off the product and taped on the outside of a bag or box. The food itself, or the wrapping, should be placed inside the corresponding bag or box. Finally, the bags or boxes should be secured and numbered 1 to 10.
- Duplicate the What Is That? worksheet (Worksheet 4.3), one for each student.
- Create ten stations around the room and place one bag or box at each station.

Procedures

1. Pass out a What Is That? worksheet to each student. Divide the class into groups of two or three, depending on how large the class is.
2. Send each pair or group to a station. Before anyone does anything, point out that each pair or group is standing at a different station. Each bag or box is numbered 1 to 10. Only the students standing at station #1 will write their answer on the first line of the worksheet. *If a pair or group starts at station 8, they write their first answer on line #8.* Each pair or group will rotate so that everyone will have a chance to be at every station.
3. No one is allowed to touch the bag or box at his or her station.
4. Allow the class to begin inspecting the list of ingredients at their station. They have to guess what the food product is by reading the list of ingredients on the outside of the bag or box. When the teacher gives the switch signal (flips the lights, rings a bell, or yells "Switch!"), the pairs or groups rotate to the next station.

5. When every pair or group has finished, the teacher reviews each station, one by one, and allows students to share what they guessed was in the bag or box. After all groups have offered their guesses, the teacher can reveal the true product and then move on to the next station.

6. After the teacher reveals what is in the last bag or box, use the following process questions to lead a class discussion:

   - Why was it so hard to guess what was in the bags or boxes?
   - How do you feel about not even knowing the ingredients in the foods that you are eating?
   - Why do you think the lists of ingredients of these products are so confusing?
   - What are the ingredients of an apple, of orange juice, of milk?
   - Which foods are healthier—apples, orange juice, and milk, or the products in the bags?
   - Why do people eat the products in the bags if they are so unhealthy?
   - Are there healthier options that people could choose? What are they?

7. Conclude by stating that although processed foods may be very convenient to eat, they are not as healthy as other choices. A person does not have to sacrifice nutrition for convenience. There are many quick healthy foods people can choose to eat. Healthier foods can be prepared on the weekends and put in Tupperware containers for the rest of the week. Read the lists of ingredients of the foods you are thinking of buying before you actually purchase them. If you can't understand what it says—don't buy it!

Assessment

- Completion of the What Is That? worksheet.
- Participation in the station activity.
- Participation in class discussion.
- Alternate Activity

WORKSHEET 4.3

NAME _____   DATE _____

What Is That?

Directions

Inspect the lists of ingredients of the foods provided. Try to guess what each food is and record your guess below on the line that corresponds to the number on the bag.

1. _____

2. _____

3. _____

4. _____

5. _____

6. _____

7. _____

8. _____

9. _____

10. _____

Lesson 4: Hearty Appetites

Time Needed

One 40–50 minute class period

National Standards

- Students will comprehend concepts related to health promotion and disease prevention to enhance health.

Objectives

- Students will compare and contrast "guesstimates" of serving sizes to the true serving sizes.
- Students will discuss the relationship between obesity and excess food consumption in the United States.

Materials & Preparation

1. Duplicate the Serving Sizes handout, 1 copy per student
2. Purchase foods prior to the lesson. For each food item, prepare one small Ziploc bag with the actual serving size of the item in it and one large Ziploc bag, or some kind of container with three to five times the actual serving size in it. No bag or container should have a food label on it, or the food label should be blacked out (food labels give away the serving sizes).
3. The food used should be foods common to the age group. Below are some examples of foods that might be appropriate to use. Actual serving sizes of the foods are given in parentheses.

    grapes (*½ cup is the real serving size*)

    cereal (*1 oz. is the real serving size*)

    juice (*¾ cup is the real serving size*)

    soda (*¾ cup is the real serving size*)

    crackers (*3–4 small or 2 large is the real serving size*)

    chips and pretzels (*handful is the real serving size*)

    bananas (*1 medium banana is the real serving size*)

    salad dressing (*1 tsp. is the real serving size*)

    cheese (*1½ oz. is the real serving size*)

    nuts (*⅓ cup is the real serving size*)

4. Plates, cups, napkins, and utensils as appropriate for the food items purchased.

Procedures

1. Divide the class into small groups, three to four per group, and pass out paper plates, cups, utensils, and napkins—whatever is applicable to the products purchased.
2, Give each small group one of the pre-prepared *large portions* of a food item.

3. Ask each group to determine the serving size of their particular food item. They should take the actual food out of the container and place their "guesstimate" of one serving size on a plate, bowl, or in a cup.

4. Once all the groups have decided how much food is in one serving, take out the pre-prepared *serving size* bags.

5. Go around the room and have each group show the "guesstimates" they made about the serving sizes of their products, and compare the actual serving sizes to the small-group guesstimates.

6. Use the following discussion questions to help spark a group discussion about serving sizes.

   • Why do you think that students overestimated many of the serving sizes?
   • What is it about our country that encourages people to eat so much food?
   • Do you think people in other countries eat as much as we do in the United States?
   • Why is it important to have a correct perception of serving sizes?
   • What can students do to cut down on serving sizes?

7. Hand out the worksheet on serving sizes and review it with the class.

8. Conclude the lesson by pointing out that in this country we have a problem with obesity and overeating. Part of this problem is caused by the very large serving sizes we tend to consume. Cutting down on serving sizes can help a person have a healthier diet.

9. Remind students to be more conscious of the serving sizes and portions of the foods they eat. Reiterate that what they eat is not as important as how much they eat.

Assessment

• Identification of the serving size of the food item
• Participation in class discussion.
• Alternate suggestion: Bring real plates, bowls, cups and utensils from home—nowadays they tend to be larger than paper products. The larger cups, bowls, and plates will encourage students to "guesstimate" lower portions—correctly simulating what people actually serve themselves each day!

HANDOUT 4.2

Serving Sizes

A Fist = One Cup. *Your fist is approximately the same size as one cup. The USDA counts one-half cup of rice, cereal, or pasta as one serving size. So if you compare your fist to a bowl of cereal or spaghetti, you are probably having two servings in your dish.*

A Handful = One or Two Ounces of Tiny Snack Food. *A handful is approximately the same size as one or two ounces of small snack foods like hard candy or nuts.*

Two Handfuls = One to Two Ounces of Crunchy Snack Food. *Chips, pretzels, popcorn, and other types of crunchy snack food are more light and airy than nuts. So when trying to determine serving sizes for these types of products, two handfuls is equal to one serving size.*

A Thumb = One Ounce of Cheese. *Use your thumb to estimate how much cheese you are eating. Hard cheeses, such as cheddar, will weigh more than soft cheeses, such as mozzarella, but in general, one thumb-sized chunk is approximately one ounce. The USDA states that 1.5 to 2 ounces of cheese is one serving.*

Thumb Tip = One Teaspoon. *Products such as butter, peanut butter, and mayonnaise are very high in fat. If you smear any of these products on your food, use the tip of your thumb to estimate the equivalent of a teaspoon.*

Palm = Three Ounces. *One serving of meat is a lot smaller than you'd expect. The USDA says that 2.5 to 3 ounces constitutes a serving of meat, chicken, or fish. A person's palm, minus fingers and thumb, is approximately the same size as 3 ounces.*

Tools for Teaching Health. Copyright © 2007 by John Wiley & Sons, Inc. Reproduced by permission of Jossey-Bass, An Imprint of Wiley.

Lesson 5: Positive and Negative
Weight Loss Cards

Time Needed

One 40–50 minute class period

National Standards

- Students will comprehend concepts related to health promotion and disease prevention to enhance health.

Objectives

- Students will identify weight loss techniques as either positive or negative.

Materials & Preparation

- One set of weight loss cards (see boxes below). Write the phrases on index cards or type them out and paste them on cards and laminate them for future use.

Procedures

1. Pass a weight loss card out to each student. There should be one card for each student. If there are more cards than students, give students more than one card.

2. Break the class up into small groups and allow groups to share the weight loss techniques on the cards and determine whether the techniques are positive or negative and *why*. The small group format allows peer teaching to occur and helps to ensure that students determine the correct answer.

3. Once groups have finished discussing their techniques, ask the class to make sure each student has his or her own cards back and then ask them to move back to their seats.

4. Start with the negative techniques and ask those who think they have negative technique cards to share their answers. The teacher either can have students read their card or can keep a running list on the board and have students copy the list into their notebooks.

5. For each technique, the teacher should make sure the class understands *why* the technique is negative. Understanding the *why* is where the true learning takes place.

6. Once all the negative techniques are read, the teacher should repeat the process with the positive techniques, correcting any mistakes along the way.

7. Conclude the class by stating that the majority of people in this country go on a diet at one time in their life. People should know safe, healthy, and effective weight loss techniques. Share this information with family members to prevent them from following negative weight loss practices.

Assessment

- Identifying their card as a positive or negative weight loss technique and discussing why this is so.
- Participation in class discussion.

Weight Loss Cards

Positive Weight Loss Techniques

Don't eat right out of the bag.

Eat within one hour of waking up.

Do not eat while standing at the kitchen counter.

Increase consumption of dietary fiber.

Limit sodium (salt) intake.

Do at least 20 minutes of aerobic exercise three times per week.

Choose fruits and vegetables as snacks.

Use less dressing on your salad.

Eat a variety of foods.

Eat fewer fried foods.

Measure your food portions for a week until you can tell at a glance how big your portion should be.

Eliminate or limit alcohol intake.

Avoid eating while watching TV or talking on the phone.

Eat breakfast. It will probably help you
avoid mid-morning munchies.

Brush your teeth after every meal or snack.

Keep low-calorie, nutritious snacks on hand.

Cut down, not out. Watch your portions.

Eat when you are hungry, not out of habit.

Indulge yourself every once in a while. It will
prevent you from being obsessed with food.

Don't skip meals.

Drink six to eight glasses of water a day.

Avoid extra calories in sodas and candy.

Weigh yourself once a week.

Negative Weight Loss Techniques

Don't worry about nutrition—just take vitamins.

Take diet pills to curb your appetite.

Fast once a week to cleanse your body.

Drink only water.

Skip dinner—don't eat after 4 p.m.

Weigh yourself every day to see if you lost weight.

Eat only junk food—why waste calories
on foods you don't like?

Skip breakfast—who needs those extra
calories so early in the morning?

Eat only grapefruit, but eat as much as you want.

Use laxatives to make you go to the
bathroom. You will weigh less.

Use diuretics—they will make you weigh less.

Eat lots of cabbage, it will help you lose weight,
and that way, you can eat anything you want.

Exercise for hours every day, then you
can eat whatever you want.

Eat only one food group each day. Mondays only
breads, Tuesdays only fruits, and so on.

Don't exercise unless you have to—
it makes you hungrier.

Avoid starches—they will make you fat.

Smoke to curb your appetite.

Eat quickly.

Always clean your plate, even if you are full.

Eat slowly. Put your fork down between each bite.

Chew your food 100 times before you swallow.

Shop on an empty stomach.

Eat only ice cream.

Eat only high-protein foods; avoid carbohydrates such as pasta and fruit.

Cut fat out of your diet altogether. It's bad for you.

Buy the latest diet book at the book store and try it.

Eat standing up. Gravity will help your digestion.

Nutrition Home–School Connection

**Home–School Connection:
Favorite Family Recipe Conversion**

Time Needed to Complete

3–5 days

Time Needed to Present

20 minutes during one class period

National Standards

- Students will comprehend concepts related to health promotion and disease prevention to enhance health.
- Students will demonstrate the ability to practice health-enhancing behaviors and avoid or reduce risks.
- Students will demonstrate the ability to advocate for personal, family, and community health.

Objective

1. Students will change the ingredients of a recipe to make it healthier.

Materials & Preparation

1. Duplicate the Family Recipe Conversion worksheet (Worksheet 4.4), one copy per student.

Procedures

1. Explain to the class that they are going to have an assignment to complete with a family member. This should not be a sibling—unless the sibling is more than ten years older than the student.

2. Distribute the Family Recipe Conversion worksheet and review.

3. Assign the due date for the assignment.

4. On the day the assignment is due, students can share the results of their participation, as well as their reflections. This can take as much or as little time as is available.

5. Following are some process questions that can be asked to facilitate discussion:

    - Prior to completing this activity, did anyone ever have a conversation with his or her family member about nutrition?

    - Which family member did you choose to speak to? How many of you spoke to many family members at the same time?

    - What were some of the suggestions your family members had for recipe conversion?

- How did the recipe come out? Did the food taste the same or better?
- What did you learn from this activity? What did your family member(s) learn?
- Are there any other comments or questions?

Assessment

Submission of the completed Family Recipe Conversion worksheet.

Extension Activities

1. Students can bring in their food dishes for an in-class taste test!
2. Students can be asked to change the recipes to make it healthy in a specific way—for example, decrease sodium, decrease saturated fat, or decrease simple sugars.
3. Students can be asked to make a food of cultural significance.

WORKSHEET 4.4

Home-School Connection: Family Recipe Conversion—Up Close and Healthy

Due Date: _____

Directions

With a parent or guardian decide on a favorite family recipe that you would like to share. Place all the ingredients necessary on the left of the activity sheet.

   After you finish, with your parent or guardian make whatever changes you can to increase the healthfulness of the recipe (for example, decrease salt intake; decrease saturated fat; lower cholesterol-containing substances) on the right side of the sheet. This can include substitutions of one ingredient for a healthier one or additions—adding a healthy ingredient to improve the nutrition of the recipe.

   Finally, make the recipe the healthier way and eat it!

Name of Recipe _____

Ingredients	Changes Made to Recipe to Make It More Healthy

Tools for Teaching Health. Copyright © 2007 by John Wiley & Sons, Inc. Reproduced by permission of Jossey-Bass, An Imprint of Wiley

NAME _____ DATE

How did the changes you made make the recipe healthier?

Student: How did it taste? Would you make it and eat it again?

Parent: How did it taste? Would you make it and eat it again?

What other recipes can your family change to make them healthier?

_____   _____

Student's Signature   Family Member's Signature

Nutrition Project

Project: Food Diary and Reflection Paper

Note to the Teacher

http://nat.crgq.com/mainnat.html

The teacher may want to visit the URL prior to taking the class to the computer lab. It will be easier to instruct students on the process of using the site if the teacher has practiced using it first.

One of the benefits of this site is that it is free. One of the drawbacks is that the database does not contain all the foods students eat. Students will have to be creative when selecting food items, selecting foods that are similar to what they ate, instead of exactly the same foods.

There are two things the teacher should be aware of when facilitating this lesson. First of all, when students are entering food items, they will need to break their foods down to the "lowest common denominator", so to speak. Thus, a roast beef sandwich becomes roast beef, 2 slices of bread and mayonnaise.

The second thing the teacher should take note of is the serving size drop down bar. Students may have a difficult time identifying how many cups, ounces, or grams they have consumed. If students carefully read down to the bottom of the drop down list, there is usually a service size option (e.g. 1 apple).

There are many commercial nutrition analysis software products that can be purchased by a school district. If cost is prohibitive, however, this site can provide basic feedback that will help inform students about their eating habits

Time Needed

This assignment should be distributed at the beginning of a nutrition unit so that students have time to complete the diary. After all students have completed their food diary, arrangements should be made to take the students to the computer lab to input their data. Alternatively, students can be required to input their data on their own time. On the day the reflection paper is due, the teacher can use as much time as is available for students to share their project reflections. Sharing can take 20 minutes or an entire period.

The project may take anywhere from 4–8 days to complete, depending on how long students are given to complete the reflection paper and how quickly the teacher can get the class into the computer lab.

National Standards

- Students will demonstrate the ability to advocate for personal, family, and community health.
- Students will demonstrate the ability to access valid information and products and services to enhance health.

Objectives

1. Students will document the food they eat over a three-day period.

2. Students will enter the food they ate into a computer database that calculates various information related to diet and nutrition.

3. Students will analyze their nutrition information and write a reflection paper about what they learned and how they can improve their eating habits.

Materials & Preparation

1. Duplicate the Food Diary Project worksheet (Worksheet 4.5) and Food Log worksheet (Worksheet 4.6), one per student.

2. Reserve the computer lab.

Procedures

1. Begin the lesson by asking students about the food they eat.
   - Are their diets healthy?
   - Do they eat enough fruits and vegetables? Protein?
   - How much junk food do they eat?
   - Are they consuming enough vitamins and minerals?

2. Tell students that they are being assigned a project. They will keep a food diary for three days, inputting their food choices into a computer database and writing a reflection about what they found out about their diet.

3. Distribute the Food Diary Project worksheet and Food Log worksheet to the students and review the directions with the class.

4. Once students understand what is expected of them, give the due dates for the assignment and have students write the due dates on their project handout.

5. At the end of the three-day period, ask students to submit their food logs or simply bring them to class.

6. Bring the class to the computer lab and assign a due date for the reflection paper.

7. The teacher may want to review the etiquette for using computers—no instant messaging, no searching eBay, no checking e-mail, and so forth!

8. Provide students with the URL for the online analysis site and directions on how to input their food choices: http://nat.crgq.com/mainnat.html

9. Allow students to input their data. The teacher should be walking around the room to assist students in the process and make sure students are on task.

10. As students finish inputting their data, they should print out their results and begin work on their reflection paper.

11. On the day the reflection paper is due, have students share the results of their data entry and what they wrote about in their reflection papers.

12. Following are some process questions that can be asked to facilitate discussion:
    - Did anyone find something surprising when they received his or her nutrition printout?
    - Are you eating in a more or less healthy manner that you thought?
    - What are some nutrients you were overconsuming? Underconsuming?
    - What other things did you learn about your dietary habits?

- How can you change your dietary habits to make them healthier?
- Does anyone intend to change his or her diet? In what way?

13. Conclude by pointing out that keeping a food diary is a good way to raise consciousness about eating habits. At different times in their life, people may have different dietary needs, such as when they age, become more or less athletic, or, in the case of women, become pregnant. Although someone may not need to keep a food diary every single day, it might be a good idea to keep a log every few months or years just to make sure eating habits are providing the proper balance of nutrients appropriate for the individual lifestyle.

Assessment

- Completion of students' three-day food diary and reflection paper. See attached rubric (Handout 4.3).

WORKSHEET 4.5

NAME   DATE

Food Diary Project

Food Diary Due Date: _____

Reflection Due Date: _____

1. You will be maintaining a three-day food diary. Food diary logs will be handed out in class. (It is very important that you write down what you eat as you are eating it. If you try to go a whole day and then remember what you ate that day, the food logs will not be as accurate. Try to pick days that are average days, maybe two weekdays and a weekend day.)

2. You will be going to the computer lab to input your food intake into a computer program (Nutrition Analysis Tool II, http://nat.crgq.com/mainnat.html). After you enter your food data, this program will print out the long list of nutrition analysis results.

3. You will analyze this printout to draw some conclusions about your dietary habits. This list must be attached to the paper when it is submitted.

4. After obtaining your results you will write a paper on the current status of your diet and how it could be improved. The following issues must be included in the paper:

   • Overall analysis of your diet (how did you do?).

   • Average number of calories per day versus recommended.

   • Average percentage of diet that comes from protein, fat, and carbohydrates versus national recommendations.

   • Mention of nutrients that you have too much of and how you can reduce consumption (what can you cut out of your diet). Discuss the danger of having too much of these nutrients.

   • Mention of nutrients that you don't have enough of and how you can increase consumption. Discuss the importance of having these nutrients in your diet.

   • Three specific nutritional changes that will improve your diet that you will commit to making over the next few months.

WORKSHEET 4.6

Food Log

Directions

Use this worksheet to keep track of all the foods and drinks you consume for the next three days.

Keep the worksheet and a pen or pencil with you at all times, so you do not forget to record what you are consuming.

Day 1

_____

Breakfast:

_____

Lunch:

_____

Dinner:

_____

Snack:

_____

NAME _____ DATE _____

Day 2

Breakfast:

Lunch:

Dinner:

Snack:

Day 3

Breakfast:

Lunch:

Dinner:

Snack:

Rubric for Food Diary and Reflection Paper

	Excellent (18–20 Points)	Good (10–17 Points)	Poor (9 or Fewer Points)
Food Diary	Student maintained an excellent food diary for three complete days. All foods eaten are written out in the appropriate spaces. The food diary was submitted as part of the completed assignment.	Student maintained a food diary, but it didn't cover three full days or the entries were incomplete or too brief. The food diary was submitted as part of the completed assignment.	Student did not keep a food diary or did not keep a food diary for three complete days. The quality of the food diary is extremely poor. The food diary was not submitted as part of the completed assignment.
Data Entry	Student entered all the items from the food diary into the Nutrition Analysis Web site. All foods were entered prior to the end of the class period.	Student entered most of the items from the food diary into the Nutrition Analysis Web site. Most foods were entered prior to the end of the class period.	Student failed to enter all the items from the food diary into the Nutrition Analysis Web site. Few or no foods were entered prior to the end of the class period.
Printout	The student completed the printout of the nutrition analysis and included it as part of the completed assignment. The printout reflects all food items in the food diary.	The student completed the printout of the nutrition analysis and included it as part of the completed assignment. The printout does not reflect all food items in the food diary.	The student did not complete the printout of the nutrition analysis and did not include it as part of the completed assignment. The printout does not reflect all food items in the food diary.
Reflection Paper	The reflection paper is clearly written and answers all 5 questions posed in the direction sheet in essay format. The student writes responses to the questions in an in-depth fashion. The quality of the student's writing is excellent.	The reflection paper answers only 4 out of 5 of the questions posed in the direction sheet in essay format. The student's responses to the questions could be fleshed out more. The quality of the student's writing is good.	The reflection paper is poorly written and answers fewer than 3 of the 5 questions posed in the direction sheet. The paper is not completed in essay format. Responses are completed in a cursory fashion. The quality of the student's writing is poor.
Spelling/ Grammar	No spelling or grammar mistakes in the reflection paper.	Minimal spelling and/or grammar mistakes in the reflection paper.	Noticeable spelling and grammar mistakes in the reflection paper.

Tools for Teaching Health. Copyright © 2007 by John Wiley & Sons, Inc. Reproduced by permission of Jossey-Bass, An Imprint of Wiley

Nutrition Assessment

Assessment: Functional Knowledge and Skills Exam

Time Needed

One 40–50 minute class period.

National Standards

- Students will analyze the influence of family, peers, culture, media, technology, and other factors on health behaviors.

Objective

1. Students demonstrate knowledge and skills related to nutrition.

Materials & Preparation

1. Duplicate the Functional Knowledge and Skills Exam, one per student.
2. Arrange the classroom desks as needed for exam format.

Procedures

1. As students enter the room, advise them to take their seats, put their books and notebooks under their chairs, and place a pen or pencil on their desk.
2. Explain the test-taking rules to the class. Following are some suggestions:
   - No talking!
   - No "borrowing" answers from a neighbor—if caught cheating, students will receive a zero and a phone call to home.
   - If students have a question, they should raise their hand. The teacher will come to them, not the other way around.
   - When students are done, they should pass in their test and work quietly on a different assignment or read a book while waiting for the rest of the class to finish.
3. Students take varying amounts of time to complete exams. It may be advisable to have some type of activity for quick test takers to work on while they are waiting for slower test takers to finish.
4. Be prepared with an activity for the entire class in case all students finish the test prior to the end of the period. The *Kids' Book of Questions* by Gregory Stock provides wonderful questions to spark class discussion on topics related to self-esteem, mental health, and other health-related issues. Students enjoy talking about answers to the questions, and it may be a relaxing way to conclude an otherwise stressful class period for them.

Assessment

Score on exam.

Answers to Multiple Choice Questions

1. D
2. B
3. D
4. A
5. A
6. C
7. B
8. B
9. A
10. D
11. B
12. D
13. C
14. C
15. B
16. A
17. D
18. A
19. C
20. B

Possible Answers: Content

Replace regular chips with "baked," regular soda or sweetened teas with a diet variety, sugary snacks with protein bars or trail mix.

WORKSHEET 4.7

NAME   DATE

Nutrition: Functional Knowledge and Skills Exam

Directions

This exam consists of twenty multiple choice questions and two constructed response (essay) questions. Please complete all questions.

Multiple Choice

Please circle the correct answer.

1. Excess fat intake increases the risk of all of the following except

   a. obesity

   b. heart disease

   c. stroke

   d. acne

2. Which of the following foods has no cholesterol?

   a. eggs

   b. peanut butter

   c. milk

   d. tuna

3. Functions of food additives include

   a. adding nutrients, flavor, color, or texture

   b. preventing spoilage

   c. improving taste and appearance

   d. all of the above

4. A serving of meat is about the size of

   a. a deck of playing cards

   b. a baseball

   c. a 16-ounce steak

   d. a half dollar

5. Iron and calcium are

   a. minerals

   b. vitamins

   c. electrolytes

   d. found in almost all foods

(Continued)

NAME   DATE

6. The substance that is essential for body growth and repair is

   a. vitamins

   b. fats

   c. proteins

   d. carbohydrates

7. Foods from this group are generally low in fat and calories.

   a. meat, poultry, fish, eggs

   b. vegetable

   c. dairy

   d. bread and cereal

8. One gram of carbohydrate has 4 calories. How many calories are in 1 gram of fat?

   a. 6

   b. 9

   c. 10

   d. 20

9. On the Nutrition Facts Label, the Percentage Daily Values are based on a diet of how many calories?

   a. 2,000

   b. 3,000

   c. 4,000

   d. 5,000

10. Laura has a basal metabolic rate of 1,500 calories and burns up an extra 1,000 calories per day from her activities. If she eats 2,000 calories a day, she will

    a. gain weight quickly

    b. gain weight slowly

    c. lose weight quickly

    d. lose weight slowly

11. As part of a healthy weight-loss plan, you should

    a. take diet pills

    b. plan to lose about 1 or 2 pounds a week

    c. fast for one day every week

    d. weigh yourself every day to see your progress

12. How many calories have been consumed in a meal with 10 grams of fat, 10 grams of carbohydrate, and 10 grams of protein?

    a. 100

    b. 120

    c. 160

    d. 170

Tools for Teaching Health. Copyright © 2007 by John Wiley & Sons, Inc. Reproduced by permission of Jossey-Bass, An Imprint of Wiley

NAME   DATE

13. Approximately how many days would it take to lose 1 pound if you took in 100 fewer calories per day than you needed?

    a. 10

    b. 25

    c. 35

    d. 100

14. Which of the following is an example of empty calories?

    a. apple

    b. whole-grain bread

    c. a can of soda

    d. a bag of peanuts

15. Whole-wheat bread has a nutritional advantage over enriched white bread because whole-wheat flour has

    a. more beta-carotene

    b. more fiber

    c. less cholesterol

    d. less fat

16. Anorexia and bulimia are

    a. psychological disorders

    b. genetic disorders

    c. degenerative disorders

    d. often related to schizophrenia

17. A fast food meal consisting of a super-size burger, super-size fries, and super-size regular soda would be unhealthy to eat on a daily basis because

    a. it contains too much fat

    b. it contains too much salt

    c. it contains a very high number of calories

    d. all of these

18. Which of the following ingredients on a food label indicate that it contains sugar?

    a. high fructose corn syrup

    b. aspartame

    c. ascorbic acid

    d. vitamin A

19. Which of the following is most likely to be a reliable source of information on foods and nutrition?

    a. an advertisement in a magazine

    b. a Web site with the URL www.buyourfood.com

    c. a nutritionist or registered dietician

    d. the guy with the biggest muscles at your gym or health club

(Continued)

20. The most healthful way to maintain your weight is

    a. skip breakfast and lunch and eat one big meal at night

    b. eat a balanced diet and exercise regularly

    c. eat mostly carbohydrates and fats, and limit protein

    d. go on two-day fasts, then eat as much as you want for the next week

Constructed Response Question

Scenario

You became interested in healthy and unhealthy food choices as a result of the nutrition information and skills you learned in your health education class. As a result, you have decided to make a presentation to the food service director about the lack of healthy snacks in the school vending machines. You do not necessarily want to eliminate all the snack items presently in the machines. You simply want to have some healthier choices added to the selection. Many students find it difficult to find healthy snacks, especially if they have to stay after school for club activities, sports, and so forth.

List three (3) typical snack foods or beverages that are high in fat, sugar, cholesterol, or salt that are presently sold in most school vending machines. For each, come up with a healthier alternative that you feel would still be appealing to students. Explain why each one is a healthier choice.

_____

_____

_____

_____

_____

_____

_____

_____

_____

_____

Tools for Teaching Health. Copyright © 2007 by John Wiley & Sons, Inc. Reproduced by permission of Jossey-Bass, An Imprint of Wiley

CHAPTER 5

SEXUALITY EDUCATION

Sexuality Education Icebreaker

Icebreaker: Abstinence Bingo

Time Needed

10–20 minutes

National Standards

- Students will comprehend concepts related to health promotion and disease prevention to enhance health.
- Students will demonstrate the ability to use interpersonal communication skills to enhance health and avoid or reduce health risks.

Objective

1. Students will find classmates who can answer questions on their worksheet.

Materials & Preparation

1. Duplicate a sufficient number of Worksheet 6.1: Abstinence Bingo for each student.
2. Pencils.
3. A healthy prize (for example, a protein bar or box of raisins).

Procedures

1. Explain to the class that they will be playing Abstinence Bingo today. A prize will be awarded (healthy prize) to the first student to get bingo. Three signatures in a row or a diagonal will constitute bingo. (If time permits, the teacher can require all the boxes to be signed to win the game.)

2. Hand out the Abstinence Bingo worksheets (Worksheet 6.1).

3. Advise students to write their name on top of their worksheet so that they do not lose it in the shuffle.

4. Tell students to read over the statements in the boxes. The object of the game is to obtain signatures in all nine boxes.

5. Review the rules of the game:

   - A person can only sign a box if they can answer "know how to" or fall into the category indicated. *No cheating!*

   - No person may sign more than one box on a page. Students may not sign any of their own boxes.

6. Tell students that they will circulate around the room and greet their classmates. Tell students to find out whether the classmates they speak to can sign any of their boxes, or vice versa. Remind students not to forget to find out the answer to the box they sign. The first student to get bingo wins!

7. Tell the students to start collecting signatures. (The teacher may want to consider telling them they cannot obtain their first signatures from people sitting next to them. This will encourage them to get up out of their seats and circulate.)

8. Continue the activity until the first student yells "Bingo!" At this point all students should sit down. The winner must read off the boxes that were signed, point out who signed them, and share the answers.

9. The teacher should go through the other boxes and have students take turns sharing what they learned from other students.

10. As each box is read, the teacher should discuss relevant information.

11. Conclude by reminding students that abstinence is the only 100 percent sure way to prevent pregnancy, HIV, and sexually transmitted infections.

Assessment

- A completed or partially completed Abstinence Bingo worksheet.
- Active participation in the Abstinence Bingo game.

Abstinence Bingo

Write the name of someone who . . . (you may not use the same person more than once)

Has discussed abstinence with their mother	Has discussed abstinence with their father	Feels oral sex is still abstinence
Feels discussing abstinence with teens is a waste of time	Can tell you three advantages of being abstinent	Knows what secondary virginity is
Has discussed abstinence with their boyfriend or girlfriend	Has discussed abstinence in your health ed class	Can name one alternative to sex that shows you care for someone

Sexuality Education Lessons

Lesson 1: Sexuality Brainstorm

Time Needed

One 40–50 minute class period

National Health Education Standards

- Students will comprehend concepts related to health promotion and disease prevention to enhance health.

Objectives

1. Students will list terms associated with the word *sex.*
2. Students will analyze and discuss the broad spectrum of terms related to *sexuality.*

Materials & Preparation

1. Duplicate the Alphabet Taxonomy worksheet (Worksheet 6.2), one copy per group.

Procedures

1. Write two words on the board: *Sex* and *Sexuality.*
2. Explain that *sex* is only one part of *sexuality.* When people think of sexuality they tend to think of just that one aspect, but there are many topics and concepts that are part of a sexuality unit.
3. Explain to the class that they are going to participate in a small-group brainstorm about sexuality. Students will work together to write words that come to mind when they hear or see the word *sexuality*—one word for each letter of the alphabet. (*Note:* the teacher may want to tell students they are only allowed to write anatomical words for parts of the body and for sexual behaviors, not slang names.)
4. Hold up a copy of the alphabet taxonomy worksheet to illustrate what you would like the students to do. Give an example, for instance, *puberty* for the letter *P* or *testicles* for the letter *T.*
5. Break the class into small groups, distribute one taxonomy worksheet per group, and give them 6–8 minutes to brainstorm.
6. After groups have had some time to work, bring the small groups back to the large group formation and have the students share their terms by asking what were some terms people had for the letter *A.* After all groups have shared *A* words, move on to the letter *B,* and so forth.
7. You may choose to record a master list of terms on the board, ask the students to copy terms in their notebook, or simply listen to the terms. Some terms that students may have written may be slang or street names. The instructor has the discretion of letting the students say the word as is, or asking students to mod-

ify their words to anatomical words. A practice that many sexuality educators use is to say the term once out loud, but then ask students if anyone knows a more acceptable term for the same word.

8. When all the terms have been read and recorded, the teacher should ask students to think about the terms that were just read or examine the master list on the board.

9. Some potential processing questions may be:

- What terms were mentioned the most?

- What terms have a positive connotation? Negative connotation? Neutral?

- What terms were related to males? Females? Both sexes?

- Were there any terms that someone never heard of before?

- Conclude by pointing out that sexuality is not just having sex. It is a part of who we are as human beings. It can be a positive part of your life (love, intimacy, caring) or negative (STDs, unwanted pregnancy, rape). This unit will teach you more about yourselves, your sexuality, relationships, and the positive and negative aspects of what it means to be a sexual person.

Assessment

- Completed, or partially completed, alphabet taxonomy worksheet.

WORKSHEET 5.2

NAME _____   DATE

Sexuality Alphabet Taxonomy

A _____   N _____

B _____   O _____

C _____   P _____

D _____   Q _____

E _____   R _____

F _____   S _____

G _____   T _____

H _____   U _____

I _____   V _____

J _____   W _____

K _____   X _____

L _____   Y _____

M _____   Z _____

Lesson 2: That's My Line

Time Needed

One 40–50 minute class period

National Standards

- Students will comprehend concepts related to health promotion and disease prevention to enhance health.
- Students will demonstrate the ability to use interpersonal communication skills to enhance health and avoid or reduce health risks.
- Students will demonstrate the ability to practice health-enhancing behaviors and avoid or reduce risks.
- Students will demonstrate the ability to advocate for personal, family, and community health.

Objectives

1. Students will identify persuasive "lines" that are commonly used to persuade someone into sexual activity.
2. Students will practice refusal and peer pressure–resistance skills.

Materials & Preparation

1. Strips of paper measuring approximately 16 by 4 inches.
2. Markers.
3. Invite a "judge" to come in—preferably someone with a sense of humor. Alternatively, the teacher can judge.
4. Prizes or awards for judge to present. Healthy snacks work well, as do silly prizes from the dollar store.

Procedures

1. To set the tone of the lesson, start with this fun activity. Read from a list of established "pick-up lines" and ask the class to rate them on a scale of 1 to 10. The lines can be clichés, humorous, or just plain pathetic—the idea is to infuse some laughter and reduce potential awkwardness about the subject of sex. Suggested "pick-up lines" are

   - Can I borrow your library card? I wanna check you out!
   - Are you from Tennessee? 'Cause ten is all I see!
   - Are your feet tired? 'Cause you've been running through my mind all day.
   - Are you Jamaican? 'Cause Jamaican me crazy!
   - Hi. You'll do.
   - Do you have a map? Because I'm totally lost in your eyes.
   - Well, here I am. What were your other two wishes?
   - I bet you 20 bucks you're gonna turn me down.

2. After you've rated the lines, begin a brief discussion about persuasion:

    *   What is the point of persuasion?
    *   What makes someone a good persuader? A poor persuader?
    *   What types of persuasion work best on you? Examples: humor, honesty, argument.
    *   Why might it be difficult to turn down someone who's trying to persuade you to do something?

3. Explain that today's lesson deals with "lines"—persuasive statements used to encourage students into certain sexual behaviors. Many lines have been used very successfully for generations, and were successful because the person receiving the line was unaware, unprepared, or not well-equipped to say no.

4. Tell students that we will be thinking of possible lines that could be given as a means of persuasion, as well as lines given back to refuse them.

5. Put the class into small groups (three to four per group). Assign half the groups the job of writing lines that a teenager could use to try to persuade another teenager into certain sexual behaviors: for instance, kissing, touching, intimate contact, having sexual intercourse. Assign the other half of the groups the job of writing lines that could be used to say "No" to the persuasive lines.

6. Distribute a number of strips of paper to each group, and indicate that there are more strips in the front of the room if needed.

7. Announce that this is a competition. Encourage the students to be creative, original, and comment that humor is permissible (as long as it is in good taste). Tell them that you will bring in a "judge" to determine the winners.

8. When students have completed their lists, tell them to select about 5–7 of their best lines and write each one on a paper strip and tape it to the board. Put all the lines of persuasion on one side and the refusal lines on the other.

9. Have a teacher, principal, or other authority (who has a good sense of humor) come to classroom to judge.

10. The judge selects the winners according to various categories of lines for persuasion, such as:

    *   Most original.
    *   Most often used.
    *   Most effective when participants are in love.
    *   Most obviously a line.

11. The judge selects the winners according to various categories of lines for refusal, such as:

    *   Most original.
    *   Most effective, least embarrassing.
    *   Least sincere.
    *   Least effective; it will never work!
    *   Most effective way to say "No."

12. The judge could award stickers or other small prizes.

13. This activity will help students understand the purpose (and sometimes insincerity) of persuasion, and how to stay in control of it.

14. Have students put their lines to use with skills practice.

    • *Option 1.* Divide students into groups to write and act out skits that use the award-winning lines, encouraging them to be creative yet realistic. Skits can be centered around just one line or use multiple lines; leave it up to the students. Groups then present their skits to the rest of the class.

    • *Option 2.* Create a song, rap, or poem using the lines and perform for the class. Students might rewrite the lyrics to an existing song of their choice.

15. Conclude by pointing out that the first step in making a good refusal is to be able to recognize lines. The next step is practicing that refusal so it easily "rolls off" the tongue when needed. The hope is that today's lesson will be a good start for students, but it should not be an ending. Students should continue to be aware and on the lookout for lines and should continue to practice refusals, so they are armed and ready in a real-life situation.

Assessment

• Submission of "lines" or refusals on strips of paper.

• Participation in class discussion.

• Participation in skills practice activity.

Extension Activities

1. For reinforcement, have a standing assignment that encourages the students to bring in any new "lines" that they hear, and have the class come up with new refusal lines for them.

2. Have students conduct an interview with students at school who have chosen to remain abstinent. Ask them what lines have been used on them and what refusals they used in return. Have students report to the class the results of the interviews. Remind them not to use real names or give identifiable information.

3. Have students write their own refusal lines that they would be comfortable with to use in a situation where assertiveness would be needed. Practice the lines with a fellow student or teacher.

4. Put some "risky" behaviors on slips of paper and have students draw a slip and give a refusal. *Examples:* "Would you like a ride home?" "Would you take off your shirt?" "If you really wanted to be my girlfriend, you would have sex with me."

Lesson 3: Raw Oysters Have Feelings Too!

Note to the Teacher

This is an excellent activity, but one that can raise uncomfortable or painful feelings, especially if there are only one or two students of the group about which a stereotype is raised. The teacher can help alleviate the pressure of these feelings if the teacher makes a conscious effort to encourage students to brainstorm stereotypes about all groups of people, especially the groups that the majority of students belong to. In addition, the teacher should stress the difference between stereotypes and generalizations and help the class examine where the stereotypes come from.

Time Needed

One 40–50 minute class period

National Standards

- Students will analyze the influence of family, peers, culture, media, technology, and other factors on health behaviors.
- Students will demonstrate the ability to use interpersonal communication skills to enhance health and avoid or reduce health risks.

Objectives

1. Students will define the words *prejudice* and *stereotype*.
2. Students will discuss situations where prejudice and stereotypes may occur.
3. Students will share how they felt when they were a witness to or a target of prejudice.

Materials Needed

1. Newsprint
2. Markers
3. Tape

Procedures

1. At the very beginning of class, before students even know what the lesson for the day will be, get their attention and announce: "Stand up if you do not like raw oysters."
2. Then request that all those standing who have never actually tasted raw oysters move to the back of the room (this will generally be a majority of them). Next, confirm that the students who are standing up at their seats have tried raw oysters and do not like them.
3. Those students sitting down either like raw oysters or they are not sure if they like raw oysters. Herein lies the point of the exercise.
4. Announce to the class that this was a surprise "Prejudice Test." Discuss the meaning of prejudice. Prejudice is prejudging—judging others on the basis of stereotypes, second-hand impressions, rumors, and so forth.

5. Ask them to explain which group is the most prejudiced against raw oysters. (Obviously, it is the group standing in back). Why? (They don't like raw oysters even though they have never actually tried them.)

6. Ask several students in the back why they do not like raw oysters. They will usually say things like "they look ugly, slimy, yucky, " or "they smell disgusting," or "I tried clams and I didn't like them," or "I don't like any seafood."

7. At this point, allow students to sit down and make the analogies to why we all have prejudices. Prejudices are learned behaviors, and people prejudge things all the time.

8. Next lead the group in a brainstorm on *stereotypes* and *labels.*

9. Explain to the class that this activity may feel uncomfortable, especially if names or labels may be offensive to people in the class. Explain that in order to change beliefs and attitudes the class needs to be honest about current prejudices and stereotypes. Advise students to try to keep an open mind. Sharing names and labels does not indicate a person's prejudices, it only reflects things that are being said and thought by people in general.

10. Break the class up into groups, with four to five students in each group. Give each group a piece of newsprint and magic marker. They must select a group leader based on who they think is the most intelligent member of the group. Instruct them to brainstorm within their group about any and all stereotypes or labels that you hear people call each other based on race, sex, age, physical appearance, clothes, nationality, religion, sexual orientation, intelligence, economic status, type of music they listen to, personality, interests, and so forth.

11. Tell groups that they are to try to list as many stereotypes and labels as they can in four (4) minutes.

12. When time is up, ask group leaders to tape their list to the board, quickly read off items, and put the total on the bottom of the newsprint.

13. Discuss where the names or labels come from. Where do we learn about these things? Are there any that you never heard of before?

14. Ask the following process questions to lead class discussion:
    - Are the labels harmless, or not?
    - Where do you cross the line; is it up to the individual to decide when the line is crossed, or is there a standard?
    - Does it depend on who says it? Or how they are saying it?
    - Does it depend on whether or not they know the person it is being directed to?
    - Does it depend on whether they belong to the group they are making the stereotype about?
    - If the topic has not already been brought up, bring up the issue of labels against those who are thought to be lesbian, gay, bisexual, or transgender. What about the labels of whore, gigolo, virgin. . .?
    - Why are labels related to sexuality particularly offensive?
    - Did the small groups make stereotypes when picking the most intelligent person?!

15. Ask the class what they can do to combat stereotypes—in their personal lives and in society as a whole.

16. Conclude the lesson by going around the room and asking students to share one thing they learned during the day's lesson.

Assessment

- Participation in class discussion.
- Responses provided during small group brainstorm on stereotypes.

Lesson 4: Contraceptive Commercials

Time Needed

One to two 40–50 minute class periods

National Standards

- Students will comprehend concepts related to health promotion and disease prevention to enhance health.
- Students will demonstrate the ability to access valid information and products and services to enhance health.

Objectives

1. Students will identify different methods of contraception.
2. Students will make a "commercial" for a specified method of contraception.
3. Students will identify advantages and disadvantages of different methods of contraception.

Materials & Preparation

1. Contraceptive Method worksheet for each small student (Worksheet 6.3).
2. Brown paper lunch bags.
3. Gather written materials about each birth control method for the small group work. (These materials can be printed out from http://www.plannedparenthood. org/birth-control-pregnancy/birth-control-4211.htm.) A local family planning agency or the health department can provide you with brochures or information sheets about these methods.
4. Birth control samples (male condom, female condom, IUD, spermicides [foam, jelly, film]), diaphragm, contraceptive sponge, contraceptive ring, oral contraceptives, emergency contraception, cards with the words "Abstinence," "Withdrawal," "Vasectomy," "Tubal ligation," or "Calendar/rhythm method" written on them). If samples of birth control methods cannot be obtained, the name of the method can be listed on a card as well.
5. Put each of the contraceptive methods mentioned above in its own brown paper bag along with at least one easy-to-read brochure that explains how to use that method.

Procedures

1. Tell the group that they are now going to learn about some specific methods of birth control.
2. Divide the class into groups of two or three. Give each small group a bag that contains a sample of a contraceptive method, along with written information about that method.
3. Review the following instructions with the class:
    - Each team will focus on one of the contraceptive methods.

- Read the information about your team's method and answer the questions listed on the worksheet.

- Pretend you work for an ad agency that promotes your method of contraception. Design a one-minute television commercial to market your contraceptive method to teens. Be sure to emphasize what makes the method effective and easy to use.

- Similar to a real ad, your commercial must contain the warnings about the product. The warnings your group creates should include any health risks for your particular method, as well as any disadvantages to using your particular method.

4. Have teens work on their worksheet and commercials.

5. Walk around the room to observe student progress and keep students on task.

6. After 10–12 minutes, ask each group to come to the front of the room and present their method (two minutes per group). The teacher should listen carefully to each group's presentation in order to correct or complete the information about each method.

7. After the presentations are completed, ask the class to vote on the best advertisement and the method that they think is the healthiest to use.

8. Ask the class when conversations about birth control should take place. Emphasize that these conversations should take place *before* the "heat of the moment." Advance discussions show maturity and responsibility and allow partners to be "prepared" and avoid pregnancy.

9. List names and phone numbers of local clinics and agencies that provide reproductive health education and services (such as local health department, Planned Parenthood, school clinic, community-based agency) on the board. Encourage students to write these numbers down. Even if they don't need the numbers now, they may need them in the future, and they may want to share them with friends.

10. Use the questions below to spark class discussion:

- What is the most effective method?
- What is the biggest difference between condoms and other methods of birth control?
- Why do you think people avoid condoms?
- How can someone encourage a partner to use condoms?
- How old must someone be to buy a condom without a parent's permission?
- What can someone do if she or he is too embarrassed to buy condoms in the store?
- How does a person decide which method of contraception to use?
- Which methods prevent pregnancy and STD/HIV?
- What makes a method easy for teenagers to use?
- Can teens avoid disadvantages of contraceptives? How?

11. Conclude by pointing out that abstinence is the only 100 percent sure way to prevent pregnancy, and that male and female condoms are the only way to prevent pregnancy, HIV, and other STDs when a person is sexually active. However, there are enough methods of contraception that all sexually active people should be able to find a method that works for them. No one who is sexually active should put himself or herself at risk for an unwanted pregnancy.

Assessment:

- Completion of the Contraceptive Method worksheet (Worksheet 6.3).
- Participation in class discussion.

Contraceptive Method Worksheet

Method: _____

How do you obtain this method?

How does this method work?

Who uses this method and how is it used?

What are the advantages of this method?

What are the disdvantages of this method?

Lesson 5: What Are They Selling?

Time Needed

One 40–50 minute class period

National Standards

- Students will analyze the influence of family, peers, culture, media, technology, and other factors on health behaviors.

Objectives

1. Students will analyze advertisements to try to determine what product is being sold.

2. Students will discuss the impact of sexuality in advertising on their own behaviors.

Materials & Preparation

1. Before class, select a series of advertisements for mundane products that use sex in the advertisements. Students will be expecting items such as lingerie, perfume, and shampoo to be advertised with sex. Try to find advertisements for things like gum or candy, cellular phones, and laundry detergent. You'd be surprised how easy it is to find such ads!

2. Once you have the advertisements, use paper and tape to cover words and any other identifying factors on the ad—so the students just see the images and cannot tell by reading the text what the product is that is being sold.

3. Set up the classroom as a series of stations, with one advertisement at each station (ten stations are recommended).

4. Duplicate Worksheet 6.4: What Are They Selling?! one copy per student.

5. Masking tape.

Procedures

1. At the beginning of class, point out the stations on the walls in the classroom.

2. Distribute one copy of Worksheet 6.4: What Are They Selling? to each student.

3. Divide the class into pairs or small groups, depending on the size of the class and the number of stations.

4. Explain to the class that they will go to a station with their partner or team. At each station they will examine the advertisement at that station and guess what product the advertisement is marketing. They will record their guess on the worksheet *on the line that corresponds with the station number.* Students will remain at their station until they receive the signal to move to the next station. Students should go to the next station that is one number higher than the one they are on (if they are at #12, go to #1).

5. After the students have rotated to all of the stations, ask them to take their seats while you go to each station, allowing students to share their guesses at the product before revealing what the product really is.

6. Use the following process questions to lead the class in a discussion about the lesson:

   - What was the similarity among all the advertisements?
   - Do you think these advertisements are an aberration or are they examples of the type of advertising that is "out there?"
   - Why do you think companies use sexuality in their advertising?
   - What is the impact of all the sexuality on young people's lives, if any?

7. Conclude by pointing out that the media is all around us. Some say that Americans are exposed to more than 3,000 advertising images in one single day. Many advertising companies use sexuality in their marketing campaign. The overwhelming number of advertisements that use sexuality may subconsciously encourage premature sexuality among young people. If people are aware of the influence of the media in their lives, it is the first step in preventing the media's powerful influence.

Assessment

- Participation the advertising analysis activity.
- Participation in the class discussion.

WORKSHEET 5.4

What Are They Selling?!

Directions

- Go to a station with your partner or team.

- Examine the advertisement at that station and guess what product the advertisement is marketing.

- Record your guess on this worksheet *on the line that corresponds with the station number.*

- Remain at your station until you receive the signal to move to the next station.

- Go to the next station that is one number higher than the one you are on (if you are at #10, go to #1). Repeat the process above.

Station 1:

_____

Station 2:

_____

Station 3:

_____

Station 4:

_____

Station 5:

_____

Station 6:

_____

Station 7:

_____

Station 8:

_____

Station 9:

_____

Station 10:

_____

Sexuality Education Home–School Connection

Home–School Connection: Hopes and Fears

Time Needed to Complete

1–3 days

Time Needed to Present

20 minutes during one class period

National Standards

- Students will comprehend concepts related to health promotion and disease prevention to enhance health.
- Students will demonstrate the ability to use interpersonal communication skills to enhance health and avoid or reduce health risks.

Objective

1. Students will talk with a family member about human sexuality.

Materials & Preparation

1. Duplicate Worksheet 6.5: Hopes and Fears, one copy per student.

Procedures

1. Explain to the class that they are going to have an assignment to complete with a family member. This should not be a sibling—unless the sibling is more than 10 years older.
2. Distribute Worksheet 6.5: Hopes and Fears and review.
3. Assign the due date for the assignment.
4. On the day the assignment is due, students can share the results of their participation and reflections. This can take as much or as little time as is available.
5. Following are some process questions that can be asked to facilitate discussion:
   - Prior to completing this activity, did anyone ever have a conversation with his or her family member about human sexuality?
   - Which family member did you choose to speak to? How many of you spoke to many family members at the same time?
   - What was it like talking to family members about this topic?
   - What were some of the fears your family members had for you?
   - Were you able to alleviate any of their fears? In what way?

- What were some of the hopes your family members had for you?
- Are you looking forward to some of the same hopes? Which ones?
- Did anything surprise you during your conversation?
- Did any other issues come up during your conversation?
- What did you learn from this activity? What did your family member learn?
- Are there any other comments or questions?

Assessment

- Submission of completed Worksheet 6.5: Hopes and Fears.

NAME

DATE

Hopes and Fears

Due Date: _____

Dear Family Member,

One of the most important areas of our Health Education curriculum deals with issues of *human sexuality and healthy relationships.* We strongly believe that families, through their thoughts, words, personal values, and actions, are the primary sex educators of their children. The role of the school is to supplement parental teachings by providing students with accurate, up-to-date information, by creating an atmosphere of mutual respect and trust in the classroom, by engaging students in learning activities that encourage a positive view of human sexuality, and by encouraging them to become well-informed, caring, and responsible adults.

With these guidelines in mind, please take a few minutes to complete the following assignment with your child. A minimum of *five* (5) responses in each column and an adult's signature are needed to complete the assignment. (You may certainly list more than five if you wish.)

Directions. As your child passes through adolescence into adulthood, what are some of your hopes and fears with regard to human sexuality and relationships?

Hopes	**Fears**
1. _____	1._____
2. _____	2._____
3. _____	3._____
4. _____	4._____
5. _____	5._____
6. _____	6._____
7. _____	7._____

_____   _____

Student Name   Adult Signature

Tools for Teaching Health. Copyright © 2007 by John Wiley & Sons, Inc. Reproduced by permission of Jossey-Bass, An Imprint of Wiley

Sexuality Education Project

Project: Music with a Message

Time Needed to Complete

3–5 days

Time Needed to Present

20 minutes during one class period

National Health Education Standard

- Students will analyze the influence of family, peers, culture, media, technology, and other factors on health behaviors.
- Students will demonstrate the ability to use interpersonal communication skills to enhance health and avoid or reduce health risks.

Objectives

1. Students will analyze the effect of the media on health.
2. Students will interpret messages relating to sexual health and sexual issues in popular music.

Materials & Preparation

1. Duplicate and distribute the project prior to this class. Assign the due date. This lesson will occur on the due date when students bring in their musical selections. (*Note:* Depending on your district or school policy you may want to tell the students that they may not use songs with profanity or graphic sexual language.)
2. CD player.
3. Audiocassette player.

Procedures

1. Collect the written assignments from the students.
2. Explain to the class: "One of the areas we will be discussing this year is the effect of media, such as TV, newspapers, radio, magazines, and the Internet, on our health. Media can influence our decisions, both positively and negatively."
3. Explain: "One important media form for teens is *music*. Music can relax, energize, relieve stress, inform, and entertain. Writers and musicians use lyrics and rhythms to share their feelings and insights about life. Many people are personally influenced by the messages in a song. What makes music especially interesting is that the same song can be interpreted in different ways by different people."
4. Ask for a volunteer to begin. This student should distribute the lyrics to the song to each classmate.

5. Put the song in the appropriate machine and play a verse or two. (Unless you have a small class there will not be enough time to play the entire song from each student.)

6. After the class has heard part of the song, first ask students whether anyone else chose the same song. If yes, allow both students to discuss the song together.

7. Then ask the student to share the reason they chose this song, what they think the message is, and whether they think the message is positive or negative.

8. If other students in the class are familiar with the song they may have something to contribute—or after reading the lyrics, discussion may ensue. When the discussion is over, repeat the procedures for the rest of the students in the class.

9. After all students have had a chance to share their music and discuss, use the following process questions to spark discussion:

   • Do you think teens are affected by the media?

   • Do the messages in songs or in the movies or TV influence teens regarding sexual attitudes and behavior?

   • If not, what *does* influence their feelings and decisions about sex? Friends? Parents? Teachers?

10. Conclude by pointing out that people's sexuality-related decisions are influenced by a number of factors, one of which is music. Sometimes people are not aware of how much influence something has over their lives until they take a critical look at it. The hope is that today's lesson helped to increase awareness of the influence of music in a person's life.

Assessment

• Submission of music lyrics and reflection. See Music with a Message rubric.

WORKSHEET 5.6

Music with a Message

Due Date: _____

One important media form for teens is *music*. Music can relax, energize, relieve stress, inform, and entertain. Writers and musicians use lyrics and rhythms to share their feelings and insights about life. Many people are personally influenced by the messages in a song. What makes music especially interesting is that the same song can be interpreted in different ways by different people.

Instructions

1. Think about and select a song that has a message about sex. This may include lyrics about love, relationships, breaking up, cheating, stereotypes, sexual violence, and so forth. It can be any form of music; for instance, new, old, rock, rap, metal, country, or Broadway. You should obtain a copy of the song on audiocassette, CD, or digital file if your teacher has access to the technology needed to play it in class.

2. On a separate sheet of paper, type the complete words to the song (you can find the lyrics to many songs online). Also include the artist(s) who recorded it, the album or CD it came from, and the year recorded.

3. Make copies of the lyrics for everyone in the class, including your instructor.

4. On a second sheet of paper, which be handed in to the teacher, answer the following questions (minimum of 1 page long):

   • What do you think the song is about?

   • Why did you choose the song for the assignment? What does it mean to you?

   • What is the message(s) you get from this song? Do you think this song sends a *positive* or *negative message* about sexuality? Why?

   • Cite at least *three specific lines* from the song that reflect this message.

   • How do you think young people react when they hear this song? Are they persuaded by the song? Do they take comfort in the song? Are they uplifted? What emotions and/or behaviors are affected?

   • How do you think adults react when they hear this song? Do they react the same way as young people?

   • Other comments, reactions?

5. Be prepared to play and talk about your song in class.

Music with a Message

	Superior 15–17 Points	Good 12–14 Points	Needs Improvement 11 or Fewer Points
Lyrics	The complete lyrics to the song are included.	Partial lyrics to the song are included.	No lyrics are included.
Message	The message of the song is entirely related to sexuality education.	The message of the song is partially related to sexuality education.	The message of the song is not related to sexuality education.
Reflection	In-depth reflection on all 7 bullets on the direction sheet for the assignment. The student elaborates on opinions without being redundant. The reflection is thoughtful and insightful and clearly demonstrates a connection between the assignment and the sexuality education unit.	Reflection on 5–7 of the bullets on the direction sheet for the assignment. The student discusses opinions without being redundant. The reflection is thoughtful and demonstrates a connection between the assignment and the sexuality	The reflection does not demonstrate thoughtfulness or insight. The student responds to 4 or fewer of the bullets on the direction sheet for the assignment. The reflection is redundant and does not show evidence of understanding the connection between the assignment and the sexuality education unit.
Writing Style	Paper is well written: written in own words in interesting style. Focused and on-topic. Good sentence structure.	Parts of paper are difficult to understand. Some evidence of copying. Writing is not completely focused on topic. Difficult to follow because of sentence and paragraph structure.	Paper is poorly written and difficult to understand. Much evidence of copying. Writing is unfocused and off topic.

Tools for Teaching Health. Copyright © 2007 by John Wiley & Sons, Inc. Reproduced by permission of Jossey-Bass, An Imprint of Wiley

Tools for Teaching Health. Copyright © 2007 by John Wiley & Sons, Inc. Reproduced by permission of Jossey-Bass, An Imprint of Wiley

NAME _____   DATE

	Superior **15–17 Points**	**Good** **12–14 Points**	**Needs Improvement** **11 or Fewer Points**
Editing	Paper is neatly done; creative and organized, great deal of attention is paid to detail, writing or word processing is neatly done. Evidence of proofreading and editing. Legible; neatly typed (12 or 14 point size, double spaced). Good grammar, spelling and punctuation.	Paper is somewhat neatly done. Some attention is paid to detail, some white-out cross-outs. Some evidence of proofreading and editing. Somewhat legible; typed (12 or 14 point size, double spaced). Some mistakes in grammar, spelling, and punctuation.	Paper is done in messy and careless manner: no attention is paid to detail. Too many white-out cross-outs. Little evidence of proofreading and editing. Illegible; not neatly typed. Many grammar, spelling, and punctuation errors.
Page Length	One full page or longer.	Three quarters to one page long.	One-half page long or less.
Timeliness	Paper is on time.	Paper is one day late.	Paper is more than two days late.

Sexuality Education Assessment

Assessment: Functional Knowledge and Skills Exam

Time Needed

One 40–50 minute class period

National Standards

- Students will comprehend concepts related to health promotion and disease prevention.
- Students will demonstrate the ability to use interpersonal communication skills to enhance health and avoid or reduce health risks.

Objective

1. Students demonstrate knowledge and skills related to sexuality education.

Materials & Preparation

1. Duplicate the Functional Knowledge and Skills Exam, one copy per student.
2. Arrange the desks as needed for exam format.

Procedures

1. As students enter the room, advise them to take their seats, put their books and notebooks under their chairs, and place a pen or pencil on their desk.
2. Explain the test-taking rules to the class. Following are some suggestions:
   - No talking!
   - No "borrowing" answers from a neighbor—if caught cheating, students will receive a zero and a phone call home.
   - If students have a question, they should raise their hand. The teacher will come to them, not the other way around.
   - When students are done, they should pass in their test and work quietly on a different assignment or read a book while waiting for the rest of the class to finish.
3. Students take varying amounts of time to complete exams. It may be advisable to have some type of activity for quick test takers to work on while they are waiting for slower test takers to finish.
4. Be prepared with an activity for the entire class in case all students finish the test prior to the end of the period. The *Kids' Book of Questions* by Gregory Stock provides wonderful questions to spark class discussion on topics related to self-esteem, mental health, and other health-related issues. Students enjoy talking about answers to the questions, and it may be a relaxing way to conclude an otherwise stressful class period.

Assessment

Score on the exam.

Answers to Multiple Choice Questions

1. B
2. D
3. A
4. A
5. D
6. D
7. A
8. C
9. C
10. C
11. D
12. C
13. A
14. C
15. D
16. A
17. D
18. D
19. D

WORKSHEET 5.7

Sex Education: Functional Knowledge and Skills Exam

Directions

This exam consists of nineteen Multiple Choice questions and two Constructed Response (essay) questions. Please complete all questions.

Multiple Choice

Please circle the correct answer.

1. The only 100 percent sure way to prevent pregnancy is . . .

   a. condoms

   b. abstinence

   c. oral contraceptives

   d. Norplant

2. Norplant is effective for

   a. six months.

   b. one year.

   c. three years.

   d. five years.

3. Depo-Provera

   a. is an injectable contraceptive that needs to be given once every 12 weeks.

   b. is implanted in a woman's arm and is effective for three years.

   c. is taken orally on a daily basis.

   d. is inserted into a woman's vagina.

4. The only temporary method of birth control for men is

   a. condoms.

   b. vasectomy.

   c. sterilization.

   d. male birth control pills.

5. According to various sources, a woman may insert a diaphragm as long as _____ prior to intercourse and have it be effective.

   a. one-half hour

   b. one hour

   c. three hours

   d. six hours

NAME _____ DATE

6. The diaphragm should remain in the vagina for at least _____ following intercourse, but not more than _____ .

   a. one hour; eight hours

   b. two hours; ten hours

   c. four hours; fifteen hours

   d. six hours; twenty-four hours

7. All of the following are presently available types of vaginal spermicides *except*

   a. vaginal contraceptive ring.

   b. vaginal contraceptive film.

   c. vaginal suppositories.

   d. vaginal foam.

8. In order to confirm that the IUD is in place, the length of the _____ should be checked.

   a. "T"

   b. copper wire

   c. string

   d. plastic rim

9. Vasectomy involves cutting and tying the

   a. corpus cavernosum.

   b. testes.

   c. vas deferens.

   d. fallopian tubes.

10. Condom usage rules include all but which one of the following?

   a. Never reuse a condom.

   b. If it breaks, replace it immediately.

   c. You may wish to fill a condom with water to test for leaks.

   d. Use only water-based lubricants with condoms.

11. What should you consider when selecting a contraceptive method?

   a. The effectiveness of the method in preventing pregnancy.

   b. The ability to use the method consistently and correctly.

   c. The safety of the method.

   d. All of the above.

(Continued)

12. Since starting to take oral contraceptive pills, a student has started to have severe headaches that prevent her from doing anything until they go away. What should she do?

   a. Take a pain reliever regularly to get some relief.

   b. Ignore them. Headaches are common in her family.

   c. Report the headaches to her health care provider and see him or her as soon as possible.

   d. None of the above

13. The point of persuasion is . . .

   a. to get someone to do something he or she does not want to do.

   b. to get someone to volunteer to help others.

   c. to get someone to do their homework.

   d. none of the above.

14. You are at a party and an upperclassmen says to you, "Hey baby, let's go upstairs for some privacy." What is the best refusal for this "line?"

   a. "I don't think that is such a good idea."

   b. "Umm. . . . Well. . . ."

   c. "There is no way I am going upstairs with you. Leave me alone before I get really angry!"

   d. All of the above.

15. One of the dangers of labels and stereotypes is that . . .

   a. they often reflect prejudices.

   b. they don't allow people to get to truly know one another.

   c. they assume that everyone is the same.

   d. All of the above.

16. Advertisers often use sex and sexuality to sell products because . . .

   a. Sex in advertising gets people's attention.

   b. Sex in advertising makes people embarrassed.

   c. Sex in advertising decreases sales.

   d. Never, the FDA has said that using sexual images in advertising is illegal.

17. In relation to sexuality, music . . .

   a. often provides a platform for discussion of social topics like relationships, dating, and break-ups.

   b. allows for expression of emotions and feelings that might otherwise be difficult for people to express.

   c. may reflect a change in social norms or actually change social norms.

   d. All of the above.

Tools for Teaching Health. Copyright © 2007 by John Wiley & Sons, Inc. Reproduced by permission of Jossey-Bass, An Imprint of Wiley

NAME   DATE

18. What contraceptive method prevents pregnancy, HIV transmission, is endorsed by all major religions, and is free of cost?

   a. Spermicidal foam.

   b. Contraceptive sponge.

   c. Oral contraceptives.

   d. Abstinence.

19. All of the following are related to good refusals except. . .

   a. recognizing a "line" when you hear one.

   b. practicing refusals so they roll off your tongue.

   c. using body language and tone of voice that match your refusal.

   d. continuing to talk with someone who gives you a "line" because they are popular.

Constructed Response Questions

Please write your answer in the space provided. Use the back of this test if you do not have enough room to complete your answer.

You really like a person from school and have been trying to get this person to notice you for the past few months. You think you have finally made some headway; the other day, this person came up to you at your locker and talked to you before homeroom and again at lunch. You found out that this person's parents are away for the weekend. Later that night, you get a phone call from the person asking you to come over.

   Discuss three (3) reasons that going to someone's house when there are no adults present is a bad idea.

_____

_____

_____

_____

_____

   Describe three (3) refusals you could give to avoid going to this person's house when there are no adults around.

_____

_____

_____

_____

_____

CHAPTER **6**

VIOLENCE PREVENTION

Violence Prevention Icebreaker

Icebreaker: What Do I Want to Be When I Grow Up?

Note to the Teacher

This can be a very emotional activity, especially with younger students and those who have already been affected by violence. Be sensitive to students' reactions in your class as you complete this activity. Consider carefully whose tie you choose to rip. The lesson makes a strong impact on some individuals.

Time Needed

10–20 minutes

National Standard

- Students will demonstrate the ability to use goal-setting skills to enhance health.

Objectives

- Students will draw images representing their goals and dreams for the future.
- Students will watch as the goals and dreams of some students are figuratively destroyed by violence.
- Students will discuss the impact of the activity on their health-related attitudes and behaviors.

Materials

1. Markers
2. Scissors
3. Tape

Preparation

1. Duplicate the Tie Diagram (Figure 7.1), one copy per student.
2. Prepare a sample tie as a visual aid for students *(optional)*.

Procedures

1. Distribute Figure 7.1: Tie Diagram.
2. Instruct students to draw pictures on their ties. The pictures will represent their goals and dreams for the future. No words, letters, or numbers are allowed.
3. *Optional.* Show an example of a finished tie so students see what is expected of them.
4. Pass out markers and scissors and allow students approximately 6–8 minutes to work on their tie. When students are done drawing they should cut out their tie. Meanwhile, the teacher is handing out tape to each student. (*Optional:* Pre-cut the ties to save time or if there are not enough scissors to distribute among the class.)
5. When time is up, the teacher will ask students to tape their tie to their chest and get up and make a circle in the middle of the room. Students should be facing the middle of the circle.
6. Students should then share what they drew on their tie and what it represents for their future.
7. When all students have completed the sharing activity the teacher should apologize to some of the students and say "I'm very sorry, but you never got to . . . *(whatever they drew on their tie).* As the teacher is apologizing, the teacher should literally rip the tie in half, crumple it up, and toss it on the floor. The teacher explains that the student was killed while speeding down the highway in a fit of road rage.
8. Rip the ties of a few students in class using various fatal violence-related scenarios, such as killed in a gang-related drive-by, killed in a fight against students from a neighboring town after a ball game, killed in a drunken bar fight, killed by accident when fooling around with a parent's gun, and so forth.
9. Once the ties are ripped on a number of students, ask the class to sit down. Move on to the process questions:

   • How did it feel to think about your goals and dreams? How often do you do that? When was the last time you thought about what you wanted out of life?

   • How did it feel when I ripped your tie?

   • How did you feel when you saw me ripping other people's ties?

214

Figure 6.1. Tie Diagram

- What was the point of this activity?

- How can you make changes in your life so your "tie is not ripped?"

10. Point out that over the course of the unit, students will be studying issues, concepts, and skills related to violence prevention.

11. Conclude by stating: "Oftentimes we don't think about the impact of our behaviors on our goals and dreams for the future until it is too late. Sometimes we make choices that are irreversible—we wish we could turn back the clock, but we can't. When you think back on this activity, I hope it will remind you to start to think toward the future when you make decisions. Ask yourself: *What will the consequence of this decision be? Will it help or hurt my chances for my goals?*"

Assessment

- Completion of the tie.

- Participation in class discussion.

Violence Prevention Lessons

Lesson 1: Violence Match Game

Time Needed

One 40–50 minute class period

National Standards

- Students will comprehend concepts related to health promotion and disease prevention to enhance health.

Objectives

- Students will arrange themselves in a continuum of violent behavior.
- Students will discuss issues related to violence in their lives and society.

Materials & Preparation

- Write or type terms for various types of violence on 8½-by-11 pieces of brightly colored cardstock or paper and laminate each piece of cardstock or paper or slip it into a pocket protector to create a set of Violence Match cards.
- Tape (optional)

Arson	Biting	Bombing
Bullying	Child abuse	Cursing
Drive-By	Elder abuse	Fight
Vandalism	Genocide	Hazing
Homophobia	Kicking	Knifing
Multiple homicide	Murder	Pinching
Pushing	Rape	Sexual harassment
Shooting	Spitting	Sports
Spreading rumors	Stealing	Suicide
War	Yelling	

Procedures

1. Explain to the class that they are about to begin a unit on violence.
2. Tell the class that they will each be receiving a card with a violent action on it.
3. Explain that students should arrange themselves in order, in a circle, from the least violent act to the most violent act.
4. Allow the class approximately 10 minutes to try to complete this task. Once students have arranged themselves in some semblance of order, either have them take a seat where they are or distribute pieces of tape to each student and have students tape their card on the wall in the appropriate order. Once students have taped their card on the wall, have them take their original seats.

5. Use the following process questions to spark discussion:

   - Did you have difficulty placing the cards in an order? What gave you difficulty?

   - Are there any actions on the cards you did not consider violent? Why?

   - Is there anyone in the class who has not participated in any of the actions on the cards?

   - Can you think of other violent actions that might have been placed on cards?

   - What is the relationship between the actions considered least violent and the actions considered most violent? Do any of the most violent actions occur without other lesser violent actions leading up to it?

   - How does violence negatively affect a person's life? What are some of the consequences of the violent actions we are looking at? (For example, punishment from parents, suspension from school, kicked off athletic teams, jail, guilty conscience.)

6. Conclude by pointing out that violence occurs in a continuum. It is impossible to reach the most violent actions without first starting a chain reaction with less violent actions. If people focus on decreasing lesser violent behaviors in their lives, they could prevent more destructive violence in their own life and in society as a whole.

Assessment

- Participation in the match card activity.
- Participation in class discussion.

Lesson 2: Where Do You Stand?

Time Needed

One 40–50 minute class period

National Standards

- Students will comprehend concepts related to health promotion and disease prevention to enhance health.

Objectives

- Students will identify their opinion by standing under the sign that best represents their opinion.
- Students will debate differing opinions with their classmates.

Materials & Preparation

The teacher will prepare for the lesson by taping five signs up on the wall, evenly spaced around the room. The signs will read as follows:

- Strongly agree
- Kind of agree
- Neither agree nor disagree
- Kind of disagree
- Strongly disagree

Procedures

1. As students enter the room, point out the signs on the walls.

2. Explain that the teacher will be reading some statements, one at a time. The students are to listen to the statement and then get up and stand under the sign that best represents their opinion about that statement.

3. Read the first statement and then ask questions based on where the students are standing. There are no specific process questions for this game; the questions will differ depending on how the game is played and the questions asked. Process each question as it is asked, instead of asking all the questions and going back to process them. Depending on how enthusiastic your class is, three to five questions may take up the entire period.

4. Allow students to debate each other and challenge classmates as to why they are standing under a sign different from their own.

5. Play the "devil's advocate" and try to get students to shift where they are standing.

6. Once all the discussion about one statement has been exhausted, read the next statement and repeat the process above.

7. Following are several statements that can be used as part of a violence unit. Feel free to create statements as they fit into the curriculum or as they relate to the district or community.

   - Some people are genetically programmed to be more violent than others.
   - If someone hits you it is acceptable to hit them back.
   - Sports are a socially sanctioned form of fighting.
   - Children should be disciplined without spanking or any use of physical force.
   - Watching a fight and doing nothing is supporting the fight.
   - Refusing to fight is more courageous than fighting.
   - Watching violence on television and playing violent video games promotes violence among youth.
   - The amount of violence in television and the movies reflects the violence in society.
   - It is human nature to be violent.

8. Conclude by telling the class that there are no right or wrong answers to the questions posed today. Students should think more about what was discussed and think about sharing what they talked about with their families. They should remember to value and respect the fact that people may have opinions that differ from their own.

Assessment

- Physical placement under the signs as each statement is read.
- Participation in class discussion.

Lesson 3: Managing Anger Round Robin

Time Needed

One 40–50 minute class period

National Standards

- Students will comprehend concepts related to health promotion and disease prevention to enhance health.
- Students will demonstrate the ability to use interpersonal communication skills to enhance health and avoid or reduce health risks.
- Students will demonstrate the ability to practice health-enhancing behaviors and avoid or reduce risks.

Objectives

- Students will describe anger and its effects on them.
- Students will identify options with which they can cope with their anger.
- Students will discuss G.R.E.A.T. Anger Management Tips (Handout 7.1).
- Students will participate in an anger management technique.

Materials & Preparation

- Seven pieces of large poster or easel paper taped up around the room with the following headings: "Synonyms for anger," "Things that trigger your anger," "How your body feels when you are angry," "How people cope with anger," "How it feels when someone is angry with you," "Positive ways to deal with anger," "Negative ways to deal with anger."
- Create an overhead transparency from Handout 7.1: G.R.E.A.T. Anger Management Tips.
- Overhead projector.
- Tape.
- Markers.

Procedures

1. Begin the lesson by asking students to think about the last time they felt really angry. Ask some students to share the cause of their anger.

2. Explain that the topic of the day will be what happens when people get angry, as well as appropriate ways to manage anger.

3. Explain to the class that they will be asked to brainstorm about several issues related to anger. Review the headings on the poster paper taped around the room.

4. Break the class into seven groups and send each group with a marker to one poster paper station. Explain to the class that each group will have 1–2 minutes at a station before they are given the signal to rotate stations. No groups should rotate until the signal is given by the teacher.

5. Allow the students to begin the activity. Walk around to monitor progress and make sure students stay on task. When all the groups have rotated to each station, ask students to return to their original seats.

6. Review student responses to the synonyms for angry feelings, such as frustration, rage, and disappointment. Ask the class why they believe there are so many words that relate to anger.

7. Review student responses to the triggers for anger. Examples are when parents treat you unfairly, when someone steals something from you, when someone spreads rumors about you, and so forth. Ask the class whether they consciously do things to avoid their personal triggers.

8. Review student responses to what happened to students' bodies when they got angry. Examples: face turned red, headaches, yelling, crying, and so on. Ask the class whether everyone reacts to anger in the same way. How can you analyze someone else's body language, tone of voice, and gestures to determine whether they are angry?

9. Review student responses to how they felt when another person was angry with them. What did they do in reaction to the other person's anger?

10. Ask the class whether there is any one correct way to handle anger.

11. Review student responses to negative ways to cope with anger. Examples of inappropriate venues of venting anger are physical fighting, punching walls, and so on. *Keep in mind that often a physical fight is admired within certain peer groups, and often children are instructed by their parents and peers to only take so much before standing up for themselves physically. Listen and divert to more positive options, rather than challenging the method.*

12. Review student responses to positive ways of coping with anger. Examples of positive anger management methods are exercise, talking with someone, journaling, going into a room and listening to music, separating yourself to a quiet place, talking to a friend or adult, talking in a calm way to the person you're angry with, going for a walk, and talking to your dog.

13. Put up the overhead on G.R.E.A.T. Anger Management Tips and have the students take notes, or distribute the tips as a handout (Handout 7.1). Review the tips with the class.

    • G: Give thought to what triggers your anger.

    • R: Recognize the signs of anger.

    • E: Elect to control your anger.

    • A: Actively do something to cool off.

    • T: Try to avoid the situations that trigger your anger the next time.

14. Lead the class in a discussion using the following questions:

    • Why is it important to identify things that trigger your anger?

    • Why is it important to identify the physical signs and feelings that indicate anger?

    • Think about the consequences of anger and the benefit of controlling anger. Will these make you think twice before you allow yourself to react to anger in the future?

15. Point out that thinking about anger when you are calm and logical will help you to decide that anger can get you into a lot of trouble. If you figure this out before you are angry, and figure out what makes you angry, then you can try to prevent yourself from being in a situation that sets you off.

16. Explain to the class that they are going to learn an important anger management technique. Explain that when people are angry, they start to take quick, shallow breaths. They may not even realize they are doing it, it just happens naturally. If you are angry, one of the things you can do is to practice deep breathing techniques. They can help you to "cool off."

17. Lead the class through the following deep breathing activity:
    * Sit up straight in your chair, keeping your spine straight.
    * Roll your shoulders back and keep your arms long and relaxed.
    * Drop your chin slightly so that the back of your neck is lengthened.
    * Close your eyes *(optional)*.
    * Breathe in slowly through your nose counting slowly from one to five.
    * *Teacher counts 1 . . . 2 . . . 3 . . . 4 . . . 5*
    * Breathe out slowly through your nose, counting slowly from five to one.
    * *Teacher counts 5 . . . 4 . . . 3 . . . 2 . . . 1*
    * Repeat steps five and six eight more times and then instruct the students to continue breathing on their own for a few more moments.

18. When the exercise is over, lead the class in a discussion by using the following questions:
    * Have the students ever done anything like this before?
    * How did the students feel after the technique? Were they more relaxed than when they began?
    * Could students imagine themselves doing this exercise if they were angry?

19. Conclude by asking some students to reiterate what anger management is. Emphasize that even though we may not be able to prevent all anger in our lives, deep breathing can help us to cool off when we do get angry.

Assessment
* Participation in the anger round robin.
* Note taking on the G.R.E.A.T. Anger Management Tips.
* Participation in the deep breathing activity.

Great Anger Management Tips

Give thought to what triggers your anger.

Recognize the signs of anger.

Elect to control your anger.

Actively do something to cool off.

Try to avoid the situations that trigger your anger the next time.

Lesson 4: Crossing the Line

Time Needed

One 40–50 minute class period

National Standards

- Students will demonstrate the ability to use interpersonal communication skills to enhance health and avoid or reduce health risks.
- Students will demonstrate the ability to practice health-enhancing behaviors and avoid or reduce risks.

Objectives

- Students will role play situations where sexual harassment may occur.
- Students will analyze and discuss how different factors play a role in sexual harassment.

Materials & Preparation

1. Bring or make a Stop sign with a handle.
2. Prepare the chalkboard or index cards with each of the following statements and nonverbal directions on them (a list on the board or one statement per card):
   a. "I like your new jeans" (casually, making eye contact).
   b. "You look nice in those jeans" (still casually, but you actually look at her jeans).
   c. "I like the way you look in those jeans" (a bit more familiar).
   d. "Those jeans look *really good* on you!" (emphasis on "really good").
   e. "You look *fine* in those jeans!!!" (body language is more sexual, leering).
   f. "Nice butt!!!" (eyes wink, hand gestures, etc.).

Procedures

1. Begin the activity with two volunteers. Explain that they will face each other, approximately 10 feet apart, with an imaginary "line" drawn between them. The line represents a "boundary." Tell the Stop sign holder to hold up the Stop sign and say "Stop!" when he or she feels uncomfortable.
2. Ask the volunteers whether they are comfortable standing this close (10 feet apart) to someone they do not know (generally they will not have a problem). Ask the non-stop sign holder to take a step forward. Ask the stop sign holder if this distance is still OK. Take another step. Still OK? Another. Another. When the non-stop sign holder is too close the stop sign holder will tell the person to "Stop!!!" and will hold up the Stop sign.
3. Discuss how it felt when personal space was invaded (tense, tightening stomach, uncertain as to what would happen next, strong desire to move away, and so forth).

4. Explain to the class that recognizing these uncomfortable feelings when some-one crosses the line is the first step in protecting ourselves against sexual harassment.

5. The next step is to take action, and this usually means telling the person to stop. This is sometimes difficult to do because we may worry about hurting other people's feelings. However, your own safety and civil rights need to come before another person's feelings.

6. Thank the volunteers and ask them to sit back down.

7. In the next part of the activity, ask for some volunteers to help illustrate when someone "crosses the line," not with their physical closeness, but with what they say or do.

8. Explain the next activity. Crossing the Line! is an improvisation activity. Two people will role play given situations, and the class will discuss their reactions to the activity. When one person says something that makes the other feel uncomfortable he or she will say "Stop" and hold up the stop sign.

9. Explain each situation below and ask for two volunteers to role play the situa-tion. Assign one volunteer the harasser role and one volunteer the victim role. Point to or hand the harasser the statements, one by one, in order, and have the volunteers act out each nuance of the list or index cards, *a* through *f*. The class should observe and discuss how the implications change with each situation.

    Situation A. Two people are in math class together. They do not know each other very well. One says to the other . . .

    Situation B. New volunteers, but this time they are total strangers. One says to the other . . .

    Situation C. New volunteers, but they have been going out for over a year. One says to the other . . .

    Situation D. New volunteers, student and middle-aged teacher. Teacher says to student . . .

    Situation E. New volunteers, boss and employee. Boss says . . .

    Situation F. New volunteers, coach and athlete. Coach says . . .

10. Repeat the process for situations B–F.

11. Discuss and process the activity. Why does the "line" get crossed at different times? What does it depend on? (*Answer:* prior relationship, sex of both peo-ple, difference in age or stature, personal tolerance for comments or behavior, if it is done repeatedly, and so forth.)

12. Conclude the activity by pointing out that many incidents of sexual harassment develop over time, often beginning with the offender repeatedly invading the victim's personal space.

13. Explain that one way to protect yourself against sexual harassment and abuse is to recognize when someone is invading your "personal space," both literally and figuratively.

14. Remind students that personal space is an "invisible boundary" that we all have. We usually aren't aware of it until someone crosses it. People's boundaries may be different and may vary for different relationships. Once a person identifies his or her boundaries, he or she will be in a better position to tell others when behavior is unwelcome and inappropriate.

Assessment

• Participation in class discussion and volunteering for in-class activities.

Follow-Up Activity

Define *sexual harassment* with the class. Discuss types of harassment in schools, statistics related to sexual harassment, school policy on harassment, and when to report harassment.

Lesson 5: Conflict Resolution

Time Needed

One 40–50 minute class period

National Standards

- Students will comprehend concepts related to health promotion and disease prevention to enhance health.
- Students will demonstrate the ability to access valid information and products and services to enhance health.
- Students will demonstrate the ability to practice health-enhancing behaviors and avoid or reduce risks.

Objectives

- Students will list the negative consequences of fighting.
- Students will define conflict resolution.
- Students will differentiate among problem solving, avoidance, and confrontation.
- Students will identify people they can ask for help with a conflict.

Materials & Preparation

- Create an overhead transparency from the attached Conflict Styles handout (Handout 7.2).
- Duplicate the attached How Does This Scenario End? worksheet (Worksheet 7.1), one copy per student.

Procedures

1. Ask the class whether anyone has ever gotten in a verbal or physical fight before. Ask for a show of hands.

2. Ask the class to think about the consequences of the fight. As the class is brainstorming, the teacher will write their ideas on the board. Following are some consequences that students might come up with: *Get upset or in a bad mood, lose friends, get grounded, lose privileges, get hurt, get detention or suspended from school.*

3. Explain to the class that since there are so many negative consequences to fighting, it makes sense to avoid fighting whenever possible.

4. Explain that trying to work things out and prevent fights is called *conflict resolution*. Give the definition of conflict resolution to the class and write the definition on the board.

   Conflict resolution   A process by which problems are solved without resorting to a verbal or physical fight.

5. Remind the class of how many people raised their hands when asked if they had ever gotten into a fight.

6. Ask the class whether anyone resolved their disagreements without actually fighting. The hope is that some students will raise their hands. Ask those students what they did to prevent the fight from occurring. Following are some examples: *Talked things out, listened to their side of the argument, compromised, agreed to disagree.*

7. Explain that certain conflict styles can prevent fights from occurring, while other conflict styles can actually cause fights to occur.

8. Give the definition of conflict styles to the class and write the definition on the blackboard.

    Conflict style The way a person reacts when he or she faces a problem.

9. Tell the class that there are three primary conflict styles that a person can use to resolve a conflict. Put up the overhead related to conflict styles. Ask for student volunteers to read the definitions out loud or have students read along with teacher.

10. Ask the class when would be a good time to use *problem solving*. Call on students and write their answers on the board. Following are some examples: *When the argument is caused by miscommunication, when you are disagreeing with a friend you do not want to lose, when you know the consequences of fighting are negative, when the argument is over something silly like rumors, when the argument is not a big deal, when you are not sure what you are fighting about.*

    Ask the class when would be a good time to use *avoidance*. Call on students and write their answers on the board. Following are some examples: *When the person who wants to argue with them has been drinking or using drugs, when the person who wants to argue with them is irrational, when the person who wants to argue with them has a weapon, when the person who wants to argue with them has a gang of friends to back them up.*

12. Ask the class when would be a good time to use *confrontation*. Call on students and write their answers on the board. Following are some examples: *When defending yourself if someone else starts a fight, when your civil rights are being violated (such as segregation, women's rights, apartheid).*

13. The teacher should emphasize that there are different ways to solve a conflict. Different conflict styles should be used in different situations. The best conflict style to use in most situations is *problem solving*.

14. Tell the class that now that they have reviewed conflict styles, they will have a chance to apply and analyze conflict styles with partners.

15. Divide the class into pairs and distribute the How Does This Scenario End? worksheet to each student (Worksheet 7.1). Give the pairs a few minutes to complete the worksheet.

16. When all pairs have finished the worksheet, ask partners to share their responses to the scenarios. Discuss the first scenario with the entire class. Then move on to the second and third scenarios.

17. Following are some questions to help facilitate discussion:
    - Are these scenarios realistic? Have things like this ever happened to you or people you know?

- What are the best conflict styles to use in each scenario?

- What are the consequences of using the other conflict styles?

18. Point out to the class that kids cannot always deal with their conflicts on their own. Sometimes they need to ask other people for help.

19. Ask a few students who they can ask or where they can go for help with a conflict. Write student responses on the board. Following are some examples that can be used: parents, teachers, spiritual advisors, guidance counselors, family members, a police officer.

20. Lead the class in a discussion. Following are some discussion questions to help facilitate the discussion:

- When are some times when a person might need help from other people?

- Can you ask anyone for help? How do you know who is a good person to ask for help?

- Could different people be better helpers in different situations? Examples?

21. Emphasize that it is important to identify who you can go to for help ahead of time. That way, when you are really in trouble, you don't have to think about who you can ask—you already know.

22. Conclude by pointing out that we all get into disagreements, arguments, and conflicts, but those conflicts do not have to end up in verbal or physical fights. When students are faced with a conflict, they can choose to use whatever conflict style they wish. However, if students think calmly and logically, they will admit that *problem solving* is usually the best choice. Most of the time problem solving can help solve a disagreement and prevent it from escalating into a full-blown fight.

23. If a student is having a conflict with another person and needs help, there are many people and places they can go to for help. They are not alone.

Assessment

- Note taking.

- Completion of the How Does This Scenario End? worksheet.

- Participation in class discussion.

NAME   DATE

Conflict Styles

Problem Solving. Talking out your problems with the person you are disagreeing with to find a solution to your conflict.

Avoidance. Not dealing with the conflict by ignoring the problem or changing what you do so you do not cross paths with the person that you are arguing with.

Confrontation. Causing a verbal or physical fight with the person you disagree with by acting aggressively, yelling at them, getting "in their face," or actually hitting them.

NAME _____   DATE

How Does This Scenario End?

Directions

Read the situations below. With your partner, write how each person could have dealt with the conflict by confronting, avoiding, or problem solving about the situation. Also write what would happen, or the outcome, of using each conflict style technique. Finally, write the best way to deal with each situation.

Maxine hears that her best friend is spreading rumors about her.

Confrontation: _____

What outcome would the confrontation lead to? Why? _____

Avoidance: _____

What outcome would the avoidance lead to? Why? _____

Problem Solving: _____

What outcome would the problem solving lead to? Why? _____

What is the best thing for Maxine to do in this situation? _____

Paul is at the mall waiting for the bus to take him home. A group of boys from another school start throwing rocks at him.

Confrontation: _____

What outcome would the confrontation lead to? Why? _____

Avoidance: _____

What outcome would the avoidance lead to? Why? _____

Problem Solving: _____

What outcome would the problem solving lead to? Why? _____

What is the best thing for Paul to do in this situation? _____

Antonio's little brother keeps taking his stuff out of his room. Antonio has told him many times not to, but his brother won't stop.

Confrontation: _____

What outcome would the confrontation lead to? Why? _____

Avoidance: _____

What outcome would the avoidance lead to? Why? _____

Problem Solving: _____

What outcome would the problem solving lead to? Why? _____

What is the best thing for Antonio to do in this situation? _____

Violence Home–School Connection

Home–School Connection: Television Violence

Time Needed to Complete

1–3 days

Time Needed to Present

20 minutes during one class period

National Standards

- Students will comprehend concepts related to health promotion and disease prevention to enhance health.
- Students will analyze the influence of family, peers, culture, media, technology, and other factors on health behaviors.

Objectives

- Students will view a television drama with a family member.
- Students will document acts of violence they observe while watching the television show.
- Students will discuss the implications of watching such violence with their family member.

Materials & Preparation

1. Duplicate the TV and Violence worksheet (Worksheet 7.2), one copy per student.

Procedures

1. Explain to the class that they are going to have an assignment to complete with a family member. This should not be a sibling, unless the sibling is more than 10 years older than the student.
2. Distribute Worksheet 7.2: TV and Violence and review.
3. Announce the due date for the assignment.
4. On the day the assignment is due, students can share the results of their participation and reflections. This can take as much or as little time as is available.
5. Following are some process questions that can be asked to facilitate discussion:
   - Prior to completing this activity, did anyone have television viewing rules in their house? What types of rules?
   - How many have televisions in your house? How many of you have a television in your room?
   - Who thinks they observed the most acts of violence? How many acts?

- Did the number of violent acts they observed surprise anyone? Did it surprise anyone's family member?
- Were you watching television shows that you normally watch, or did you pick a show especially for this assignment?
- What were some of the violent acts you observed?
- Did anyone not observe any violence? What was the name of that show?!
- What did you learn from this activity? What did your family member learn?
- Did anyone's family create new television viewing rules after completing this activity?
- Are there any other comments or questions?

Assessment

- Submission of the completed TV and Violence worksheet.

Extension Activities

Students and family members can listen to and analyze violence in music. They can play and observe violence in video games. They can read and document violence in the newspaper.

WORKSHEET 6.2

Home-School Connection: TV and Violence

Due Date: _____

Directions

• Choose a family member and select one drama TV show which both of you will watch together.

• Using scrap pieces of paper, both student and family member should keep a list of each incident of violence they observed during the show.

• After the show compare your results and make a master list of incidents in the table below.

• Answer the following questions:

The name of the show we viewed was: _____

Time: _____   Date of Viewing: _____

Time of Incident _____

Description of Incident _____

Who Observed the Violence? Student, Adult, or Both? _____

1. How many acts of violence were observed in total?

2. Was there a difference among the acts considered violent by the student versus the family member? If so, why do you think this happened?

NAME   DATE

3. Were there any acts of violence that either one of you omitted because, on second thought, you didn't consider it an act of violence? Explain.

4. What was the most prevalent act of violence you both viewed?

5. What conclusion can you both draw from this activity?

_____   _____

Student's Name   *Family Member's Signature*

Violence Prevention Project

Project: Production Company

Time Needed

This assignment should be distributed at the beginning of a violence prevention unit so that students have time to complete the project. On the day the assignment is due, the teacher can use as much time as is available for students to share their project selections and outcomes. Sharing can take 20 minutes or an entire period.

National Standards

- Students will demonstrate the ability to advocate for personal, family, and community health.

Objective

- Students will create a video that can be used to help young children learn how to react appropriately to a lure (see Handout 7.3).

Materials & Preparation

1. Duplicate the Production Company student worksheet (Worksheet 7.3), one copy per student.
2. Duplicate the Child Abduction Distribution List (Handout 7.3), one copy per student.
3. Duplicate the Production Company Rubric (Handout 7.4), one copy per student.

Procedures

1. Begin the lesson by asking students whether they know what a lure is. Can they name any lures?
2. Explain that a lure is something used to convince someone to do something; for example, a lure used in fishing is intended to convince the fish to bite the hook.
3. Describe lures as they relate to child abduction. Explain that in this instance, child abductors use lures to isolate children from others, or to get children close enough that they can get them in a car and drive off with them.
4. Ask students to give some ideas of lures that child abductors commonly use to try and lure young children. Following are some examples to share in case students cannot think of any examples on their own:

   Do you want some candy?

   Can you help me find a lost pet?

   Can I have directions please—come closer . . .

   Are your parents home?

   Do you need a ride home?

   Your mom told me to come and pick you up . . .

5. Explain to students that they are going to produce short video segments to help young children become aware of lures that are used. The hope is that this will help prevent young children from being susceptible to lures.

6. Divide the class into groups of four and assign production company roles to each group member, or allow group members to select their own roles.

7. Distribute and review the Production Company student handout and the corresponding rubric.

8. Assign a grade level and type of lure to each small group—see Child Abduction Distribution List (Handout 7.3).

9. Once students understand what is expected of them, give the due date for the assignment and have students write the due date on their project worksheet (Worksheet 7.3).

10. On the day the assignment is due have students share their video with the class.

11. Use the following process questions to lead discussion:

    • What was creating a video like?

    • What did you learn from completing the project?

    • Do you think your project would prevent young children from being susceptible to lures? Why or why not?

12. Conclude by pointing out that the only way to prevent violence is to be aware of it! There is a saying that "It takes a village to raise a child." This means that we all must look out for one another in today's society to be safe.

Assessment

• Completion of the video and screenplay. See Production Company Rubric (Handout 7.4).

NAME   DATE

Child Abduction Distribution List

Kindergarten   Emergency Lure—Your Mom told me to come and pick you up—she is in the hospital (no name).

Kindergarten   Lost Pet Lure—Will you help me find my lost pet? He ran into the woods. . . .

First Grade   Directions Lure—Can I have directions? Come closer, I can't hear you. . . .

First Grade   Name Recognition Lure—Your parents told me to come and pick you up—abductor sees a child's name on a lunch box, book bag, or jacket and pretends to be a friend of the parents.

Second Grade   Ride Home Lure—Do you want a ride home? C'mon, hop in. . . .

Third Grade   Bribery Lure—I have this job I need done in my backyard—I'll pay you $20 bucks to come and help. I need it done right away, no time to tell your parents, we'll be back before you know it. . . .

Fourth Grade   Ego/Fame Lure—you are so beautiful, you should come to my studio—I will do a photo shoot, you will be a star! Or, you are so talented, you should come to my gym, you could be the best!

Fifth Grade   Chat Room/Online Lure—child is lured by someone on the Internet pretending to be another child. The abductor asks the child to meet in person.

Sixth Grade   Authority Lure—someone dresses up like a police person or security guard and tells the child that they are in trouble and to come with them. They lure the child to a secluded place.

Tools for Teaching Health. Copyright © 2007 by John Wiley & Sons, Inc. Reproduced by permission of Jossey-Bass, An Imprint of Wiley

Production Company: Preventing Violence
in Your Community

Due Date: _____

My group members are:

_____   _____

_____   _____

Our scenario is: _____

Our grade level is: _____

My group is (check the group assigned):

_____   *Screenwriter.* This company member is in charge of writing, editing, and typing the final script before submitting it to the teacher. The screenwriter should collaborate with other members of the production company to develop ideas for the script but is the ultimate person responsible for taking notes and creating the final product.

_____   *Prop Master.* This company member is responsible for identifying, gathering, and coordinating props and costumes for the production. The prop master should collaborate with the other members of the company to help select appropriate items for the script but is the ultimate person responsible for all the props and costumes.

_____   *Producer.* This company member puts all the pieces together by coordinating the work of the screenwriter, the prop master, and the director. The producer is in charge of coordinating dates and times for rehearsals and filming, obtaining actors to act in the film, and securing an appropriate film location.

_____   *Director.* This company member is responsible for the filming and editing of the video. The director should collaborate with other members of the production company to approve the final product but is the ultimate person in charge of lighting, obtaining video equipment and supplies, and actually filming the sequence.

(Continued)

WORKSHEET 6.3 (Continued)

NAME   DATE

Group Directions

The ultimate goal of this project is to create a child abduction prevention video to be used for children in your district. Groups will be submitting two final products, a video and a typed script.

Each team, or production company, will be writing, producing, and directing a video that will help younger children in their district avoid becoming victims of violence. Each team will develop a two to three minute scenario for a specified grade level in which the various lures that are used by perpetrators are demonstrated. The video should illustrate the lure attempt and then stop so the children in the classroom can be asked, "What would you do in this situation?" A teacher will lead a discussion on the topic and then finish the video, which will portray the children making the *right choice.*

Production companies are responsible for writing a script, obtaining children to act in the video, using appropriate props and costumes, and filming the video. The video should be age appropriate for the age group assigned by your teacher.

Use the rubric distributed to assist you in completing the assignment.

Tools for Teaching Health. Copyright © 2007 by John Wiley & Sons, Inc. Reproduced by permission of Jossey-Bass, An Imprint of Wiley

NAME   DATE

Rubric: Production Company

	Five Stars 11–13 Points	**Three Stars** 7–10 Points	**One Star** 6 or Fewer Points
Role Responsibilities	Roles are assumed, and all students complete tasks. Cooperation and collaboration are routine.	Roles are assumed, and most students complete tasks. Cooperation is evident, but collaboration is weak.	Roles are assumed, but students do not complete tasks. No cooperation or collaboration evident.
Screenplay	Screenplay is created with notes about proposed shots and dialogue. A working script is used in the video.	Screenplay is created with notes about proposed shots and dialogue.	No evidence of a script being used. No screenplay is submitted.
Preparation	All necessary supplies and equipment are located and scheduled well in advance. All equipment is checked to ensure it is operational. A backup plan is developed to cover problems caused by technical difficulties.	Almost all necessary supplies and equipment are located in advance. Equipment is checked to ensure it is operational.	Little evidence exists to document gathering supplies and equipment and checking their condition.
Technical Elements	Additional lighting is used. Almost no shadows or glares are apparent. The video is steady with few pans and zooms. Close ups are used to focus attention. Video shows evidence of attention to technical detail.	Additional lighting is used. Few shadows or glares are apparent. The camera is held steady. Pans and zooms are limited. The main subject is located slightly off center.	Only ambient (available) light is used. Scenes are too bright or too dark. The camera is not held steady and excessive panning and zooming distracts the viewer.

(Continued)

243

NAME _____   DATE _____

Storyline	The video tells a compelling story in a style or mood which suits the content. Motion scenes are planned and purposeful, adding impact to the story line. "Talking heads" scenes are used only when they are crucial to telling the story.	The video tells a connected story, but the style and mood do not suit the content. The video includes some "talking heads," but backgrounds and video effects add interest. Most motion scenes make the story clearer or give it more impact.	The video is a disconnected series of scenes with no unifying story. No style or mood is apparent. The video features "talking heads" with little or no action to add interest *or* the video uses action excessively.
Content	Content is creative and compelling. Video subjects and objects always relate to the storyline. Extremely age-appropriate.	Content relates to the storyline. Random and disconnected material has been edited out. Somewhat age-appropriate.	Content is unrelated to the story. Random shots of disconnected or irrelevant content are included. Not age-appropriate.
Pace	All video clips fit the storyline. Clips are just long enough to make each point clear. The pace captures audience attention.	Most video clips move at a steady pace, fast enough to keep the audience interested and slow enough to tell the complete story.	Video clips are too long and do not advance the storyline *or* too short and leave out essential action or dialogue.
Deadline	Products are delivered on or before assigned deadlines. On-time!	Products are delivered near scheduled deadlines. One day late.	Product deadlines are missed. Two or more days late.

Violence Prevention Assessment

Assessment: Functional Knowledge and Skills Exam

Time Needed

One 40–50 minute class period

National Standards

- Students will comprehend concepts related to health promotion and disease prevention.
- Students will demonstrate the ability to advocate for personal, family, and community health.

Objective

- Students demonstrate knowledge and skills related to violence prevention.

Materials & Preparation

1. Duplicate the Functional Knowledge and Skills Exam (Worksheet 7.4), one per student.
2. Arrange desks as needed for exam format.

Procedures

1. As students enter the room, advise them to take their seats, put their books and notebooks under their chairs, and place a pen or pencil on their desk.
2. Explain the test-taking rules to the class. Following are some suggestions:
   - No talking!
   - No "borrowing" answers from a neighbor—if caught cheating, students will receive a zero and a phone call to home.
   - If students have a question, they should raise their hand. The teacher will come to them, not the other way around.
   - When students are done, they should pass in their test and work quietly on a different assignment or read a book while waiting for the rest of the class to finish.
3. Students take varying amounts of time to complete exams. It may be advisable to have some type of activity for quick test takers to work on while they are waiting for slower test takers to finish.
4. Be prepared with an activity for the entire class in case all students finish the test prior to the end of the period. The *Kids' Book of Questions* by Gregory Stock provides wonderful questions to spark class discussion on topics related to self-esteem, mental health, and other health-related issues. Students enjoy talking about answers to the questions, and it may be a relaxing way to conclude an otherwise stressful class period.

Assessment

Score on the exam.

Answers to Multiple Choice Questions

1. D
2. A
3. B
4. C
5. A
6. D
7. D
8. B
9. D
10. A
11. A
12. C

Constructed Response Question
Possible Answers: Content

Deep breathing, exercise, count to ten, guided imagery, take a walk, journaling, and so forth.

Possible Answers: Skill

*G*ive thought to what triggers your anger.

*R*ecognize the signs of anger.

*E*lect to control your anger.

*A*ctively do something to cool off.

*T*ry to avoid the situations that trigger your anger the next time.

NAME _____   DATE _____

Violence: Functional Knowledge and Skills Exam

Directions

This exam consists of twelve multiple choice questions and a constructed response (essay) question. Please complete all questions.

Multiple Choice

Please circle the correct answer.

1. An emotion that is similar to anger is
   a. Rage
   b. Frustration
   c. Irritation
   d. All of these

2. Which of the following is least likely to trigger anger?
   a. When someone apologizes for yelling at you
   b. When you are treated unfairly
   c. When someone steals something from you
   d. When someone spreads rumors about you

3. Which of the following is a common physical response to anger?
   a. Decreased heart rate
   b. Increased heart rate
   c. Decreased blood pressure
   d. Decreased pulse

4. All of the following are negative ways to cope with anger except
   a. Fighting
   b. Punching walls
   c. Going for a walk
   d. Screaming at someone

5. Which of the following is a positive way to cope with anger?
   a. Deep breathing
   b. Keeping it inside
   c. Hitting someone
   d. Yelling at a sibling or parent

(Continued)

NAME   DATE

6. Which of the following does not constitute sexual harassment?

   a. Body language

   b. Tone of voice

   c. Choice of words

   d. Choice of clothing

7. How might someone feel if they are being sexually harassed?

   a. Tense

   b. Clenched stomach

   c. Strong desire to move away

   d. All of the above

8. What should you do when you feel as if you are big sexually harassed?

   a. Just try and ignore it

   b. Tell a trusted adult

   c. Try and change your behavior

   d. None of the above

9. All of the following are consequences of getting into a fight except . . .

   a. Getting grounded

   b. Getting hurt

   c. Getting in trouble at school

   d. All of the above

10. Conflict resolution is . . .

    a. Learning how to settle a disagreement without fighting

    b. A new law related to drinking and driving

    c. A promise to make resolutions

    d. None of the above

11. Drew has a huge problem with one of the kids in his class. This kid keeps making fun of him every time he talks. The best conflict style for Drew to adopt in this situation would be . . .

    a. Problem solving

    b. Confrontation

    c. Avoidance

    d. None of the above

12. On the way home from school every day, Mara passes by a group of boys that call her names and make jokes about her. The best conflict style for Mara to adopt in this situation would be. . .

    a. Problem solving

    b. Confrontation

    c. Avoidance

    d. None of the above

Tools for Teaching Health. Copyright © 2007 by John Wiley & Sons, Inc. Reproduced by permission of Jossey-Bass, An Imprint of Wiley

NAME _____

DATE _____

Constructed Response Questions

Please write your answer in the space provided. Use the back of this test if you do not have enough room to complete your answer.

Peter has been having problems in his new school. He already has been in the principal's office twice for fighting and was told that if be misbehaves again, he will get suspended. He can't seem to control his anger and is worried that someone will get him mad.

You are Peter's friend. You have just taken health class and have learned a good way to control anger. Describe each of the steps in the G.R.E.A.T. anger management model. Then suggest three positive ways Peter can use when trying to deal with anger.

_____

_____

_____

_____

_____

_____

_____

_____

_____

_____

_____

_____

_____

_____

_____

_____

_____

_____

_____

CHAPTER 7

PHYSICAL ACTIVITY

Physical Activity Icebreaker

Icebreaker: Who's Who on the Playground?

Time Needed

10–20 minutes

National Standards

- Students will comprehend concepts related to health promotion and disease prevention to enhance health.
- Students will demonstrate the ability to use interpersonal communication skills to enhance health and avoid or reduce health risks.

Objectives

Students will practice "active listening."

- Students will share a form of physical activity or exercise that they did in the past, engage in now as teens, and hope to engage in as an adult.
- Students will act out the types of physical activity they state.

Preparation

Prepare an open area in the center of the classroom or other space where the entire class can form one large circle.

Procedures

1. Tell students to form a circle in the middle of the classroom.

2. Inform students that they are going to do an activity that involves listening carefully to what each of their classmates is saying.

3. Each student is going to come up with an answer to this unfinished sentence: "When I was younger, I used to exercise or get physical activity by . . ."

4. Explain that this seems easy to do, except, students must *act out* the physical activity they state and they *may not* repeat an activity already stated by a classmate! Explain that this is where the listening is very important! (*Alternate:* Students may repeat actions, but as students act out their action, they must act out the action of everyone who proceeded them!)

5. For example, Laura might volunteer by saying "When I was younger I used to ride my bike a lot." When Laura says "ride her bike" she simulates the action of riding a bike.

6. Go around the circle with each student stating and acting out their physical activity. When all students have gone, tell students that they are going to do it again, but they now have a clean slate. All previously stated forms of physical activity are erased and they can start from scratch. However, they have a new unfinished statement.

7. Tell the students the new unfinished statement and repeat the activity as described above. "Something I *do now* that involves physical activity or exercise is. . . ." Go around the circle in the other direction and have students act out their current physical activity. Remind them that repeats are not allowed!

8. Repeat the activity one more time with the following statement: "When I am an *adult,* I plan to get some physical activity or exercise by. . . ." Follow the same format as described above.

9. Conclude the activity with the following process questions:
    - What were some common things people did as children?
    - What are some common things that you are doing now?
    - How many of you think you were more active as children? More active now? Why?
    - What are some common things that you hope to be doing in the future?
    - Do you think you will be more or less active in the future? Why?
    - How did the types of activities change from when you were children, to when you will be adults? Why?
    - What were some not-so-common answers that surprised you?

10. Finally, explain that through the course of the unit, students will be studying fitness and the importance of staying physically fit throughout their lifetimes.

Assessment

- Participation in the icebreaker activity.
- Participation in class discussion

Physical Activity Lessons

Lesson 1: The Secret Magic Super Pill for Good Health

Time Needed

One 40–50 minute class period

National Standards

- Students will comprehend concepts related to health promotion and disease prevention to enhance health.
- Students will demonstrate the ability to practice health-enhancing behaviors and avoid or reduce risks.

Objectives

1. Students will evaluate a personal health assessment to determine their level of physical activity and fitness.
2. Students will analyze how behavior can affect health maintenance and disease prevention.

Materials Needed

1. Newsprint
2. Markers
3. Tape
4. A large prescription bottle or "pill" (plastic egg that splits apart works well)
5. A die, preferably an oversized spongy one, but any die will do.

Preparation

1. Prepare a large container that can simulate a prescription bottle. Inside the bottle should be something that simulates a large "pill." Create a label for the outside of the bottle. Following is a sample:

Rx: Secret Magic Super Pill for Good Health

Suggested Use: For best results, should be taken for the rest of your life. As with any product, please consult your physician before using.

Recommended Dosage: Take a minimum of 3–4 times per week. It should take at least 30 minutes to administer. (*Note:* For some people, this is a hard pill to swallow!)

Scientifically Proven to: Decrease blood pressure, decrease risk of cardiovascular disease, aid in digestion, aid in weight control, reduce risk of obesity, reduce stress, aid in restful sleep, release natural body endorphins, reduce risk of osteoporosis, and add quality years to your life.

Refills: Unlimited.

Caution: Do not mix with alcohol or other drugs, especially anabolic steroids.

Prescribing Doctor: Irun Daily, M.D.

---

2. Inside the large prescription bottle or the plastic egg, place a piece of paper, with the "Magic" ingredient written on it—*Exercise!*

3. Duplicate the Physical Activity Questionnaire (Worksheet 8.1), one copy per student.

Procedures

1. Hold up the large simulated prescription bottle and read the title: "Secret Magic Super Pill for Good Health."

2. Ask students whether they have ever heard of this magic pill. Do they really think there is such a thing? If there really was such a pill, do you think it would be popular? Worth a lot of money?

3. Read the information on the label. After reading the instructions, ask the class whether they believe that there is really something that can have such a positive effect on their health.

4. At that point, open the top of the bottle, take out the "pill," split it open, and reveal the "secret"—*Exercise!*

5. Brainstorm the following topics with the class:

   • What are some of the physical, mental, and social benefits of physical activity that were mentioned on the prescription label?

   • What are some other benefits of physical activity and sports?

   • What are some of the activities and exercises that they enjoy and engage in? (organized sports, pick-up games, walking, biking, and so forth)

6. Read the following quote by the Centers for Disease Control and Prevention (CDC):

   All adolescents should be physically active daily, or nearly every day, as part of play, games, sports, work, transportation, recreation, physical education, or planned exercise.

   Adolescents should engage in three or more sessions per week of activities that last 20 minutes or more at a time and that require moderate to vigorous levels of exertion.

7. Explain to the class that one of the very big concerns in the United States in the last few years has been an "epidemic" of overweight and obese adults. Recent surveys find that many children and adolescents are also becoming overweight and out of shape.

8. Tell the class that what they are going to do next is take a Physical Activity Questionnaire that will ask them questions related to how much physical activity they get each day. They will not have to share the results of this questionnaire with anyone, but they will be using the results to create a Physical Activity Improvement Plan for themselves, so they should please be truthful and accurate in their answers.

9. Distribute the Physical Activity Questionnaire and instruct students to complete it. Tell students to keep it in their health notebooks or folders for future reference.

10. Divide the class into groups of three to five students. Give each group a sheet of newsprint, marker, and tape. Explain that one of the biggest reasons people give for not exercising regularly is that they are "too busy" and "just don't have the time."

11. Each group should designate one person with legible handwriting to be the recorder. On top of the newsprint they should write: *Time Management: Ten Tips for Fitting More Exercise into Your Day.*

12. Groups are then given 6–8 minutes to brainstorm *ten* or more ways that teens or adults with busy schedules can find ways to get some exercise into their daily lives. Encourage students to be creative with their suggestions.

13. When the lists have been completed, have each group tape their newsprint to the board or wall and discuss their "Tips." The teacher will then collect the lists and make a master list that will be displayed permanently in the room.

14. Conclude by playing the "fuzzy dice" assessment. Roll the die, on the floor if there is ample space, or simply on a desk if not. As the die is rolling, call on a student volunteer. The student volunteer must share a number of things that they learned from the day's lesson—the number is determined by the number that is rolled on the die. After one student answers, roll the die again and call on a different volunteer. The next volunteer must also share things learned in the day's lesson, but they may not share anything already said by their class-mate(s). Continue this process for as many minutes as are left in the period—reiterating that no student may repeat what was said previously!

Assessment

- Participation in class discussion.
- Completion of the brainstorm list of ten or more ways to find time to exercise.
- Responses to the "fuzzy dice" assessment.

Extension Activity

Based on their answers to the Physical Activity Questionnaire, students can develop a short-term physical activity goal and monitor their progress for two weeks.

Physical Activity Questionnaire

Age: _____   Sex: _____   Height: _____

1. Do you enjoy participating in physical activities?   Yes _____   No _____

If you answered "Yes," describe the types of activities that you enjoy and why you enjoy them. If you answered "No," explain why you do not enjoy participating in physical activity.

_____

_____

_____

2. When you do participate in physical activity, what is the main reason(s) you do so? (check all that apply)

_____ Fun	_____ Socialize	_____ Reduce stress
_____ Stay in shape	_____ Improve my health	_____ Look or feel better
_____ Maintain weight	_____ Other _____	

3. How much time do you generally spend *daily* on physical activity?

_____ Less than 15 minutes	_____ 15–30 minutes
_____ 30–60 minutes	_____ 1 or more hours

4. How much time do you generally spend per *week* on *cardiovascular fitness?* (walking briskly, running, cycling, swimming for at least 20–30 minutes)

_____ Less than 15 minutes	_____ 15–30 minutes	_____ 30–60 minutes
_____ 1–2 hours	_____ 2 or more hours	

5. How much time do you generally spend per *week* on *muscular endurance?* (ability of muscles to contract repeatedly without becoming fatigued: cycling, climbing stairs, running, lifting light weights for many repetitions)

_____ Less than 15 minutes	_____ 15–30 minutes	_____ 30–60 minutes
_____ 1–2 hours	_____ 2 or more hours	

NAME _____   DATE

6. How much time do you generally spend per *week* on *muscular strength?* (amount of force a muscle is capable of exerting against a resistance with a single maximum effort: lifting a heavy box, lifting heavier weights with few repetitions)

_____ Less than 15 minutes   _____ 15–30 minutes   _____ 30–60 minutes

_____ 1–2 hours   _____ 2 or more hours

7. How much time do you generally spend per *week* on *flexibility?* (ability to move joints through a full range of motion; stretching exercises)

_____ Less than 15 minutes   _____ 15–30 minutes   _____ 30–60 minutes

_____ 1–2 hours   _____ 2 or more hours

Lesson 2: Disco Aerobics

Time Needed

One 40–50 minute class period

National Standards

- Students will comprehend concepts related to health promotion and disease prevention to enhance health.
- Students will demonstrate the ability to practice health-enhancing behaviors and avoid or reduce risks.

Objectives

1. Students will define and compute their target heart rate.
2. Students will analyze and compute their resting heart rate.
3. Students will participate and calculate their individual fitness results.
4. Students will review conclusions of their cardiovascular health.

Materials Needed

1. Cassette or CD player.
2. A stopwatch or wristwatch with a second hand.
3. Bring a recording of a fast-paced song such as "Everybody Dance Now" or "Saturday Night Fever." (The song you use should be approximately 5 minutes long. Ask students about their current favorite songs.)

Preparation

1. Get approval from your administrator to bring the class to the bleachers or to the steps in front of the school.
2. Make copies of the Disco Aerobics worksheet (Worksheet 8.2), one copy per student.
3. Make sure you have extra pencils for students who forget to bring a writing utensil.
4. Prior to the activity, as a safety factor, ask whether any student has a medical exemption or consult with the school nurse.

Procedures

1. Bring the class to the designated location in the school where students can use the steps to step up and down.
2. Review the benefits of physical fitness (decreases risk of obesity, high cholesterol, high blood pressure, cardiovascular disease; improves body image, flexibility; is a stress management technique).
3. Review how to take a pulse. (Take your pulse on the carotid artery on the side of your neck or on the radial artery on the thumb side of the wrist. Do not use the thumb to take the pulse because the thumb has its own pulse.)

4. Have students find their pulse.

5. Hand out the Disco Aerobics worksheet (Worksheet 8.2).

6. Explain *resting heart rate* (RHR) to the class. RHR is the number of times the heart beats in one minute. RHR is always calculated in beats per minute. To obtain your RHR you can count your pulse for 60 seconds. You can also count your pulse for 30 seconds multiplied by 2, or 20 seconds by 3, or 15 seconds by 4, or 10 seconds by 6, or 6 seconds by 10.

7. Have students calculate their RHR together. The teacher should tell the class when to begin counting, and when to stop. Have the student write their RHR on the worksheet.

8. Explain *maximum heart rate* (MHR) to students. MHR is the highest rate your heart can safely attain during exercise. It is a general figure—some people can exercise safely at higher rates, and some people should never get close to that heart rate.

9. Share the formula for MHR with the class, have them calculate their own MHR, and write it on the worksheet.

MHR = 220 – age

For example, if you are 15 years old:
- MHR = 220 – 15
- MHR = 205

10. Explain *target heart rate* (THR) to students. THR is a pulse range in which a person can safely exercise while still achieving cardiovascular benefits. A person does not really want to have their pulse at the MHR level, but they still want the pulse high enough to achieve benefits.

11. Share the formula for THR with the class, have them calculate their own THR, and write it on their worksheet.

THR = 60 percent to 80 percent of MHR

If you use the above example:
- 60 percent of 205 = 123 beats per minute
- 80 percent of 205 = 164 beats per minute
- So your THR zone is between 123 and 164 beats per minute

12. Explain that the students will participate in Disco Aerobics to determine whether they can get their heart rate into the THR zone. Students will be stepping up and down on steps for approximately 5 minutes. This game will attempt to measure how much the heart rate increases when called upon to work harder.

13. Demonstrate the method of the activity on a step (up left foot, up right foot, down left foot, down right foot).

14. Have the students place their worksheets and pencils on the side and practice for a few seconds (correct any students who are performing improperly).

15. Explain to students that the activity will take place throughout the entire song and perhaps into a new song! Students should try to stay with the beat.

16. At the end of each minute, stop students, lead them through taking their pulse, and have them mark their sheets. At the end of five minutes, have the students take their pulse and then walk for a few minutes to decrease their heart rate back to normal.

17. Discuss questions on sheets and the results students receive after the activity.

    • What did you think about this activity?

    • Are you in better or worse shape than you thought?

    • How many of you reached your THR zone?

18. Conclude by pointing out that physical activity can help prevent many chronic diseases, help with stress management, and help us feel better about our bodies. However, it is important to participate in cardiovascular exercise to achieve those benefits. In addition, when working out, people should make sure they are reaching their THR zone.

Assessment

• Completion of the Disco Aerobics worksheet (Worksheet 8.2).

• Participation in class discussion.

Disco Aerobics Worksheet

Directions

- Before you begin Disco Aerobics you should complete the first three calculations below.

- You should make every attempt to step up and down at a constant pace. Music will be playing to help you keep the beat.

- If you have a problem with your legs or become short of breath or dizzy at any time, stop the exercise immediately and inform the instructor of your problem.

My Resting Heart Rate (RHR) = _____

My Maximum Heart Rate (MHR) = _____

   220 – (Your Age)

My Target Heart Rate (THR) = _____

   MHR × 60% to MHR × 80%

Heart Rate After One Minute = _____

Heart Rate After Two Minutes = _____

Heart Rate After Three Minutes = _____

Heart Rate Immediately after Exercise = _____

Did you reach your "Target Heart Rate" at any time during the activity? If so, when and what was the rate(s)? _____

Based on your results, what conclusions can you make about your cardiovascular health?

_____

_____

_____

_____

_____

_____

Lesson 3: Physical Activity and Goal Setting

Time Needed

One to two 40–50 minute class periods

National Standards

- Students will demonstrate the ability to use goal setting skills to enhance health.
- Students will demonstrate the ability to practice health-enhancing behaviors and avoid or reduce risks.

Objectives

- Students will evaluate a Physical Activity Questionnaire done in a previous lesson to determine their level of physical activity and fitness.
- Students will implement a plan for attaining a Physical Activity Goal.

Materials & Preparation

1. Duplicate the Physical Activity Myth-Fact Quiz, one copy per student.
2. Duplicate and prepare a packet for each student stapled together. The packet should include:
   - Physical Activity Wellness Plan (Worksheet 8.3)
   - Physical Activity Goal (Worksheet 8.4)
   - Two-Week Physical Activity Journal (Worksheet 8.5)
   - Goal Reflection (Worksheet 8.6)
3. Physical Activity Questionnaire completed in previous lesson.

Procedures

1. Distribute the Physical Activity Myth-Fact Quiz (Worksheet 8.7) and have the students complete the quiz individually.
2. When all students have completed the quiz, discuss the answers and clarify any misinformation the students believe. Answers to myth-fact quiz are as follows:

1. Fact (YRBS 2001)	7. Myth (testosterone)
2. Myth	8. Myth (every other day is recommended)
3. Myth	9. Myth
4. Fact	10. Myth
5. Myth	11. Fact
6. Myth (7 vs. 12 percent)	12. Fact

3. Instruct students to take out their Physical Activity Questionnaire, which was completed in a previous lesson.

4. Tell students to look over the questionnaire and try to find one or more areas of physical activity that they can begin to work on or improve upon.

5. Explain to students that whether they are a competitive athlete or couch potato, evaluating the results of the Physical Activity Questionnaire can help them investigate some physical activities or types of health-related fitness that they think they might enjoy and that will help them achieve their goal of becoming more active and physically fit.

6. Distribute Worksheet 8.3, Physical Activity Wellness Plan, and Worksheet 8.4, Physical Activity Goal. Have students follow along on the worksheets as you review the instructions.

7. Tell students that they have two days to determine what their goal is and to complete the Wellness Plan.

8. If there is time before the end of class, have students begin work on their wellness plan.

Day Two

1. On the day the Wellness Plan is due, tell students to take their plan out and share what they chose to focus on. Some students may wish not to share their goal in public, but they should make time after class to share their plan with you so that you know their goal meets the five criteria outlined on their instruction sheet.

2. Explain that you will be reminding them of their goal each day in class. After one week, they should be prepared to share their Physical Activity Journal with you so that you can monitor their progress and make positive suggestions if necessary. They will hand in their project on a date specified by the instructor.

3. After explaining the project, read the Tips to Help You Succeed (listed below), which are included on their task sheet.

4. Tell students that in a survey of Professional fitness trainers, these were some of their "Tips for Success" for beginning an exercise program:

   • *Have a goal and a plan.* Check with your doctor if you have any possible health concerns about starting an exercise program. Then ask a physical education teacher or coach or trainer to help with your plan. Why do you want to exercise? What do you hope to get from regular physical activity?

   • *Time management.* Make regular exercise a planned activity. Schedule a half hour walk, for example, each day at a convenient time.

   • *Drink plenty of water.* Drink water before, during (if possible), and after exercise. Comfortable clothing and good athletic shoes are also important.

   • *Listen to music you enjoy or other appropriate "diversions."* Music helps the time pass more quickly. Many people use a portable music device with headphones while walking or jogging. If you are indoors on a treadmill or stationary bike, watching TV or reading can also help to pass the time.

   • *Learn and apply the safety guidelines appropriate to your activities.* For weight training, start with lighter weights and more repetitions. When the reps and sets become easier, increase the weight slightly.

- *Have a positive, realistic attitude.* Most people who are unsuccessful and give up their physical activity plan have unrealistic expectations about how soon they will see positive results. Losing ten pounds or getting those "six pack" abs in just a few weeks is simply not going to happen. Slow, steady progress should be your ultimate goal.
- *Try finding a workout buddy.* Some people do not enjoy working out by themselves. With a partner, you can give each other encouragement on those days when you just may not feel like exercising.

Assessment

- Submission of the two-week physical activity journal.
- Submission of the Physical Activity Wellness Plan (Worksheet 8.4).
- Submission of the Goal Reflection worksheet (Worksheet 8.6).

Physical Activity Myth = Fact Quiz

Separating Myths from Facts

Take this myth-or-fact quiz to see how much you already know about exercise and physical activity. Read each statement. Decide whether it is a *myth* (untrue) or *fact.* Write your answer on the line provided.

1. _____ Male students are more likely to get sufficient moderate-to-vigorous physical activity than female students.

2. _____ On the 2001 National Youth Risk Behavior Survey, 30 percent of adolescents reported that they did not participate in *any* physical activity in the 7 days prior to taking the survey.

3. _____ American teenagers are more physically active now than they were 25 years ago.

4. _____ In general, people who are physically active live longer than those who are inactive.

5. _____ Spot-reducing (that is, working the abs by doing crunches) is possible.

6. _____ On the average, high school juniors and seniors get more exercise than high school sophomores and freshmen.

7. _____ All women who lift weights will get big, bulky muscles.

8. _____ If you do strength training, you should exercise the same muscle groups every day for quickest results.

9. _____ The best way to get really fit and improve your physique and performance is by taking supplements and anabolic steroids.

10. _____ Teenagers exercise more often than adults who are over the age of 55.

11. _____ Running a mile in 10 minutes burns about the same number of calories as walking a mile in 15 minutes.

12. _____ Exercise may be as effective as drugs for treating depression.

Physical Activity Wellness Plan

Name _____

Directions

Based on our class discussion about the benefits of regular exercise, you will be required to develop a short-term goal (two weeks) that will increase your level of physical activity. Use the Physical Activity Wellness Plan handout to develop your two-week *goal.* When writing your goal, please keep the following in mind:

1. It should be important to you.

2. It should be clear, specific, and measurable.

3. It should be realistic for the time period.

4. It should be reasonable and under your control.

5. It should be positive and health-promoting.

Losing 15 pounds or running a four-minute mile might be important and measurable but for most people certainly would not be realistic. Losing 2 to 4 pounds and walking two miles in under 30 minutes would be much more under your control and realistic, given the two-week time frame.

Tips to Help You Succeed

1. Have a goal and a plan.

2. Schedule time to exercise.

3. Drink plenty of water.

4. Listen to music you enjoy or other appropriate "diversions."

5. Learn and apply the safety guidelines appropriate to your activities.

6. Have a positive, realistic attitude.

7. Try finding a "Workout Buddy."

Tools for Teaching Health. Copyright © 2007 by John Wiley & Sons, Inc. Reproduced by permission of Jossey-Bass, An Imprint of Wiley

Exercise in any form—mild, moderate, or intense—is good for your health. It can reduce your risk of many diseases and keep your heart, lungs, and bones healthy. You do not have to be a great athlete to reap the health benefits of exercise. If you have been inactive and would like to start an exercise program, regular moderate exercise like walking, biking, or skating is a great way to ease into the routine.

Slow and steady exercise (remember the story of the *Tortoise and the Hare*?) can increase your level of fitness and help you maintain a healthy weight.

If you are already active with an individual or team sport or other type of program, be very specific in your journals. For example, a soccer player may warm up with a jog around the field, followed by stretching for a given amount of time. Then list drills, skill practice, wind sprints, or game-situation exercise you are getting.

Good Luck and Get Moving!!!!

Physical Activity Goal

Name _____

My Overall Physical Activity Goal: (This might involve only one area of Health-Related Fitness or all four)

Steps to Achieve My Goal:

	Frequency	Intensity	Time	Type
Cardiorespiratory Endurance	(Ex: 3–5 times per week)	(Ex: 70% of max)	(Ex: 20–30 min)	(Ex: Jog around the school track)
Muscular Strength				
Muscular Endurance				
Flexibility				

Who will support me in reaching my goal? How?

What might prevent me from reaching my goal?

How will I reward myself for reaching my goal?

My Two-Week Physical Activity Journal

Name _____

Based on My Physical Activity Goal, I Will . . .

List the activities I participate in, list how often I participate in them, list the duration (how long) I spent on each activity, and list the intensity (easy, moderate, vigorous) for each activity.

Write the times on the calendar below. I will keep my calendar for two weeks.

Week One Dates: Monday _____ to Sunday _____

Mon
Tues
Wed
Thurs
Fri
Sat
Sun

(Continued)

My Two-Week Physical Activity Journal

Name _____

Week Two Dates: Monday _____ to Sunday _____

Mon
Tues
Wed
Thurs
Fri
Sat
Sun

WORKSHEET 7.7

Goal Reflections

Complete the goal reflection questions below and hand in to instructor after the two-week period, along with your Physical Activity Plan and Two-Week Calendar.

Goal Reflection

Name _____

1. Did you achieve your goal? Completely or partially?

_____

_____

_____

_____

2. Was achieving your goal easy or hard? Why?

_____

_____

_____

_____

3. How do you feel about achieving your goal or not achieving your goal?

_____

_____

_____

_____

4. What changes would you make to your goal with what you know now?

_____

_____

_____

_____

Lesson 4: "Counterfeit Fitness"—The Dangers
of Using Anabolic Steroids and Other
Performance-Enhancing Substances

Note to the Teacher

This assignment can be completed as an out-of-class assignment if the computer lab is unavailable during class time.

Time Needed

Two 40–50 minute class periods

National Standards

- Students will comprehend concepts related to health promotion and disease prevention to enhance health.

- Students will demonstrate the ability to access valid information and products and services to enhance health.

- Students will demonstrate the ability to use interpersonal communication skills to enhance health and avoid or reduce health risks.

Objectives

- Students will research how getting involved with performance-enhancing drugs can impact their health.

- Students will evaluate the validity on the Internet regarding the potential health consequences of performance-enhancing drugs.

Materials & Preparation

1. Reserve a computer lab for this lesson.

2. Handout 8.1, How to Evaluate the Reliability of a Web Site, one copy per student.

3. Worksheet 8.8, Finding Answers to Some Questions About Performance-Enhancing Drugs and Supplements, one copy per group.

Procedures

1. Begin class by asking students the following questions:

   - Can you always tell how healthy people are just by looking at them? Why?

   - Why might some people not show the effects of an unhealthy habit or lifestyle?

   - Do the effects of an unhealthy lifestyle always show up right away?

   - Why do some people take chances with their health by using harmful substances?

2. Explain that for the next two days, students will be working in groups to research information on steroids, supplements, and other performance-enhancing sub-

stances. Along with trying to access information, groups will also be evaluating the Web sites that they are assigned.

3. Explain that although the Internet is a great research tool, there are many sites that have incorrect or biased information. There are also many Web sites that sell or attempt to sell products and services. After doing this activity, students will have a better understanding of how to access accurate, unbiased information that may affect their health.

4. Divide the class into groups of three to five students. After groups have been formed, give each student a copy of Handout 8.1, How to Evaluate the Reliability of a Web Site. Students should read through the information, as a group, before attempting to go online.

5. Hand out Worksheet 8.8: Finding Answers to Some Questions About Performance-Enhancing Drugs and Supplements. Assign individuals different tasks so that each member of the group plays a role in accessing information.

6. Student groups should then log on to their first Web site. On their worksheet, they should make sure to write down the complete, accurate URL for the site. They should then attempt to answer worksheet questions from the information on that site.

7. When they have completed the questions from the first Web site, they should follow the same procedure for the second site. Allow 20–30 minutes for students to complete the worksheet.

8. Based on the information regarding the credibility of a Web site, groups should rate the site, from 1 (Poor) to 10 (Excellent) in the five categories listed.

9. Have each group present their findings from their worksheets. When all groups have presented, ask the following discussion questions:

   • Which types of Web sites seemed to be accurate sources of information?

   • What qualities did these sites seem to have in common? (.org, .edu, .gov)

   • Which did not seem to be able to provide you with accurate sources of information? (.com sites that often try to sell you something or are biased in their opinions)

   • What generalizations can you make about accessing information on the World Wide Web?

   • Can accessing the wrong type of information affect your health? Give examples.

Assessment:

   • Completion and submission of the two group worksheets.

How to Evaluate the Reliability of a Web Site

The URL can usually give you a clue as to the reliability of a site. *URL* stands for "uniform resource locator," and is the "address" that serves as a pointer to a resource on the World Wide Web.

1. *Sites that end in ".com" are generally individual Web sites and/or companies that want to sell you something.* What to look for: Is the information one-sided? Does the author use words like "best" or "worst" or "always" or "never?" If there are opinionated statements or biased language, this is a warning sign. If there is advertising on the site, you should be skeptical of its informational accuracy. If the grammar or spelling is poor, this is a definite indication that the site is questionable.

2. *Sites that end in ".org"* Community organizations, such as the American Cancer Society, generally end in ".org" and are pretty reliable.

3. *Sites that end in ".edu"* These sites are usually educational institutions and universities and are usually (but not always) reliable. If the site ends in ".k12," these are public or private schools or school districts. Their information may or may not be reliable, depending on several variables listed on the "Other Things to Look for on a Site" below.

4. *Sites that end in ".gov"* These sites tend to be the most reliable, since a government agency is in charge of maintaining the information. An example might be the Centers for Disease Control and Prevention Web site, listed as "CDC.gov".

Other Things to Look for on a Site

1. Who is the author of the article? Is this person's name in the article or byline? Is this person qualified? An expert? Degrees held? Are credentials for the author given? Is a contact person or address available so the user can ask questions or verify information?

2. Is the site current? When was it last updated? How current are the links to other sites? Are the links working properly? The more current and updated, generally the more reliable the site.

3. Quality of information—The purpose of the site should be clear on first glance. Is it informational, business and commercial, news, or personal? The content should be well organized. The information should be accurate based on the user's previous knowledge of the subject. Does it contradict something you found somewhere else? The information should be consistent with similar information in other sources. Is a bibliography of print sources included?

Tools for Teaching Health. Copyright © 2007 by John Wiley & Sons, Inc. Reproduced by permission of Jossey-Bass, An Imprint of Wiley

Group Worksheet

Finding Answers to Some Questions About Performance-Enhancing Drugs and Supplements

Group Members

_____   _____

_____   _____

Based on your information obtained from the site, answer the following questions:

URL of Site #1 _____

1. What is the name and source (man-made or natural) of the substance?

2. Are there any common or street names for the substance?

3. How is this substance used? (pill, injection, liquid, powder, herbal, cream?)

4. What are the effects sought? (Why do people take them?)

5. Are there any dangers or health problems associated with taking this substance? If so, list two or more.

Based on the information given, how would you rate this site? 1 = Poor 10 = Excellent

- Scientifically Accurate: 1 2 3 4 5 6 7 8 9 1 0

- Credible Source of Information: 1 2 3 4 5 6 7 8 9 1 0

- Overall Evaluation of Site: 1 2 3 4 5 6 7 8 9 1 0

Looking at all of the questions above and the information you were given in How to Evaluate the Reliability of a Web Site, your group should construct a response of at least *two paragraphs* that explains why your group believes that this site is valid or invalid. Include in your evaluation aspects related to author and credentials, technical content, bias, advertising, if it's updated, references you can check, and so on.

_____

_____

_____

_____

(Continued)

Group Worksheet: Finding Answers to Some Questions About Performance-Enhancing Drugs and Supplements

Group Members

_____   _____

_____   _____

Based on your information obtained from the site, answer the following questions.

URL of Site #2 _____

1. What is the name and source (man-made or natural) of the substance?

2. Are there any common or street names for the substance?

3. How is this substance used? (pill, injection, liquid, powder, herbal, cream?)

4. What are the effects sought? (Why do people take them?)

5. Are there any dangers or health problems associated with taking this substance? If so, list two or more.

Based on the information given, how would you rate this site? 1 = Poor 10 = Excellent

- Scientifically Accurate: 1   2   3   4   5   6   7   8   9   1 0

- Credible Source of Information: 1   2   3   4   5   6   7   8   9   1 0

- Overall Evaluation of Site: 1   2   3   4   5   6   7   8   9   1 0

Looking at all of the questions above and the information you were given in How to Evaluate the Reliability of a Web Site, your group should construct a response of at least *two paragraphs* that explains why your group believes that this site is valid or invalid. Include in your evaluation aspects related to author and credentials, technical content, bias, advertising, if it's updated, references you can check, and so on.

_____

_____

_____

_____

Lesson 5: A Pound of Fat—Doing the Weight-Loss Math

Note to the Teacher

If it is not possible to spend two days on this topic, the teacher can show the legitimate and questionable sites to the class prior to assigning the homework and simply collect and assess the homework without reviewing it together as a class.

Time Needed

One to two 40–50 minute class periods

National Standards

- Students will comprehend concepts related to health promotion and disease prevention to enhance health.
- Students will demonstrate the ability to access valid information and products and services to enhance health.
- Students will demonstrate the ability to practice health-enhancing behaviors and avoid or reduce risks.

Objectives

- Students will discuss the concept that to maintain a healthy weight, the intake of calories must equal the output of energy, and to lose weight, the energy output must exceed the calorie intake.
- Students will calculate the number of calories that must be expended to lose one pound.
- Students will compare and contrast credible and non-credible sources of weight loss information.

Materials Needed

1. 1-ounce bag of chips.
2. 20-ounce bottle of cola.
3. Computer with Internet access and large screen that can be viewed by the entire class.

Preparation

1. Arrange to have a computer with Internet access delivered to your classroom or arrange to bring your class to the computer lab.
2. Duplicate Handout 8.2, Dietary Guidelines: Tips for Healthy Eating, one copy per student.
3. Duplicate Handout 8.3, Secret Formula for Losing a Pound a Week: An Ounce of Chips, a Bottle of Soda, and a 30-Minute Walk, one copy per student.
4. Write the following "Do Now" on the board: "Write down one food or beverage that you consume on a regular basis that you think is *Healthy,* and briefly describe why you feel it is a healthy food. Then write down one food that you

consume on a regular basis that you feel is *Unhealthy,* and briefly describe why you feel that it is not a healthy food."

Procedures

1. Begin class with a "Do Now" written on the board (item 4, above). Allow students two minutes to write their answers in their notebooks.

2. Have the class "whip" around the room, whereby each student quickly states their "healthy" food. Then do the same with their "unhealthy" food.

3. Continue discussion by having students tell why (and give reasons) their choices are healthy or unhealthy. On the board, compile a list in two columns and ask students to duplicate the list in their notebooks. Following are some samples:

Foods We Think Are Healthy	*Foods We Think Are Unhealthy*
Spinach	Peanut butter
Apples	Butter
Whole wheat bread	Ice cream
1 percent milk	Cookies
Cheese	Chips
Water	Soda
Salad	Double cheeseburger
Sweet potatoes	French fries
Pasta	Sugary candy
Rice	Fried chicken nuggets
Turkey	Sausage and pepperoni pizza
Eggs	Iced tea with sugar added
Chocolate	

4. Clarify any myths about the foods on their lists. Students will generally have appropriate answers but often cannot explain just why a food is healthy or unhealthy.

5. Explain that, unless they are allergic, there are no foods that should *never* be eaten. For example, treating yourself to "fast food" of a burger, fries, and soft drink from time to time is not going to do lasting harm to your health. However, if this same type of diet is consumed every day, it can *start* to become unhealthy if you are getting too much salt, fat, cholesterol, and calories. This same theory holds true for most foods that they may have listed on the "unhealthy" side.

6. Clarify some items on their "healthy" food list. For example, although cheese and rice and pasta are fairly nutritious foods, the type and quantity of these foods can sometimes have an adverse effect on a weight management program. Whole grain rice and whole grain pasta would be better choices than white rice

or regular pasta because of extra fiber. Low or reduced-fat cheese would generally be a better choice than regular cheese products.

7. Explain that the other problem with some type of so-called "healthy" foods is portion size. Very few people actually eat a half cup of rice or pasta, which is considered one serving. They may think that a "bowl" of pasta is one serving, when in reality, it is most likely three or four "servings."

8. Distribute Handout 8.2: Dietary Guidelines: Tips for Healthy Eating. Discuss.

9. Distribute Handout 8.3, Secret Formula for Losing a Pound a Week! A Bag of Chips, a Bottle of Soda, and a 30-Minute Walk. Discuss tips for decreasing calorie intake. Then discuss Exercise tips for weight control.

10. Demonstrate the "Secret Formula" by showing the bag of chips and the bottle of soda and reading the calorie content of each. Demonstrate approximately how fast you would have to walk to maintain a 4 mph pace (about 20 steps every 10 seconds).

11. After reading through the handout and doing the demonstration, ask the class:

    Q: *If it seems so simple to lose weight by modifying the diet slightly and increasing daily physical activity, why are there so many diets out on the market?*

    A: People want a quick fix and usually don't want to change their lifestyle. Also, people respond better to different types of programs. Some people like to exercise alone, while others like to exercise with others, such as with a running partner or at a gym or club.

    Q: *What can I do to continue to motivate myself to exercise?*

    A: Make exercise a regular, planned activity. No matter how busy you are, schedule a half hour of exercise into your daily routine. Instead of going home and eating cookies in front of the television, take a walk. Instead of staying on the computer or talking on the phone for an extended period of time, restrict your time, and schedule some time on a bike or exercise equipment.

    Q: *If we now know so much about diet and exercise and the role that each of these play in maintaining a healthy weight, why are so many children, teens, and adults overweight in this country?*

    A: Modern living has made us less active. We take cars and busses everywhere. We sit and play video games instead of playing outside. We do not have to perform manual labor to get the food that we eat. And the fast-food industry has actually promoted unhealthy eating, through advertising campaigns like "Super-Size" portions and so-called "Value Meals."

12. Conclude discussion for the day and assign homework. Over the next two days, each student is to go online and attempt to find two different Web sites.

    • One should be a legitimate, credible site that has research-based information about diet, healthy eating, physical activity, and weight loss.

    • The other should be a site that has questionable information, biased or opinionated information, or is trying to sell you something.

13. Explain that students are to log on to these sites, decide whether they are legitimate or not, write down the URL for the site, and give at least three reasons that each site gets the "Thumbs Up" or "Thumbs Down" based on criteria given in a previous lesson on accessing credible information on the Web.

Optional Day Two

1. Check student homework. Review their site evaluations. Then ask for volunteers to give you the address (URL) for some legitimate sites.

2. Log on to some of these sites, show on large screen, and discuss characteristics of each site.

3. Then log on to some sites of questionable value. Again, discuss characteristics of why these sites should be scrutinized carefully, especially if they are trying to sell a product.

4. Following are some legitimate and questionable sites to use as examples if students have a difficult time locating appropriate sites:

Legitimate Sites

www.cnpp.usda.gov
www.calorielab.com
www.mypyramid.gov
www.teamnutrition.usda.gov

Questionable Sites

http://www.foolproof-diet.com/?hop=pageload
www.vitadigest.com/hollywood-48-hr.html

5. Conclude by pointing out that by following the dietary guidelines and increasing daily physical activity, you can slowly but steadily lose weight and keep it off.

Assessment

- Class participation
- Submission of URL addresses of Internet sites.

Dietary Guidelines: Tips for Healthy Eating

1. *Reduce fat.* Gram for gram, fat has more than twice as many calories (9) than either carbohydrates or proteins (4). Go easy on butter, salad dressings, fried foods, and whole-fat dairy products. Small amounts of unsaturated fats such as nuts, olive oil, or peanut butter are better choices.

2. *Limit added sugar.* Foods with a lot of added sugar, such as soda, candy, and most desserts, are mostly empty calories and provide little, if any, nutritional value.

3. *Watch portions of* all *foods.* Too much of almost anything will turn to body fat and cause weight gain.

4. *Drink a lot of water.* Water is calorie-free and helps keep you hydrated.

5. *Eat more fruits, vegetables, and whole grains.* These are loaded with nutrients and fiber, but are generally low in calories.

6. *Low-fat, protein-rich foods.* Examples are skinless turkey breast, fish, beans, eggs, and low-fat dairy. Protein makes you feel full longer so you're less likely to snack between meals.

7. *Eat several small meals throughout the day.* Not having breakfast and skipping lunch means that you may not have "fueled" your body for 12 hours or more. If you go an extended period of time without eating, your body tries to compensate by slowing down your metabolism, thus burning fewer calories. Eating a large dinner or late-night snacks, then going to bed, tends to make your body store body fat much easier.

Secret Formula for Losing a Pound a Week!

A Bag of Chips, a Bottle of Soda, and a 30-Minute Walk

Exercise Tips for Weight Control

Research has shown that regular physical activity, with healthy eating habits, is the most efficient and healthy way to control your weight. It doesn't matter what types of activity you do—sports, aerobics, walking, yard work—all are beneficial. Studies show that even the most inactive people can benefit if they accumulate 30 minutes or more of physical activity per day.

How Does Physical Activity Help in Weight Management?

Physical activity helps control your weight by using excess calories that otherwise would be stored as fat. Balancing the calories you use through physical activity with the calories you eat will help you achieve or maintain your desired weight.

How much exercise is enough? It is recommended that you do 20–30 minutes of aerobic activity three or more times per week, along with some muscle-building or weight training 2 or 3 days per week. The more muscle you have, the more efficiently your body burns calories.

Calories in foods > Calories used/burned = Weight gain

Calories in foods < Calories used/burned = Weight loss

Calories in foods = Calories used/burned = Weight maintained

Q: *How many calories need to be reduced to lose one pound of fat?*

A: It takes a reduction of 3,500 calories to lose one pound of fat.

Q: *What is a safe amount of weight to lose per week?*

A: Weight loss should generally not exceed one to two pounds per week. That's a caloric deficit of 3,500 to 7,000 calories. The average person consumes between 2,000 and 3,000 calories per day. If you want to lose one pound a week this corresponds to a caloric decrease of 500 calories per day (500 × 7 = 3,500). This can be accomplished by eating 500 calories less per day, or by exercising more and eating 200–300 calories less per day.

For example: a 1-ounce bag of chips has about *150 calories.* A 16-ounce bottle of soda has about *200 calories.* If you walk at a brisk pace (2 miles at 15 minutes per mile), you will burn up approximately *150 calories* (based on your body weight—a 180-pound person would burn more than 150 calories, while a 110-pound person may burn slightly less than 150 calories). If you do the math, not eating the chips (-150) and not drinking the soda (-200) you have consumed 350 fewer calories. By burning up the extra 150 calories by your 30-minute walk, you have now reduced your total caloric intake/usage by 500 calories. If you simply did this each day for a week (7 × 500), you would lose *a pound of fat,* or *3,500 calories!*

That's 4 pounds per month, 12 pounds in three months, and 24 pounds in 6 months!

Tools for Teaching Health. Copyright © 2007 by John Wiley & Sons, Inc. Reproduced by permission of Jossey-Bass, An Imprint of Wiley

Home–School Connection: Physical Activity

Time Needed to Complete

1–3 days

Time Needed to Present

20 minutes, one class period

National Standards

- Students will comprehend concepts related to health promotion and disease prevention.
- Students will demonstrate the ability to advocate for personal, family, and community health.

Objective

- Students will interview family members about physical activity.

Materials & Preparation

- Duplicate Worksheet 8.9, Family Interview on Leisure Time and Physical Activity, one copy per student.

Procedures

1. Explain to the class that they are going to have an assignment to complete with a family member. This should be a parent or caregiver—not a sibling—unless the sibling is more than ten years older than the student.
2. Distribute the Family Interview on Leisure Time and Physical Activity worksheet and review.
3. Assign the due date for the assignment.
4. On the day the assignment is due, students can share the results of their interviews and reflections. This can take as much or as little time as is available.
5. Following are some process questions that can be asked to facilitate discussion:
   - Is physical activity a large part of anyone's family activities? In what way?
   - How many of you frequently participate in physical activity with your family? What types of activity?
   - Did completing the interview raise awareness of physical activity as a health issue with your family member?
   - Has anyone's family changed their behavior as a result of the interview?
   - What did you learn from this activity? What did your family member learn?
   - Are there any other comments or questions?

Assessment

- Submission of the completed worksheet.

Home–School Connection: Family Interview on Leisure Time and Physical Activity

Due Date: _____

Student Name: _____

Name of Person Being Interviewed: _____

Relationship to Student: _____

Choose an adult member of your immediate or extended family and write down their answers to the questions below. *(The person being interviewed is allowed to "Pass" on any question they may find too personal or difficult to answer.)*

1. What are some examples of leisure activities that you enjoy in your everyday life?

2. Which of your leisure activities provide you with some form of exercise?

3. In your opinion, do you believe that regular physical activity is important for maintaining a healthy body? Why or why not?

4. Which of your physical activities listed above, if any, maintain your overall level of fitness and keep you in "good shape?"

NAME _____   DATE _____

5. The Surgeon General of the United States has issued a warning that a high percentage of children, teens, and adults are overweight. What do you feel you can do as a parent to encourage your children to maintain a healthy weight?

6. Additional comments:

Thank you for the interview!

_____   _____
Signature of Interviewee   Date

Project: Student-Created Public Service Announcements

Note to the Teacher

If possible, identify students adept at using a video camera prior to creating groups. Then assign one of the selected students to each of the groups as the producer. This will allow for a higher-quality public service announcement.

Time Needed

This assignment should be distributed at the beginning of a physical activity unit so that students have time to complete the project. On the day the assignment is due, the teacher can use as much time as is available for students to share their public service announcements (PSAs) with the class. Sharing can take 20 minutes or an entire period.

National Standards

- Students will demonstrate the ability to use interpersonal communication skills to enhance health and avoid or reduce health risks.

- Students will demonstrate the ability to advocate for personal, family, and community health.

Objectives

- Students will obtain information on the benefits of physical activity on health.

- Students will create a public service announcement (PSA) that encourages the viewer to engage in physical activity, extols the benefits of physical activity, or gives some specific examples of physical activities that most adolescents can engage in for little or no cost or special equipment.

Materials & Preparation

1. Access to video camera.
2. Duplicate a storyboard (Handout 8.4), one per group.
3. Duplicate a packet of four rubrics (Handout 8.5), one packet per group.
4. Sample PSAs (on any topic), if available.
5. Television.
6. VCR or DVD player.

Procedures

1. Introduce the assignment by explaining that the class will be getting involved in a group project. Each group will create a public service announcement, or PSA.
2. Explain what a PSA is. The purpose of a PSA is to encourage or convince someone to *do* something positive, such as exercise more, or *stop* doing something negative, such as smoking. PSAs can be done in a variety of ways, but most have one thing in common; they use *facts* to try to get their message

across to the audience. PSAs sometimes also use humor, a catchy phrase or jingle, famous people, or other creative methods to make their point.

3. Ask whether students can give you some examples of PSAs that they have seen on television or heard on the radio.

4. Show students some examples of public service announcements. Many can be downloaded from the Internet. If you have done other activities in which students created PSAs, you can show them these examples.

5. Tell students that the public service announcements that they will be creating will be on Physical Activity and Health.

6. Groups will need to incorporate a minimum of 7–10 facts related to the health benefits of physical activity and exercise in their PSA. The length of the PSA should be approximately 30–60 seconds and should be targeted to children and teenagers.

7. Divide the class into groups of four students. Tell students to assign themselves roles within the groups. One student will be the researcher, one will be the storyboard writer, one will be the producer, and the fourth student will be the sales associate. Explain the roles as follows:

   - *Researcher.* The researcher is in charge of locating and selecting accurate facts for the PSA.

   - *Storyboard writer.* The storyboard writer is in charge of developing and writing the script for the PSA.

   - *Producer.* The producer is in charge of videotaping the PSA.

   - *Sales associate.* The sales associate is in charge of "selling" the PSA to the class.

8. Distribute a set of rubrics (Handout 8.5) to each group, one per role. Direct students to the rubrics to learn more about the responsibilities of their role.

9. Tell the class that they will have the remainder of that class period to share their facts within the group and begin thinking about developing their PSA.

10. Explain to the class that once they have decided on a theme for their PSA, and have an outline of a script, they should complete the storyboard. The storyboard is a scene-by-scene visual and written description of what is going on in the video. Distribute a storyboard handout (Handout 8.4) to each group.

11. In the box on the storyboard, the storyboard writer should draw a simple picture of what or who the audience will *see.* In the lines underneath the box, the storyboard writer should write in the words (if any) that the audience will *hear.*

12. Explain to the class that once storyboards are completed, producers will be responsible for filming their PSAs. If no one in the group has a video camera, students can arrange to stay after school and videotape under the teacher's supervision.

13. On the day the assignment is due, plan to show each PSA to the entire class. Have the sales associates introduce their PSAs and "sell" them to the class. Sales

associates are also responsible for answering any questions that their class-mates or teacher have.

14. Conclude by pointing out that physical fitness is a crucial component of well-ness. If young people become and remain physically active at their age, they will live a longer, more productive life.

Assessment

Completion of public-service announcement (Handout 8.5).

Storyboard

Researcher Rubric

4	3	2	1
Student demonstrates thorough understanding of how to locate and apply factual information to support an opinion.	Student demonstrates an adequate understanding of how to locate and apply factual information to support an opinion.	Student demonstrates an inadequate understanding of how to locate and apply factual information to support an opinion.	Student demonstrates no understanding of how to locate and apply factual information to support an opinion.
• All statements of fact in the presentation are factually correct.	• Most statements of fact in the presentation are factually correct.	• Some statements of fact in the presentation are factually correct.	• Many statements of fact in the presentation are not factually correct.
• Seven or more significant facts support the main idea.	• Five or more significant facts support the main idea.	• Three or more significant facts support the main idea.	• No significant facts support the main idea.
• One or more graphs or tables are used effectively to display factual information.	• One or more graphs or tables are used somewhat effectively to display factual information.	• A graph or table is used to display factual information, but it does not support the main idea.	• No graphs or tables are used effectively to display factual information.

Tools for Teaching Health. Copyright © 2007 by John Wiley & Sons, Inc. Reproduced by permission of Jossey-Bass, An Imprint of Wiley

Producer Rubric

4	3	2	1
Student demonstrates exemplary skill in portraying facts and a persuasive message through the medium of video.	Student demonstrates adequate skill in portraying facts and a persuasive message through the medium of video	Student demonstrates inadequate skill in portraying facts and a persuasive message through the medium of video.	Student demonstrates no skill in portraying facts and a persuasive message through the medium of video.
• Video moves smoothly from shot to shot.	• Tape is edited throughout with only quality shots remaining.	• Tape is edited in a few spots, but several poor shots remain.	• Tape is unedited and many poor shots remain.
• The audio is clear and effectively assists in communicating the main idea.	• The audio is clear, but only partially assists in communicating the main idea.	• Transitions from shot to shot are choppy.	• Audio is cut off and inconsistent.
• Students communicate ideas with enthusiasm, proper voice projection, appropriate language, and clear delivery.	• Students communicate ideas with proper voice projection, adequate preparation and delivery.	• There are many unnatural breaks and/or early cuts.	• Students have great difficulty communicating ideas, with poor voice projection.
• The color scheme for backgrounds and clothing is selected to suit the mood of the video.	• The color scheme used for backgrounds and clothing enhances the presentation.	• The audio is inconsistent in soft/garbled) at times and insufficiently communicates the main idea.	• No color scheme is apparent.
• All scenes have sufficient lighting for viewer to easily see action.	• Few shadows or glares are apparent.	• Students have difficulty communicating ideas due to weak and/or lack of preparation.	• Most scenes are too dark or too light to determine what is happening.
• All shots are clearly focused and well framed.	• Most scenes have sufficient lighting to tell what is happening.	• Backgrounds and clothing distract from the presentation and are not suited to the mood of the video.	• Many shots are unfocused and poorly framed.
• The video is steady with few pans and zooms.	• The camera is held steady.	• Some scenes are too dark or too light to determine what is happening.	• The camera is not excessive panning and zooming distracts the viewer.
	• Most shots are clearly focused and well framed.	• The motion shots are fairly steady.	
		• Some shots are unfocused or poorly framed.	

(Continued)

Storyboard Writer Rubric

4	3	2	1
Student demonstrates thorough understanding of how to organize and present writing and images to support an opinion.	Student demonstrates an adequate understanding of how to organize and present writing and images to support an opinion.	Student demonstrates an inadequate understanding of how to organize and present writing and images to support an opinion.	Student demonstrates no understanding of how to organize and present writing and images to support an opinion.
• The language and imagery of the PSA is extremely appropriate for children and adolescents.	• The language and imagery of the PSA is appropriate for children and adolescents.	• The language and imagery of the PSA demonstrates little understanding of children and adolescents.	• The language and imagery of the PSA demonstrates no understanding of children and adolescents.
• The written and spoken parts of the PSA presentation are organized for greatest persuasive effect: a hook and conclusion are effective, and the factual support is organized from least important to most important reasons.	• The written and spoken parts of the PSA presentation are organized for adequate persuasive effect. The announcement contains an adequate hook and conclusion, but the factual support of opinions could be improved.	• The written and spoken parts of the PSA presentation are not organized for greatest persuasive effect. Hook or conclusion is missing or ineffective, and organization of support is ineffective.	• The written and spoken parts of the PSA presentation are organized for greatest persuasive effect (hook, least important to most important reasons, conclusion).
• No errors in spelling, punctuation, grammar exist in the written or spoken parts of the PSA.	• Few errors in spelling, punctuation, grammar exist in the written or spoken parts of the PSA, and they do not seriously limit the effectiveness of the PSA.	• Errors in spelling, punctuation, grammar exist in the written or spoken parts of the PSA and limit the effectiveness of the PSA.	• No errors in spelling, punctuation, or grammar exist in the written or spoken parts of the PSA.
• The images in the PSA are extremely effective in conveying the message of the written and spoken portion.	• The images in the PSA are mostly effective in conveying the message of the written and spoken portion.	• The images of the PSA do little to help the group's attempt to persuade the audience.	• The images in the PSA distract from or prevent the group's attempt to persuade the audience.
		-	

NAME   DATE

Sales Associate Rubric

4	3	2	1
Student demonstrates a thorough understanding of how the PSA will persuade young viewers to be physically active and demonstrates an excellent understanding of the needs of the audience. • The sales presentation is organized for greatest persuasive effect. The hook and conclusion are effective, and the factual support is organized from least important to most important reasons. • Five or more significant facts about the PSA or examples support the student's sales presentation. • The speech effectively addresses the needs and desires of the audience.	Student demonstrates an adequate understanding of how the PSA will persuade young viewers to be physically fit and demonstrates a sufficient understanding of the needs of the audience. • The sales presentation is organized for persuasive effect. The hook and conclusion are adequate, but the organization of factual support could be improved. • Three or more significant facts about the PSA or examples support the student's sales presentation. • The speech adequately addresses the needs and desires of the audience.	Student demonstrates an inadequate understanding of how the PSA will persuade young viewers to be physically active and demonstrates an insufficient understanding of the needs of the audience. • The sales presentation is not organized for persuasive effect. The hook and conclusion are missing or ineffective, and factual support is disorganized. • Opinions in the presentation are not adequately supported by facts or examples. Fewer than three significant facts about the PSA or examples support the student's sales presentation. • The speech inadequately addresses the needs and desires of the audience.	Student demonstrates no understanding of how the PSA will persuade young viewers to be physically active and demonstrates no understanding of the needs of the audience. • The sales presentation is not organized for persuasive effect. The hook or conclusion is missing, and factual support is disorganized. • Opinions in the presentation are not supported by facts or examples. No significant facts about the PSA or examples support the student's sales presentation. • The speech does not address the needs and desires of the audience.

Assessment: Functional Knowledge and Skills Exam

Time Needed

One 40–50 minute class period

National Standards

- Students will comprehend concepts related to health promotion and disease prevention.
- Students will demonstrate the ability to use goal-setting skills to enhance health

Objective

- Students demonstrate knowledge and skills related to physical activity.

Materials & Preparation

1. Duplicate Worksheet 8.10, Physical Activity and Fitness: Functional Knowledge Exam—one per student.
2. Arrange the desks as needed for exam format.

Procedures

1. As students enter the room, advise them to take their seats, put their books and notebooks under their chairs, and place a pen or pencil on their desk.
2. Explain the test-taking rules to the class. Following are some suggestions:
   - No talking!
   - No "borrowing" answers from a neighbor—if caught cheating, students will receive a zero and a phone call to home.
   - If students have a question, they should raise their hand. The teacher will come to them, not the other way around.
   - When students are done, they should pass in their test and work quietly on a different assignment or read a book while waiting for the rest of the class to finish.
3. Students take varying amounts of time to complete exams. It may be advisable to have some type of activity for quick test takers to work on while they are waiting for slower test takers to finish.
4. Be prepared with an activity for the entire class in case all students finish the test prior to the end of the period. The *Kids' Book of Questions* by Gregory Stock provides wonderful questions to spark class discussion on topics related to self-esteem, mental health, and other health-related issues. Students enjoy talking about answers to the questions, and it may be a relaxing way to conclude an otherwise stressful class period.

Assessment

Score on exam.

Possible Answers: Content

Physical benefits: improve endurance, flexibility, strength, reduce risk of heart disease, diabetes, obesity, improved sleep, lower blood pressure, lower cholesterol

Social benefits: meet new friends, share enjoyable activities with others, get involved with formal or informal sports or games

Mental and emotional: enhanced self-esteem, enhanced body image, improve mood, and relieving of stress

Possible Answers: Planning and Goal-Setting Skills

Choose an activity that you like and that is easy to fit into your schedule, like walking outside or on a treadmill.

Start an exercise log or journal and write down short-term and long-term goals. Short term may be to walk a mile three times per week to start, and then slowly increase frequency, intensity, and time (duration) of workout. Begin slowly and gradually build.

Long-term goal may be to eventually walk-run or jog two miles without stopping to rest. Another short-term goal may be to lose 5 pounds in one month, making sure that there has been an increase in muscle tone and mass, and a decrease in body fat.

Make exercise enjoyable by finding a partner, listening to music, or watching TV while on a treadmill.

Slowly incorporate strength training and flexibility into your workouts.

Rubric

Commits to making a personal goal and develops realistic plan

Lists specifics steps for reaching goal

Identifies positive and negative influences on achieving the goal

Reflects on overall goal and adjusts if necessary

WORKSHEET 7.10

Physical Activity and Fitness: Functional Knowledge Exam

Directions

This exam consists of twenty multiple choice questions and one constructed response (essay) question. Please complete both sections.

Multiple Choice

Please circle the correct answer.

1. Which of the following activities is most likely to develop cardiorespiratory fitness?

    a. golf

    b. soccer

    c. weight training

    d. stretching

2. Although many teens and adults want to lose weight, Rick wants to gain weight. What would be the recommended way to gain some weight in the most healthful way?

    a. take steroids

    b. eat a balanced diet with a slight increase in total calories and begin a weight training program

    c. eat a lot of high-carbohydrate foods, like cakes, cookies, and soda

    d. instead of meals, take protein shakes and other supplements

3. Which of the following is *not* true about regular exercise?

    a. it improves the function of the heart, lungs, and circulatory system

    b. it reduces the chance of developing brain and lung cancer

    c. it reduces the risk of colon cancer and osteoporosis

    d. it helps to increase "good" cholesterol (HDLs) and decrease "bad" cholesterol (LDLs)

4. American teens today are

    a. more physically active than 25 years ago

    b. less physically active than 25 years ago

    c. are about equally as active as they were 25 years ago

    d. have a lower incidence of overweight and obesity than 25 years ago

5. If you do strength training, you should exercise the same muscle group

    a. every day

    b. every other day

    c. twice per day

    d. once per week

6. Which of the following is not a component of health-related fitness?

   a. muscular strength

   b. flexibility

   c. cardiorespiratory endurance

   d. speed and agility

7. If you are a healthy 15-year-old, your maximum heart rate would be approximately

   a. 220 beats per minute

   a. 205 beats per minute

   c. 180 beats per minute

   d. 150 beats per minute

8. Which of the following activities would be considered aerobic?

   a. sprinting a short distance

   b. weight lifting

   c. cycling for 20 minutes or more

   d. shooting 50 foul shots in basketball practice

9. Scott wants to encourage Todd to start a physical fitness program. Which of the following should Scott *not* do?

   a. find out what type of activities Todd likes to do

   b. offer to work out or exercise with Todd

   c. take Todd to his gym and start him off with a hard, intense workout

   d. encourage Todd to be realistic about his short- and long-term goals related to exercise

10. The amount of force a muscle is capable of exerting against a resistance with a single maximum effort is referred to as

    a. muscular endurance

    b. muscular strength

    c. flexibility

    d. mesomorphic displacement

11. The recommended percentage of body fat for a healthy adolescent male would be about

    a. 3–5 %

    b. 12–15%

    c. 18–21%

    d. 25–30%

(Continued)

12. The recommended percentage of body fat for a healthy adolescent female would be about
    a. 3–5%
    b. 12–15%
    c. 18–21%
    d. 25–30%

13. Exercising strenuously without replacing enough body fluids can result in
    a. cramping
    b. heat exhaustion
    c. heat stroke
    d. all of these

14. Ricardo weighs 200 pounds. His teammate, Maria weighs 120 pounds. They both warm up together by running a mile in 6 minutes. Who burned more calories?
    a. Ricardo
    b. Maria
    c. they each burned up the same number of calories
    d. it depends on who is in better aerobic condition

15. Victoria is a senior in high school. She used to play sports in middle school, but now rarely exercises and has led a sedentary lifestyle for the last couple of years. What would be the safest way for Victoria to start an exercise program?
    a. take an intermediate aerobic dance class at the "Y"
    b. swim 2–3 miles five days per week
    c. walk at a moderate pace for 30 minutes every day
    d. go out for her high school track team

16. Regular physical activity may reduce a person's risk for developing which of the following diseases or disorders?
    a. obesity
    b. heart disease
    c. high blood pressure and high cholesterol
    d. all of these

17. Which of the following would *not* be a mental or emotional benefit of regular physical activity?
    a. increased self-esteem
    b. improved mood
    c. reduced self-image
    d. stress reduction

18. The number of times per week you engage in aerobic activity would relate to which area of the FITT formula?

    a. frequency

    b. intensity

    c. time

    d. type

19. Which of the following is *not* true about stretching for increased flexibility?

    a. recommend slow and controlled stretching

    b. should be the very first thing you do before you start any workout

    c. should avoid jerky, bouncing stretches

    d. should stretch after a workout

20. Which of the following actions can you take to help your personal fitness plan succeed?

    a. start out slowly and try to find an exercise buddy

    b. have realistic expectations

    c. be committed and record your progress

    d. all of these

Constructed Response Questions

Please write your answer in the space provided. Use the back of this test if you do not have enough room to complete your answer.

Scenario

After a discussion on the benefits of physical activity, Bruce stays after class to have a private talk with his health teacher. He confides in his teacher that he has concerns about his lack of physical activity. He also is embarrassed about being overweight and would like to do something about it, but doesn't know how to start. He has started to eat healthier and has lowered his daily intake of calories, but wants to exercise to help lose the weight, get in shape, and feel better about himself.

Question: Describe one physical, one social, and one mental-emotional benefit of regular physical activity. Also, help Bruce develop a plan and/or goal that can get him started in a regular physical activity program that would be realistic.

_____

_____

_____

_____

_____